Charles Spencer Churchill, Duke of Marlborough, the Consuelo, Duchess of Marlborough, and Their Sons, the Marquess of Blandford and Lord Ivor Spencer Churchill

JERRY E. PATTERSON

THE VANDERBILTS

HARRY N. ABRAMS, INC., PUBLISHERS

Page 1: Grand Central Terminal, the most enduring legacy of the Vanderbilt family.

Page 2: John Singer Sargent. *The 9th Duke and Duchess of Marlborough with Their Sons the Marquess of Blandford and Lord Ivor Spencer-Churchill*. c. 1905. Oil on canvas, 131 × 94″. Red Drawing Room, Blenheim Palace. By Kind Permission of His Grace the Duke of Marlborough. Consuelo Vanderbilt married the 9th Duke of Marlborough in 1895.

Page 3: The Breakers in Newport, Rhode Island, was built for Cornelius Vanderbilt II by Richard Morris Hunt in 1892–1895. This is the State Dining Room at The Breakers.

Pages 4–5: The forest and gardens of Biltmore in Asheville, North Carolina, the largest Vanderbilt house. It was built for George Vanderbilt and opened in 1895. The forest was developed by Gifford Pinchot, and Frederick Law Olmsted laid out the grounds.

Page 8, Frontispiece: In his old age, the Commodore was painted wearing evening clothes by Jared B. Flagg, who had the unusual distinction of being an Episcopal clergyman as well as a portrait painter. The Commodore's portrait was exhibited at the Philadelphia Centennial Exhibition of 1876 and now hangs at Biltmore.

The genealogical charts, which precede each chapter, show only those members of the Vanderbilt family mentioned in the text. Vertical lines indicate descendants who are not listed. The charts are based on Verley Archer's *Commodore Cornelius Vanderbilt, Sophia Johnson Vanderbilt and Their Descendants* (Nashville: Vanderbilt University, 1972).

PROJECT DIRECTOR: *Margaret L. Kaplan*

EDITOR: *Mark D. Greenberg*

DESIGNER: *Dirk J. v O. Luykx*

PHOTO EDITOR: *John K. Crowley*

Library of Congress Cataloging-in-Publication Data
Patterson, Jerry E.
The Vanderbilts/Jerry E. Patterson.
p. cm.
Bibliography: p. 297
Includes index.
ISBN 0–8109–1748–3
1. Vanderbilt family. 2. Vanderbilt family—Homes and haunts.
3. United States—Biography. 4. United States—Genealogy.
5. Mansions—United States. I. Title.
CT274.V35P38 1989
929′.2′0973—dc19   88–35957

Text copyright © 1989 Jerry E. Patterson
Illustrations copyright © 1989 Harry N. Abrams, Inc.

Printed and bound in Japan

Contents

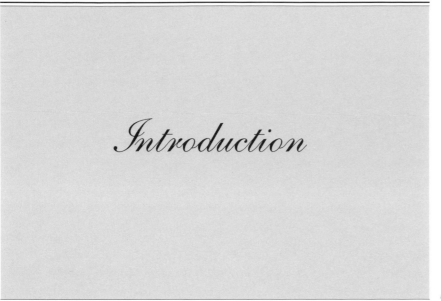

Introduction

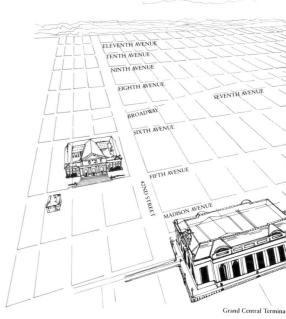

450 Fifth Avenue
New York Public Library

Grand Central Termina

VANDERBILT—the name means wealth, social position, fashion, and style. In the glittering annals of the American rich the Vanderbilt dynasty takes front rank; for over a century they fascinated contemporaries with their money and power, their magnificent homes and yachts, their extravagant entertainments, their victorious racehorses, and with their divorces, scandals, and family lawsuits, too.

The rise of the Vanderbilts from a farm on Staten Island to international standing was the result of the energy and imagination of Cornelius Vanderbilt, called "the Commodore," who began as a ferryman on New York Bay and died as the railroad king of the United States. Most American dynasties have risen in much the same way, but once having achieved wealth, the Vanderbilts used it with unparalleled style. Like the Commodore, they played to win, whether it was control over yet another railroad or the leadership of New York society.

They thought of themselves as princes. The title Head of the House of Vanderbilt was given to the eldest son, sometimes after an intrafamily struggle, and it was taken quite literally by younger members of the family and by the press. There was every justification for thinking of themselves as American princes: they went yachting with Kaiser Wilhelm II, had tea with King George V and Queen Mary at Buckingham Palace, entertained Russian

450 Fifth Avenue, southeast corner of East 40th Street, home of William Henry, later of Frederick W.

42nd Street between Vanderbilt and Lexington Avenues, Grand Central Terminal

640 Fifth Avenue, occupying full block along Fifth Avenue on west side between 51st and 52nd Streets, built by William Henry, later home of George, then of Cornelius III

642 Fifth Avenue, northern section of double house, home of Margaret Vanderbilt Shepard

2 West 52nd Street, farthest north portion of double house, home of Emily Vanderbilt Sloane

645 and 647 Fifth Avenue, east side of avenue between 51st and 52nd Streets, "The Marble Twins" built by George

660 Fifth Avenue, northwest corner of 52nd Street, home of William K.

666 Fifth Avenue, southwest corner of 53rd Street, home of William K. II

680 Fifth Avenue, between 53rd and 54th Streets, home of Lila Vanderbilt Webb

684 Fifth Avenue, between 53rd and 54th Streets, north of Webb house, home of Florence Vanderbilt Twombly

grand dukes—who were amazed at the splendor of Vanderbilt houses—and once thought a mere Battenberg probably not good enough for one of their daughters.

This remarkable family has produced not only railroad executives, yachtsmen, and society leaders, Vanderbilts have also been artists and collectors, scientists and conservationists, legislators and Suffragettes.

Their greatest accomplishment has been as builders. The Vanderbilts have left a unique architectural and decorative heritage in the eastern United States. No other American dynasty built so many distinctive houses, and of no other family have so many homes survived intact. Every year hundreds of thousands of visitors see the Vanderbilt houses in Newport, in Asheville, North Carolina, in Dutchess and Suffolk counties, New York, and in Vermont, and they leave amazed at the glimpse of a vanished way of life.

This book seeks to capture that way of life, to describe the Vanderbilts who created and enjoyed it, to show why a magazine could state solemnly in 1883 that "The Vanderbilts have come nobly forward to show the world how millionaires should live," and to show why, when many once-great American families are half-forgotten, the House of Vanderbilt is remembered.

THE VANDERBILT FAMILY I

Cornelius Vanderbilt
"The Commodore"
1794–1877

1 m. 1813 Sophia Johnson,
his first cousin
1795–1868

2 m. 1869 Frank Armstrong Crawford,
his first cousin twice removed,
circa 1839–1885

Phebe Jane
1815–1878
m. 1833 James Madison
Cross

Ethelinda
1817–1889
m. 1834 Daniel B.
Allen

Elizabeth
1818–1890sp
m. 1849 George A.
Osgood

William Henry
1821–1885
m. 1841 Maria
Louisa Kissam
1821–1896

Chart II

Emily
1823–1896
m. William Knapp
Thorn
1807–1887

Sophia
1825–1912
m. 1849 Daniel
Torrance

Maria Louisa
1828–1896
1 m. 1844 Horace
F. Clark
1815–1873
divorced 1854
2 m. 1860 Robert
J. Niven

Frances
1828–1868
unmarried

Cornelius Jeremiah
1830–1882sp
m. 1855 Ellen
Williams

George
1832–1836

Mary Alicia
1833–1902
1 m. Nicholas Bergasse
La Bau
2 m. 1878 Charles
Francis Berger

Catherine
1836–1887
1 m. 1850 Smith Barker
2 m. 1861 Gustave
LaFitte

George
1839–1863
unmarried

I

The Vanderbilts of Staten Island

PEOPLE NAMED VANDERBILT had lived modestly and inconspicuously around New York City for almost a century and a half before Commodore Cornelius Vanderbilt endowed their name with unimaginable wealth and persistent fame. Although their social rivals liked to sneer at them as upstarts, the Vanderbilts are old American stock, counting ancestors among the early settlers of the Eastern Seaboard and eligible for membership in such aristocratic New York organizations as the St. Nicholas and Holland societies.

The exact date at which the first member of the family emigrated from Holland to the Dutch West India Company's colony of New Netherland is unknown, but it must have been around 1650 because in that year the records begin to mention Jan Aertsen van der Bilt as a landowner in Flatbush, Long Island. With typical seventeenth-century indifference to spelling, the name appears in the contemporary documents as three words or two and indicates the family's origin in the little town of Bildt in Holland.

The Vanderbilts were always a numerous family, and they required much space. They seem, from the scanty records, to have been relatively prosperous as farmers in a sparse and conservative community. The change from Dutch to English rule in 1664 affected them little. They continued to speak Dutch, attend

Cornelius spent much of his childhood with his parents, five sisters, and brother in this modest farmhouse on Bay Street in Stapleton, Staten Island, where his family moved in 1795. The house had only four rooms downstairs; the upper story was a loft with dormer windows. The house had an excellent view of the Narrows leading to Upper New York Bay and Long Island. Cornelius's mother, Phebe Hand, lived in the house until her death in 1854. The house burned down in the late 19th century.

Dutch churches, and marry within the Dutch-speaking group, sometimes their own cousins. In 1715, when Jacob van der Bilt, the grandson of Jan Aertsen, married, his father deeded to him one hundred acres of land near the tiny settlement of New Dorp on Staten Island. There was plenty of room on Staten Island. Although it was the first part of present-day New York seen by a European (Giovanni da Verrazano in 1524), nothing much had happened there since. After two centuries, fewer than a thousand inhabitants were scattered in farms and little villages over the sixty-four square miles of the island.

Jacob and his wife, Neilje (the Dutch version of Elinor), cleared land and made a farm where they brought up eleven children. Like most of their neighbors, the Vanderbilts began to send their farm produce and fish to Manhattan on their own little boats. Not much is recorded of the family except that in the 1740s they became converts to the Moravian Brethren, a German evangelical sect remotely descended from John Huss, the Bohemian Protestant martyr of the early fifteenth century, and were active in building a meetinghouse in the village of New Dorp that was started on July 7, 1763. Fourteen years later, the church was burned during the American Revolution, when there was considerable armed conflict on Staten Island. The Vanderbilts also helped build a boat that was sent to Holland to bring some of their fellow Moravians to America.

By the time of the Revolution, Staten Island positively swarmed with Vanderbilts and their relations by marriage. Like most of the old Dutch families, they slowly began to intermarry with the English, who were moving westward from the English settlements on Long Island. The wife of Jacob Vanderbilt II, for instance, was born Mary Sprague. They were the grandparents of the Commodore. Among their seven children was Cornelius, a farmer who ran an irregular ferry service that took produce and a few passengers across the six miles of New York Bay to the tip of Manhattan Island. He also married a girl of English descent, Phebe (the family's spelling) Hand. She was of a somewhat higher class than the Vanderbilts: both her grandfathers had been clergymen and her uncle Edward a major general in the American forces. Her family, however, had lost its money by patriotically investing in Continental bonds during the Revolution, and at the time of her marriage to Cornelius, she was working as a hired girl on a farm at Port Richmond, Staten Island. Nine children were born to them between 1787 and 1810.

The fourth of this numerous brood, Cornelius, was born on May 27, 1794 at Port Richmond on the Kill van Kull, the narrow body of water that separates Staten Island from New Jersey. His prospects were not brilliant: his father had made no great success of either farming or ferrying, and there were many children. Cornelius (called by his family "Cornele"), who became the eldest son when his brother Jacob died at the age of seventeen, was said to be his mother's favorite. One often hears that story of the childhood of great men, and it is one that especially appealed to sentimental nineteenth-century America. Biographers have rejoiced in this relationship and have supplemented a very thin documentary record with unlikely dialogue between the sainted mother and the ambitious son. What is certain is that throughout her long life—she died only in 1854— Cornelius was a dutiful son and far more considerate to Phebe Vanderbilt than he was to his other relations.

Cornelius made plenty of enemies in his lifetime, and they were not slow to criticize; after he became rich, there were plenty of flatterers. Both gave accounts of his youth that are obviously unreliable, and the story is now so encrusted with mythic additions it is difficult to determine what really happened. The Vanderbilts were not a family given to recording on paper; indeed, earlier generations of the clan failed even to keep up the family Bible. It is clear that Cornelius was actively hostile to formal education, even the modest learning then available on Staten Island. He remained all his life virtually illiterate and even took pride in his lack of letters. He spelled "according to common sense," as he put it; the results were sometimes startling. He is said to have read no book but the Bible; if that is true, he remembered only its sterner lessons. There is more than a suspicion, however, that the canny Cornelius exaggerated his illiteracy and crudeness to disarm his numerous business opponents.

His manners, or lack of them, were noted early. "He was not conciliatory," one early biographer wrote, "and never seemed to care what people thought or said of him. He lacked the affability and suavity which are born of a love of approbation—the desire to please. He was sometimes harsh, abrupt, unceremonious, and even uncivil . . ." Throughout his life he was dour and sarcastic and terrified almost everyone who came into contact with him, not excluding his family.

He was a stalwart worker, even in early youth, proficient at heavy labor, tall and unusually strong; at the age of twelve he was driving teams of horses across Staten Island and helping to load boats. He was broad-shouldered with pink and white skin, dark hair and eyes; through his old age he was regarded as remarkably handsome.

He was obsessed with the sea. Anxious to escape both school and the family farm at the earliest possible age, he wanted to ship out as a sailor but settled on getting his own boat at the age of sixteen. His mother is said to have given him $100, a large sum in 1811, to buy a "piragua." A piragua—the Indian word was also spelled "peraguer" or even "perry auger"—was a clumsy sailboat with a shallow draft that gave boatmen easy access into the marshlands that rimmed part of the Staten Island shore. The $100 is supposed to have been given on the condition that he clear some acres of particularly intractable land on his parents' farm. The story of his mother's promise and his accomplishment of the required feat in record time for his sixteenth birthday, endlessly repeated by Cornelius himself and his sycophants, has assumed cherry-tree dimensions in the Vanderbilt family history. A skillful and strong boatman—and Cornelius was both—could handle a piragua alone and make a good living hauling freight and passengers across New York Bay. Cornelius became known for his skill in poling his boat through the most turbulent waters. He is said to have performed special services during the War of 1812 in transporting American troops to strategic locations when it was believed that the British fleet was about to force its way into New York Bay. The thought of enlisting himself in the American forces apparently never occurred to him; there was money to be made.

The New York City waterfront on which Cornelius spent his young manhood was not a genteel place, but Cornelius, strong and naturally pugnacious, more than held his own among numerous competitors for freight and passengers. Rivalry for business was so great that it often ended in fistfights, which the combative Cornelius usually won. His profanity was positively epic: he blistered the waterfront with his tongue, a gift that remained with him throughout his life. In his old age, when his second and much younger wife surrounded him with clergymen, hoping against all odds for a reformation, the reverend gentlemen were horrified by his ordinary discourse.

At the age of nineteen he married his eighteen-year-old first cousin, Sophia Johnson, daughter of his father's sister, Eleanor, on December 19, 1813. She had been born at Port Richmond, too, and also had numerous brothers and sisters. After very little schooling, she had gone out to work as a hired girl, as had her mother-in-law, Phebe, whom she is said to have resembled. Cornelius and Sophia had no honeymoon, but they did have a wedding party for their many nearby relations. They settled in a little house near the landing where Cornelius docked his piragua. Biographers have pretty much ignored Sophia Johnson Vanderbilt, to whom they ascribe only the conventional virtues—"the charm of her husband's home, the sharer of his anxieties and his labors, acquiescent and patient under the sway of his dominant will and in the presence of his trying moods." To put it more accurately, she was downtrodden and could not call her soul her own. One knowing contemporary remarked coolly, "The fact that she lived harmoniously with such an obstinate man bears strong testimony to her character." She was never his confidant, "the sharer of his anxieties and his labors"; that role was always reserved for Phebe, her son's only counselor.

Cornelius Vanderbilt became known as one of the most reliable boatmen operating in the waters around New York City, and in the second decade of the nineteenth century, he branched out, building schooners that operated on both the East and North (Hudson) rivers, hauling passengers and cargo, fish and fruit that he often peddled himself on shore. He was thrifty, not to say mean, and Sophia practiced the frugality admired in Dutch housewives. The children were brought up the same way.

The wonder of the age, although in its infancy, was the steam-powered boat. It was fashionable to laugh at the huffing and puffing of the little vessels, so lacking in dignity when compared to the quiet and majestic sailing vessels, but Cornelius took them seriously from the time they began to appear in New York waters. The results of his attention were profound, not only on his own fortunes but on the history of transportation in the United States. The steamboats on New York Bay, the Hudson River, and surrounding waters were run by Robert Fulton, their inventor (or, at least, one of their inventors), and his relation Robert R. Livingston. Through the power of the great Livingston clan, they had succeeded in getting New York State to grant them a monopoly of steam navigation on all the waters of the state. This concession, potentially of enormous value, was fiercely contested by rivals, especially Thomas Gibbons of New Jersey, who inaugurated steamer travel (the Union Line) from New York to Philadelphia: from the Battery in Manhattan to New Brunswick at the head of the Raritan River, thence by stage to Trenton and by steamer from Trenton to Philadelphia. Fulton got an injunction against this traffic, countered by other legal movements on the part of Gibbons, including an incredible New Jersey law threatening with state prison any officer of New York State who should arrest any citizen of New Jersey for steamboating in New York waters.

In 1818, the Commodore went to work for Thomas Gibbons, piloting a little steamer with the extraordinary name *Mouse of the Mountain* between the Battery and New Brunswick for the substantial salary of $1,000 a year. He constantly dodged writs brandished by New York officers of the law who tried to prevent his boat from docking in the city. So skillful was he in piloting and dodging writs that Gibbons soon gave him a bigger boat, the *Bellona,* in which Cornelius installed a secret closet where he could take refuge from law officers when the steamer arrived at the Battery.

Cornelius also took over the management of a dilapidated inn at New Brunswick called Bellona Hall, where his passengers broke the trip between Philadelphia and New York. He put the obedient Sophia in charge. With incredible labor she soon made Bellona Hall into one of the best and most profitable inns on the East Coast; the well-patronized bar was a veritable gold mine. In between her duties at the inn, Sophia bore, in the true Vanderbilt tradition of large families, thirteen children—four sons and nine daughters. Despite the hard work and the constant childbearing, Sophia always maintained that her New Brunswick years were the happiest in her life.

Inevitably, a go-ahead young man like Cornelius Vanderbilt would want to work for himself. In 1829, he resigned from Thomas Gibbons's Union Line and moved his family to New York City. He began to build steamboats that he organized into the Dispatch Line. His boats ran up the Hudson to Albany and on Long Island Sound to Norwalk and New Haven, Connecticut, Providence, and Boston. His brother, "Cap'n" Jacob Vanderbilt, was one of the most daring pilots on the sometimes perilous waters. Cornelius himself was known as the "king of Long Island Sound" from the number of his boats—there were eventually more than a hundred—and their runs. He gave good service: the Vanderbilt boats were larger and more comfortable, yet cheaper, than the competitors'. They were also speedier. Cornelius could not bear competition; when another line seemed to have become profitable, he soon drove it out of the water by offering better service at a lower rate.

Travel by steamboat, although more reliable than sailing, was quite dangerous for passengers and crew; there was a mania for speed records, especially on the Hudson between New York City and Albany, and captains were always pushing their vessels, "putting up steam" until the boilers exploded and the vessel burned, often with great loss of life. Sometimes, carried away by the competition, captains burned the cabin furniture in an effort to get more steam. The Vanderbilt boats seemed unusually fortunate, or unusually well run: Cornelius never lost a vessel, which was fortunate since he never insured them! "Good vessels and good captains are the best sort of insurance," he was quoted as

Sophia Johnson Vanderbilt managed Bellona Hall, a tavern in New Brunswick, New Jersey, the terminus of Cornelius's steamship route. In the 1820s it was one of the most popular taverns on the East Coast, and one of the most profitable; Sophia is said to have made more money than her husband at the time by sleeping three guests to a room and serving excellent food and drink. She was well known for providing special services such as heating stones for passengers in the stage to Trenton to warm their feet during cold weather.

OLD UNION LINE, FOR PHILADELPHIA.

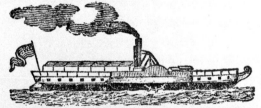

Via New-Brunswick, Princeton, Trenton, & Bristol.

Fare Through, $5.

The Vice-President's Steamboat NAUTILUS will leave New-York every day (Sundays excepted) from Whitehall Wharf,

At 11 o'clock A. M.

for Staten-Island. From her the passengers will be received without delay into the superior fast sailing Steamboat BELLONA, Capt. Vanderbelt, for Brunswick; from thence in Post Chaises to Trenton, where they lodge, and arrive next morning at 10 o'clock in Philadelphia with the commodious and fast sailing Steamboat PHILADELPHIA, Capt. Jenkins, in time to take the Old Union Line Baltimore Steamboat, which leaves at 12 o'clock every day.

For seats, apply at No. 145 Broadway; No. 5 Courtlandt-st. 2d office from Broadway; at the Steamboat Hotel, corner of Washington and Marketfield-sts; at Messrs. J. & C. Seguine's, Whitehall; or Capt. De Forest, on board Steamboat Nautilus.

N. B. This line arrives in Brunswick three quarters of an hour before the Olive Branch Line.

JAMES GUYON, jun. } Proprietors,
CALEB T. WARD, } New-York.
ROBERT LETSON, New-Brunswick.
JOHN JOLINE, } Princeton.
JOS. B. GROVER, } Princeton.
JOSEPH I. THOMPSON, } Philadelphia.
DAVID BRENTON, } Philadelphia.
WM B. JAQUES, *Agent for Proprietors.*
. All goods and baggage at the owners' risk.

Cornelius's first large vessel was the *Bellona,* a "sailing steamboat" (meaning that it had sails in case, as often happened, the steam failed) running from Staten Island to New Brunswick. On the same line was the *Nautilus,* owned by Daniel Tompkins, then Vice President of the United States, and piloted by Captain John De Forest, who was Cornelius's brother-in-law.

Determined to own the fastest and most luxurious vessel in the waters around New York, the Commodore personally designed and supervised the construction of the *Cornelius Vanderbilt*. Wheaton J. Lane, the Commodore's best biographer, says, "The vessel was a monster, over a thousand tons, and could reach a top speed of twenty-five miles an hour; with rosewood furniture, the appointments were considered the last word in luxury. The Commodore proudly enrolled her at the Custom House with himself as both owner and master." In 1847, she was portrayed proudly cruising the Hudson by the marine artists James and John Bard.

James and John Bard. *Cornelius Vanderbilt.* c. 1847. Oil on academy board, 31½ × 47¾". Shelburne Museum

saying. "If corporations can make money out of insurance, so can I." The liveliest and most cutthroat competition on the Hudson route came from Daniel Drew, who was owner and part-owner of many steamboats on the river and who was for forty years alternately Cornelius's friend, enemy, competitor, persecutor, and victim.

Between 1829 and 1850, Cornelius made a great deal of money: $30,000 a year between 1829 and 1836, it was calculated, and twice that annually after 1836. Keeping tab on the incomes of rich men was just as popular a sport then as it is now. One of the best-informed observers was Moses Yale Beach, owner of the New York *Sun* and one of the founders of the Associated Press. He figured that in 1835, when Cornelius had reached the age of forty-one, he was worth half a million dollars, which put him in the ranks of New York City's richest men. About that time, he began to be referred to as "the Commodore"—simply an honorary title, a tribute to his nautical skills.

The Commodore's wealth was not reflected in his daily

life. In New York City the family lived first on Stone Street near the Battery in a cramped tenement, then they moved to a small house on East Broadway. It must have been equally crowded with so many children, but it was close to the Commodore's business at the Battery.

Ancestral Staten Island called to the Commodore, possibly because Phebe, a widow since 1832, still lived there (the elder Cornelius, totally overshadowed by his son, had faded out of life without much comment by anybody). He built a house on the family farm halfway between Stapleton and Tompkinsville. His relations clustered around him. In early middle age, he was already the patriarch. His children were growing up and marrying. He and Sophia became grandparents for the first time in 1834 at the ages of forty and thirty-nine, respectively, when Cornelius Vanderbilt Cross, eldest child of their eldest daughter, Phebe Jane, was born. The Commodore had given jobs to many of his brothers and nephews, not to speak of the sons-in-law that were beginning to join the family.

The presence of numerous family did not indicate any warm domesticity. The Commodore's stern attitude toward his wife and offspring was well known at the time; he made no secret of it. The Commodore, a contemporary said, "was not only the incumbent of the throne, but the power behind it also. He ruled home, wife, and children with a rod of steel and brooked no disobedience or even contradiction. He manifested scant affection for his children, seldom sought their love or confidence, and treated them very nearly like anybody else's."

Cornelius Jeremiah, the ninth child and second son, was his father's despair. He was tall and cadaverously thin with a scrabbly blond beard, and he suffered from epilepsy. Quite early in his life he became addicted to the fleshpots, especially gambling. The Commodore, who regretted out loud that he had given this son his own name, denounced him as a weakling and told all and sundry that Cornelius would inherit none of his money. In 1849, Cornelius Jeremiah (known as "Corneel" to his mother, his only defender in the family) ran away to the California goldfields. He stayed there only a short time and on his return was arrested by order of his father and confined for a time to the Bloomingdale Asylum for the Insane, which then stood on Broadway between 117th and 119th streets. When he was released, on the appeal of

In the 1830s Cornelius built an imposing house on the old family farm in an area called The Clove. Other Vanderbilts gathered around the leading member of the family: his brother, the Van Duzers (his sister Elinor Jane and her husband), his daughters, Mary Alicia La Bau and Ethelinda Allen, and their husbands and children, and a cousin, John King Vanderbilt, ancestor of the 20th-century writer on etiquette, Amy Vanderbilt. The house, with its imposing portico and Corinthian columns, is still standing on Clove Road.

his brother William Henry, he took to gambling again. He was almost continually in bad health and sometimes fell into a fit at a gambling table, which only momentarily interrupted his playing; he picked up the cards as soon as the fit passed. His father gave him an allowance on the understanding that he would stay away from him, but it was never enough for the spendthrift. So he borrowed. He had a positive talent for borrowing money; one of his main supporters was Horace Greeley, the eccentric and soft-hearted editor of the New York *Tribune.* In 1855, Cornelius Jeremiah married Ellen Williams of Hartford. She was from a respectable and well-to-do family and was one of the few people who was not afraid of the Commodore; she stood up to him and got additional funds for her husband. She died without children in 1872. Cornelius Jeremiah survived his father and the fleshpots to precipitate one of the greatest scandals in the Vanderbilts' history.

The eldest son was William Henry, named after his father's hero, William Henry Harrison, the ninth president. Unlike his tall and handsome father, he was short and heavy, and also unlike him he was neither combative nor short-tempered. The Commodore found him only slightly more satisfactory than Cornelius Jeremiah, although he was dutiful to the point of self-

24

During the years that William Henry farmed on Staten Island, he and his family lived in a modest house five miles from Stapleton. In 1855, when he was reported to be earning the substantial annual income of $12,000 from his farming, William Henry enlarged his house and "Italianized" it by adding a tower.

effacement. He had evidently decided that a totally passive attitude toward his parent was the only way to coexist with him. He gave up smoking, for example, because his father declared it was a bad habit, although the Commodore himself smoked strong cigars. The result was that the Commodore, a hard man to please if ever there was one, thought him a milksop.

William Henry attended the Columbia Grammar School, which was attached to the college—he went no further in education—and for a time worked for Daniel Drew's brokerage house (Drew and the Commodore were temporarily friends at the time). Like his father and most males in his family, he married young. He was only twenty when he was united to Maria Louisa Kissam, daughter of a pastor of the Reformed Dutch Church and descended from a family of English origin that had been in New York State for six generations. They set up housekeeping, modestly, in lower Manhattan.

William Henry was a plodder, a diligent man who moved slowly and carefully and spared himself no labor. Unlike his father, he was a paper shuffler, writing innumerable business letters himself. His health broke down from this industry in 1842, much to the disgust of his father, who was never ill, and he was exiled to Staten Island by his unsympathetic parent. He and Maria Louisa, who were starting their own large family—nine children, five sons and four daughters, born between 1843 and 1862—took up residence in a two-story house facing the sea five miles from Stapleton. Their circumstances were modest, considering that his father was one of the richest men in the nation. They stayed there until 1864. William Henry was considered a "gentleman farmer," but like his father, he worked his employees hard and watched expenses. He raised and sold hay, potatoes, and oats. The soil of Staten Island was thin and poor, being mainly sandy loam. It required a lot of fertilizer, and there was an ample supply in Manhattan, where an estimated 30,000 horses were kept. William Henry got his from the stables on Fourth Avenue, which housed the horsecars that plied the city streets. After the Commodore became interested in horse railways, he made a deal with William Henry for the purchase of fertilizer from his street railways in which both sides behaved strictly as businessmen. William Henry is said to have got the better of the Commodore over this deal, which may have given the Commodore new respect for his child.

About the same time William Henry became interested in the Staten Island Railroad. It wasn't much of a line, running only thirteen miles on the eastern side of the island and limping along "without money, without credit, without materials, without organization," as W. A. Croffut, an early biographer of the Commodore and William Henry, wrote. But William Henry, by a close attention to detail and by cutting expenses and connecting the little road with a line of ferryboats running directly to Manhattan, made it profitable, impressing even his cantankerous father. It was about this time that the Commodore decided there was something in William Henry, after all. About this time, too, the Commodore must have begun planning the future of the fortune he was amassing.

That fortune was now growing by leaps and bounds. When the discovery of gold in California was announced, the Commodore immediately saw a great opportunity for his line of steamships. Most goldseekers reached California by crossing the Central American isthmus to avoid the perilous and lengthy trip around Cape Horn. For the first time since his mother had given him the famous $100 for his piragua, he was seeking investors in an enterprise. He went to England—his first trip abroad—and spoke to the great banking houses of Rothschild and Baring, but they would not invest without a firsthand report on the possibilities of the route. The Commodore decided to go it alone. In 1850, he sailed his ship, the *Prometheus*—said to be the first steamship owned by an individual—to Nicaragua as the first move in setting up his own Central American route. He was so secretive about this new venture that he didn't even inform his wife that he was going, a telling glimpse into the Vanderbilt marriage. After three weeks of frantic inquiry, Sophia heard of his whereabouts via the mail from Panama.

During that brief period, he had established a new business, transportation across the isthmus for mail and passengers that would add more than $1 million a year to his fortune for the next few years. The route lay by Vanderbilt steamship—nine days—from New York to Greytown (the locals called it San Juan del Norte), Nicaragua, thence by steamboat up a narrow and rock-strewn river to the point where passage became impossible, then by portage to Lake Nicaragua, where another Vanderbilt vessel transported the passengers across the lake to the head of another river down which a Vanderbilt steamboat took them to the Pacific coast of Central America. There they were picked up by a Vanderbilt steamship and taken up the coast to California. Many observers said that the way upriver from Greytown was unnavigable, but the Commodore proved them wrong by piloting the first boat up the river from the Atlantic. Prosperity and middle age had robbed him of none of his skills as a boatman. The Accessory Transit Company, with the Commodore as president, was soon chartered by the Nicaraguan government. Vanderbilt ships, "The New and Independent Line for California via Nicaragua," began to sail on July 3, 1851.

The line hauled thousands of goldseekers across the isthmus and on to California at a cost of $150 first class, $45 steerage. Westbound, the ships usually carried five or six hundred passengers, eastbound, considerably fewer. Some terrible marine disasters occurred, the first in the Commodore's career: one ship making its way up the coast of Baja California went down with the loss of 176 lives. And not a few travelers died of fevers in the notoriously unhealthy climate of Central America.

Believing that the traffic across Central America was beginning to thin in the fourth year of the rush, the Commodore sold his shares in the Accessory Transit at enormous profit in 1853. At that time, he said publicly that he had a fortune of more than $11 million, "invested better than any other eleven millions in the U.S.," earning more than 25 percent a year. The Commodore had become a very rich man at a time when total assets of $100,000 guaranteed one a place on the list of the great American capitalists.

He decided, uncharacteristically, to give himself and his family a vacation in Europe. To do so, he had built the *North Star,* an oceangoing steam yacht, at that time the largest ever built for a private person—2,500 tons. Accommodations were magnificent: leading off the grand salon were the family staterooms, each decorated in a different color combination, green and gold or crimson and gold, for example. Berths were fitted with silk lambrequins and hung with heavy lace curtains. Each cabin was steam heated. The traveling party consisted of the Commodore and Sophia, two sons—the disgraced Cornelius Jeremiah was left behind, as might have been expected—eight Vanderbilt daughters (one, Frances, was an invalid and remained in New York) and their husbands. One imagines that these last were given no choice about going. There were other relatives and friends, a doctor, and other attendants. A Baptist minister from Newport served as

The steam yacht *North Star* was built to Commodore Vanderbilt's orders expressly to convey his family—23 people in all—to Europe in style. The furnishings were sumptuous: in the saloon were two rosewood sofas upholstered in green-figured plush that cost a then astonishing $350 each. The dining room was faced with marble, the ceiling ornamented with portrait medallions of the Commodore's heroes, including Henry Clay and Daniel Webster. The two-month trip was reported to have cost half a million dollars!

chaplain—"The Commodore did the swearing and I did the praying," he said cheerfully.

The trip almost didn't start at all; an hour before sailing time the firemen struck for higher wages. The Commodore met this challenge with his customary resolution: he refused to discuss the matter with the strikers and simply hired new firemen; he steamed away almost on schedule on May 20, 1853. As the *North Star,* the Commodore at the helm, passed through the Narrows opposite the home of Phebe Vanderbilt on Staten Island, guns were fired and rockets let off to salute the Commodore's mother.

Southampton was reached in ten days, a phenomenally fast Atlantic crossing for the time, especially in a new ship. The British didn't quite know what to make of the yacht or the Commodore. "An American merchant has just arrived in London on a pleasure trip," wrote a puzzled reporter for the London *Daily News.* "He has come by train from Southampton and left his private yacht behind him in dock at that port. This yacht is a monster steamer. Her saloon is described as larger and more magnificent than that of any ocean steamer afloat and is said to surpass in splendor the Queen's yacht . . ." The Vanderbilt party was invited to a soiree at the Lord Mayor of London's Mansion House. They went, but the Commodore refused to make a speech, as he always refused to speak in public. The Lord Mayor and the merchants of Southampton gave a dinner for two hundred, and the Commodore offered hospitality aboard the yacht to five hundred curious visitors.

The *North Star* then sailed off to Copenhagen and St. Petersburg, where the Grand Duke Constantine, an admiral in the Russian Navy, came aboard. This was the first contact between a Vanderbilt and European royalty, who in time would treat the family almost as equals. Then they sailed to Le Havre and Paris for nineteen days of sightseeing, then through the Strait of Gibraltar to the Mediterranean. They visited various Italian cities, including Florence, where the Commodore sat to the expatriate American sculptor Hiram Powers for his portrait in marble, and Sophia was painted by Joel Tanner Hart. Then the party traveled to Constantinople and returned to America, stopping briefly in Madeira. Phebe was saluted again on the return from the trip, which had covered 15,024 miles in fifty-eight days.

When he returned to business, the Commodore engaged

One of the Commodore's few failures as a steamship owner was on the transatlantic run. In 1856, he put into service the *Vanderbilt* between New York and Southampton and Le Havre. Built at a cost of over $500,000, the ship was hailed as "the largest vessel that has ever floated on the Atlantic Ocean." Passengers were unhappy, however, about the facilities and service on the giant. An irate traveler wrote to the New York *Tribune,* "I am told that Mr. Vanderbilt is his own ship's architect. If so, I think that he would be effectually cured of his vanity, or his parsimony, by taking a first class passage in the fore saloon of his own ship . . ." At the beginning of the Civil War the Commodore got the ship off his hands by donating it to the Union. The *Vanderbilt* survived the war and for decades was used to haul coal; she was finally scrapped in 1929.

LE VANDERBILT, PAQUEBOT DU HAVRE A NEW-YORK.
5268 Tonneaux, force de 2500 Chevaux.

in a vigorous quarrel with the Accessory Transit Company, which, he claimed, had not lived up to the terms of the contract by which he sold his controlling interest. He did not sue them but took more Vanderbiltian measures. He is supposed to have told his adversaries, "The law is too slow. I will ruin you." In the event, he did: he put another fleet of steamers on the Nicaragua route, and in two years the opposition line was hopelessly bankrupt.

In 1857, the Commodore's Nicaragua overland transportation properties were seized by William Walker, an American filibuster who, with a small military force, had made himself president of Nicaragua. The Commodore sent agents to the other Central American countries and organized an effort to oust Walker, who surrendered himself on May 1, 1857 to a United States Navy officer in order to escape capture by the infuriated Nicaraguans. In 1858, the Commodore sold his New York-to-California shipping line to rivals who operated it via Panama — the future route of the Panama Canal. He had made $20 million from his Central American ventures, partly from the revenues of his company, partly from manipulating the company's stock.

At sixty-three the Commodore was set in his habits. He and Sophia lived in a narrow townhouse at 10 Washington Place between Washington Square and Sixth Avenue. Sophia had not wanted to move back to Manhattan; she preferred the bucolic atmosphere of Staten Island. The Commodore changed her mind by sending her to the Bloomingdale Asylum, which he appears to have regarded as the solution to all family problems. She had been rescued by Phebe, in one of the last actions of her life. Phebe died in 1854 and was buried in the Moravian Cemetery on Staten Island.

Neither Cornelius nor Sophia, despite their wealth, had any social ambitions at all. "Society" in New York City then consisted of the descendants of the old Dutch families into which the Astors and a few other later arrivals had gradually mixed. It was an extremely conservative society, content with its inherited fortunes made in real estate and the professions, living comfortably but quietly and uninterested in increasing its wealth, espe-

When the Commodore and Sophia moved to 10 Washington Place, west of Washington Square, in 1846, the neighborhood was only just becoming fashionable; it was still considered rather "too far uptown." The Commodore was himself indifferent to such considerations, but he lived to see the square, formerly a potter's field and later a parade ground, become the center of the most desirable residential area in New York City. In his later years, his office was behind the house on West 4th Street and his beloved trotting horses were stabled nearby.

CORNELIUS VANDERBILT, ESQ.—[FROM A PHOTOGRAPH BY BRADY.]

At the time of the Civil War, the Commodore, like so many notable Americans of the time, had himself photographed by Mathew Brady at his large "photographic gallery" at Broadway and 10th Street. The photograph was the basis of many prints and engravings of the Commodore for years to come.

cially by such methods as the Commodore's. Although the Vanderbilts were of the oldest Dutch stock themselves, this society might as well have existed on another planet so far as the Commodore and Sophia were concerned.

The Commodore despised office routine and spent very little time in the modest office space that his enterprises occupied. From 1838 to 1842 his office was at 39 Peck Slip, right at the shipping docks. After moving several times, he finally put his office at 2 West Fourth Street, which was at the rear of his town house. He hardly ever wrote letters and kept most of his business in his head. His signature on documents (always "C. Van Derbilt") rarely appeared on anything but the necessary stock certificates. He usually had only one clerk. Daniel Allen, husband of his daughter Ethelinda, was in charge of daily operations. Another son-in-law, Horace F. Clark, husband of Maria Louisa and a member of the New York bar, took care of legal business.

After glancing at the newspapers at home, the Commodore went to his office at ten or eleven o'clock in the morning, gave a few orders, bullied William Henry and his sons-in-law, and soon departed. Riches had not improved the Commodore's literacy: in one letter he asked the friend of a deceased associate "to com down and sea the widow." Nor had riches caused him to forgo his frugality: when he was making out stock certificates, he would always lump as many shares as possible together in order to save the twenty-five-cent Internal Revenue tax on each certificate.

After his office work was done, he enjoyed his principal relaxation of the day. His great weakness had always been for horses. He took a drive every afternoon, always handling the reins himself and refreshing himself occasionally with an odd combination of gin and sugar. He drove his pair of trotters Plow Boy and Mate up Fifth Avenue, then over to the Bloomingdale Road (now upper Broadway) almost to the end of Manhattan Island, and then back to Washington Place.

In 1863, he and Sophia celebrated their fiftieth wedding anniversary surrounded by no fewer than 140 descendants and relations to various degrees. The Commodore gave Sophia a little golden steamboat with musical works instead of an engine. As he entered old age, the Commodore might have been supposed to be a contented man, yet the energy and intelligence and toughness that had brought him from a hardscrabble farm on Staten Island to the position as one of the richest men in America soon carried him into an entirely new enterprise—one in which he would multiply his fortune tenfold and found one of the greatest businesses in American history and a dynasty. In the last fourteen years of his life Cornelius Vanderbilt would astonish his contemporaries by becoming the railroad king of the United States.

The Commodore's affection for fine trotting horses was well known in New York. Currier and Ives portrayed him and his rival, the newspaper owner Robert Bonner, in the forefront of *Fast Trotters on Harlem Lane*. A reporter for the New York *Herald* exclaimed, "What fine looking man is that with a segar in his mouth, who is passing all those roadsters on the right? He dashes past everybody but Bonner. His bays must be well trained; he handles the ribbons as though he was used to it. That gentleman with a white cravat you mean? Yes, sir. That is Commodore Vanderbilt. . . ."

The Commodore was honored by having trotters named for him. Currier and Ives depicted *The Celebrated Stallions George Wilkes and Commodore Vanderbilt* trotting in a "dead heat match" at the Union Course on Long Island on November 6, 1865.

FAST TROTTERS ON HARLEM LANE N.Y.

THE CELEBRATED STALLIONS GEORGE WILKES, AND COMMODORE VANDERBILT.
TROTTING "A DEAD HEAT" IN THEIR MATCH TO WAGONS.— MILE HEATS, BEST 3 IN 5.
OVER THE UNION COURSE, L. I. NOV. 6TH 1865.

JOHN CROOKS ENTERED BR. S. GEORGE WILKES   1, 2, 0, 1.
D. MACE   ENTERED B. S. COMMODORE VANDERBILT   2, 1, 0, DIST.
Time, 2:34½ 2:30 2:29½ 2:31½

THE VANDERBILT FAMILY II

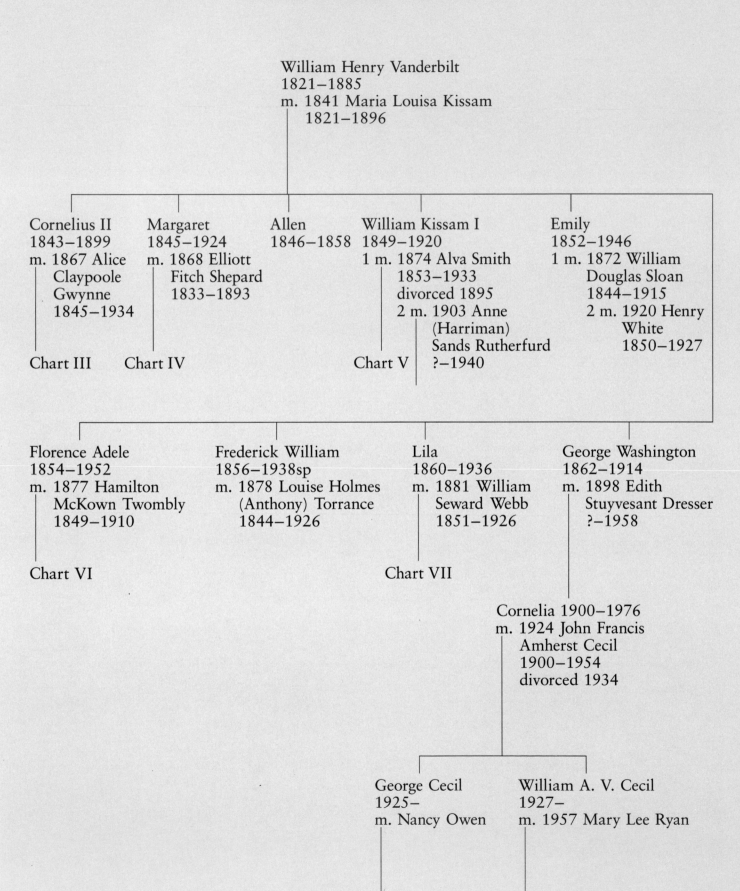

William Henry Vanderbilt
1821–1885
m. 1841 Maria Louisa Kissam
1821–1896

Cornelius II
1843–1899
m. 1867 Alice
Claypoole
Gwynne
1845–1934

Chart III

Margaret
1845–1924
m. 1868 Elliott
Fitch Shepard
1833–1893

Chart IV

Allen
1846–1858

William Kissam I
1849–1920
1 m. 1874 Alva Smith
1853–1933
divorced 1895
2 m. 1903 Anne
(Harriman)
Sands Rutherfurd
?–1940

Chart V

Emily
1852–1946
1 m. 1872 William
Douglas Sloan
1844–1915
2 m. 1920 Henry
White
1850–1927

Florence Adele
1854–1952
m. 1877 Hamilton
McKown Twombly
1849–1910

Chart VI

Frederick William
1856–1938sp
m. 1878 Louise Holmes
(Anthony) Torrance
1844–1926

Lila
1860–1936
m. 1881 William
Seward Webb
1851–1926

Chart VII

George Washington
1862–1914
m. 1898 Edith
Stuyvesant Dresser
?–1958

Cornelia 1900–1976
m. 1924 John Francis
Amherst Cecil
1900–1954
divorced 1934

George Cecil
1925–
m. Nancy Owen

William A. V. Cecil
1927–
m. 1957 Mary Lee Ryan

II

The Wealthiest Man in America

THE COMMODORE didn't acquire his naval title, honorary though it was, undeservedly. For the first fifty years of his career he sailed boats, built boats, and made millions from boats. Transportation by water absorbed most of his energies from the early days of his island youth. But by the 1860s the land-going steam railroads were obviously the future of transport for both freight and passengers. By 1860, some 30,000 miles of railroad track had been laid in the United States; every year more travelers chose the railroad over the steamboat or horse-drawn vehicles. For years the Commodore seemed to be ignoring this change. He positively disliked railroads, which he referred to in his uncouth way as "them things that go on land." Naturally, a man who loved horses and had made his money from boats would regard trains suspiciously. He had good personal reasons, too. His first trip on a railroad, made in New Jersey, on the Camden and Amboy in October 1833, ended in a wreck in which he sustained quite serious injury to his ribs, one of which punctured his lung and nearly killed him. He entered railroading indirectly and hesitantly. He owned steamboats operating on Long Island Sound and on the New Jersey coast and became an investor in the little railroads that connected with his steamers: the Stonington Line, the Central of New Jersey, and the Hartford and New Haven.

When he sold out his Central American steamship lines after having drained them of the last possible penny, he had an immense capital sum to invest. Cannily, he began buying stock in the railroads, particularly those entering New York City. His railroading activities differed greatly from his steamboating. In the waters, he was a builder, laying out routes, specifying what boats should be built, hiring captains, and often, even in late middle age, piloting them himself. On land, he was an investor and a consolidator. He bought stock in railroads that were already operating, often joining them to other lines in which he had a financial stake, improving service—if it profited him to do so, otherwise not—and, of course, doing his ruthless best to bankrupt his competition. But his great profits came not from the revenues of the railroads he gradually acquired but from speculation, actually manipulation, of their shares. The Commodore was one of the most successful stock operators in American history.

In his railroad speculations the Commodore often availed himself of the skillful but unreliable services of Daniel Drew. They were old opponents, Drew having been in the steamboat business in competition with the Commodore as far back as the Hudson River rate wars during the 1830s. He was a former cattle drover and tavern keeper who speculated in the stock of steamboats and trains. Drew was universally known as "Uncle Dan'l" in the small world of high finance in New York, but not from any kindly avuncular affection; on the contrary, he was universally distrusted and despised. He was as ruthless and flinty as the Commodore but much more unscrupulous, and where the Commodore was creative, with a coherent vision—building a lasting transportation empire—Drew saw no further than a quick profit. In all his stock operations he was naturally destructive. He delighted in selling a stock short, in watering, in depreciating; contemporaries said he was "the touch of death to companies." In any market he was always a bear, undermining while apparently encouraging and without the least scruple betraying partners and friends. He prided himself on his secretiveness—"It's the still hog that eats the most," he said.

"Uncle Dan'l" was even less literate than the Commodore and used to tell his brokers "gimme them sheers" when he wanted his stock certificates. Unlike the Commodore, who never disguised his origins or put on sanctimonious airs, Drew was a hypocrite, praying and psalm singing and wringing his hands over the wickedness of the world. A good Methodist, by his own lights at least, he founded a theological school that still exists as Drew University in Madison, New Jersey, although typically he defaulted on part of the endowment. He was cunning but not wise, a bold player but a poor loser and unacquainted with probity or loyalty. It was a bold man who took Drew either as an ally or an enemy, but Commodore Vanderbilt *was* a bold man and knew him as both.

Drew was slovenly and in the days of his greatest prosperity dressed like a cattle drover, carrying an old broken umbrella instead of the gold-headed cane that most prosperous gentlemen then sported. At the time when he entered the market for railroad shares with the Commodore, he was very prosperous himself, mainly through manipulation of stock in the Erie Railroad, a major but perennially mismanaged carrier into New York, which under the ministrations of Drew sometimes fluctuated 20 or 30 percent in a day. In the 1860s, Drew was said to command more cash than any other individual in the country, having at his disposal the almost unbelievable sum of $13 million. Such was the Commodore's business partner when he went into railroading.

In the late 1850s, the bonds and stock of the New York and Harlem (then usually spelled Haarlem) Railroad were selling sluggishly, and the Commodore picked up a few shares at bargain prices. In May 1857 he bought 1,001 shares, which surprisingly gave him a major interest. The New York and Harlem had been the first railroad to enter New York City, its tracks running from 23rd Street, then far uptown, along Fourth Avenue to 125th Street, in 1832. The first trains were drawn by horses. A steam locomotive was put into service in 1834 but promptly exploded, and the Harlem was required by the alarmed local authorities to use horses to draw the cars below 32nd Street until 1876; elsewhere the road turned permanently to steam power for its trains in 1837.

New York City at the time, as so often in its history, was in the grip of bad government. Respectable citizens tended to avoid contact with the city's politicians. "The majority of office holders of the great city are men whom a reputable citizen would not ask into his house," wrote a contemporary, "the better class of New

Yorkers have a holy horror of politics and all things pertaining thereunto." That category did not include the Commodore and Daniel Drew. On April 21, 1863, it was discovered that the New York City Common Council had given the New York and Harlem a perpetual franchise for a street railway on Broadway from the Battery to Union Square, a concession of immense potential value. The Commodore began buying stock in the road again, driving it up from $9 a share to $50. The councilmen sold short, assuming that the price would fall and intending to help the process by canceling the franchise. But Vanderbilt kept buying, pushing the stock up to $170. The short-sellers' contracts came due, and they had to pay $179 a share to fulfill them. By that time the Commodore and his partners, including Daniel Drew, owned most of the stock. The pathetic cries of the fleeced moved not the Commodore, who merely smiled grimly. Daniel Drew said, "He who sells what isn't his'n, must pay up or go to prison."

After the "Harlem corner," Wall Street respected the Commodore. He was still not a railroad man; he was an expert manipulator of railroad stock. The Commodore's Wall Street operations succeeded in part because most of the shares quoted on the New York Stock Exchange then were in the railroads; there were very few other publicly traded companies. If you speculated, you most likely speculated in the railroads. Vanderbilt and Drew could be successful, too, because of the rapid increase in rail traffic and profits. In other words, although railroad stock was oversold and watered, revenues usually justified the price before long. By 1869, the various railroads serving metropolitan New York City operated a total of 480 regularly scheduled trains on a weekday, carrying about 50,000 passengers into the city.

The next railroad ripe for picking was the New York and Hudson, which had been authorized by New York City in 1847, and which by 1851 was operating from Canal Street to East Albany. It entered the city on the west side with a depot for passengers at West 30th Street and Eleventh Avenue. All cars were drawn by horses below 30th Street until 1867; stops were made at 23rd, 14th, and Christopher streets. Despite what seemed to be its advantageous position along the Hudson, the railroad did not turn a profit until 1865 because many passengers still preferred to travel to Albany and the other Hudson River towns by the faster—and cleaner—steamboats.

The faithless Daniel Drew, although he had made millions with the Commodore in the "Harlem corner," now betrayed him over the New York and Hudson. He was constitutionally a Judas. In 1864, he and various members of the New York State Legislature, which set railroad routes and rates, began to sell the New York and Hudson short. The legislators planned to appear to pass a bill for the consolidation of the New York and Hudson and the New York and Harlem, then defeat it at the last moment, driving the stock down. They would then meet their calls at a cheaper price and great profit. But the Commodore, with his almost unlimited funds, promptly bought up all the New York and Hudson shares on the market plus another 27,000 shares that Drew issued, more or less illegally. When Drew and the Albany legislators could not deliver the stock they had sold short, there was chaos. The Commodore kindly sold them stock at $285 a share so they could deliver. He only settled for that sum when he was told piteously that every brokerage house on Wall Street would fail if he put the price any higher. By 1867, the Commodore owned 18,000,000 shares out of a total of 28,500,000 in the New York and Hudson. He was president of the line; his son William Henry, his son-in-law Horace Clark, a faithful henchman of the old man in all his railroad dealings, and William A. Kissam, an in-law of William Henry, became directors; another son-in-law, Daniel Torrance, husband of Sophia Vanderbilt, became a vice president. The Commodore permitted himself a small gloating: "We busted the whole legislature," he said, "and scores of the honorable members had to go home without paying their board bills."

For all his piracy in acquiring control of the New York and Hudson, once he had it, the Commodore set to work to improve the line. He issued much additional stock, which could only be called watered, but he improved service and managed to keep the dividend at 8 percent annually. He was able to do this largely because of the expansion of traffic and because the New York and Hudson was an important freight railroad; in fact, in 1851, the line was the first to deliver freight into New York City. The line had excellent rolling stock. In 1868, Webster Wagner's new sleeping and parlor cars began operating on the line; the first private car, said to be the first in the country, was owned by Daniel Torrance. It was inelegantly named the Shoo-Fly.

The next railroad to fall into the Commodore's hands was the one with which the Vanderbilts were to be most closely associated in the public mind, the New York Central. The Central was born in 1853 when fourteen little railroads operating in central and upstate New York were amalgamated. The result was a rather wobbly corporation that consisted mainly of debt or, as it was then jocularly called, "vapor." Although it had few assets and thin traffic, the Central's total capital obligation was no less than $89,503,840. Cynics calculated that the average watering of stock per mile on the Central between New York City and Buffalo was $110,145. But the Central had a route into New York City, and that was its attraction for the Commodore. His grand plan was beginning to emerge: the control of all the railroads entering America's greatest port city.

The Commodore's way of getting hold of the Central, although quick and effective, was not attractive to the public. Contemporaries, in fact, found it outrageous. The Central connected with Vanderbilt's Hudson Railroad at Albany, and the Commodore determined to show the public that if he were not permitted to acquire the Central, passengers would suffer. In January 1867, during a particularly brutal cold spell, the Commodore served notice that his Hudson Railroad would carry passengers and freight only to its terminus, East Albany, half a mile short of the Hudson and a mile short of any connection with the Central on the far bank. Passengers were left to make the connection by wading through snowdrifts with their baggage. Pathetic stories appeared in the press about passengers with small children struggling in blizzard conditions to board their train. The New York State Legislature, generally at the beck and call of the railroad magnates, having been well bribed to be obedient, was forced by public outcry to hold hearings on the situation. The Commodore had to appear. He spoke to the legislators in his most insolent manner:

He was asked why he had ordered his trains stopped half a mile from the river.

"I was not there, gentlemen," the Commodore replied.

"But what did you do when you heard of it?"

"I did not do anything."

"Why not? Where were you?"

"I was at home, gentlemen, playing a rubber of whist, and

I never allow anything to interfere with me when I am playing that game. It requires, as you know, undivided attention."

His scheme worked; the Commodore got the New York Central despite public indignation and legislative investigation. In 1869, he merged it with the New York and Hudson, after, of course, inflating the Central stock, issuing no less than 80 percent more. The stock of the joint company was then inflated again, and the 8 percent dividend paid for by issuing still more stock. By these moves the Commodore vastly increased his own wealth. Traffic grew steadily: in 1870, the New York Central carried over seven million passengers and over a million tons of freight into New York City.

The Commodore was certainly not loved, but his vast operations were beginning to command respect and to develop around him a mystique of infallible judgment and the golden touch. Even Charles Francis Adams of Massachusetts, who had his full share of the carping attitude common to his distinguished family, wrote with reluctant respect, "It is impossible to regard Vanderbilt's methods or aims without recognizing the magnitude of the man's ideas and conceding his abilities. He voluntarily excites feelings of admiration for himself and alarm for the public. His ambition is a great one. It seems to be nothing less than to make himself master in his own right of the great channels of communications which connect the city of New York with the continent and to control them as his private property."

The Commodore needed one more line to complete his mastery of access to New York: the Erie Railroad, which ran down the west bank of the Hudson into the city. He decided to go into the stock market and acquire control by buying all the stock necessary. In this grandiose scheme his ally again was Daniel Drew; they had made up their differences over the New York and Hudson corner. The Commodore had the satisfaction of knowing that Drew had paid dearly for his betrayal. Drew, however, was again faithless: while apparently acting for the Commodore, he was, as treasurer of the Erie Railroad, quietly issuing more stock and distributing it among his brokers so that every time the Commodore thought he had bought up all that was available and had control new certificates appeared.

Then ensued the great "Erie Railroad War," one of the most famous battles for control ever waged over an American corporation. Before he discovered that he had been tricked, the Commodore had bought no fewer than 50,000 shares of the Drew stock at a cost of millions of dollars. Erie Railroad dropped from $83 to $71 a share. The Commodore had many friends in the New York judiciary, notably Judge George G. Barnard, who was also a good friend of the Tweed Ring, which was then looting the city's treasury. He issued at the Commodore's behest various injunctions against the management of the Erie. Daniel Drew and his chief cohort, Jim Fisk, an unmitigated rascal, too, fled to Jersey City out of reach of New York injunctions and holed up in a well-guarded hotel. They were said to have carried $7 million of the Commodore's funds in their bags, representing his purchase of over 100,000 shares.

The Erie had its own favored judges, and they also issued writs and injunctions. The skies over Wall Street rained legal instruments; no sooner would one side get an injunction than the other would counter. The Erie litigation fell into such a hopeless tangle that even the lawyers—who were drawing thousands of dollars in fees—were confused. At this point, Drew, not for the first time, betrayed his associates by crossing stealthily to Manhattan on a Sunday—the only day when he could visit New York without fear of being arrested—and making his peace with the Commodore by selling out Jim Fisk and his other associates, among them the young Jay Gould, already noted even in these circles for his appalling lack of business ethics. In an extremely complicated arrangement, the Commodore was recompensed by the unfortunate Erie shareholders for most of his losses. He was relieved of the 50,000 doubtful shares of Erie at a price of $3.5 million. He also received compensation for his losses and legal expenses amounting to $1 million. He unloaded the remainder of his Erie stock. The whole battle cost him between $1 million and $2 million, the only major setback he had ever sustained in his business career. Control of the Erie passed to Fisk and Gould. Gould was the only person the Commodore was ever known to fear; he regarded Gould as too slick to deal with, a high compliment indeed.

The Commodore took little role in the Civil War other than chartering two of his vessels to the federal government, for which he was paid at the staggering rate of $2,000 a day. He lost a son to the war, however. George Washington Vanderbilt, his youngest child, was twenty-one when the war broke out. Although his brothers had not gone to college, George had been sent to West Point. He had inherited his father's strength; the sycophantic W. A. Croffut claimed that "on his twenty-second birthday [he] lifted a dead weight of nine hundred pounds." He enlisted in the Union forces and speedily became a captain, but he caught malaria in the field and was invalided out of the army. His father sent him to the south of France to recover and, when his condition worsened, dispatched William Henry to take care of him. The brothers traveled together for months—travel was supposed to have curative powers—but George died in Paris in 1863.

While the Commodore was locked in the battle for the Erie, his helpmate was coming to the end of her life. Sophia Johnson Vanderbilt died on August 17, 1868. Her husband was making his customary summer visit to Saratoga; he came back to the city by special train. Although she had lived a reclusive life, she had made some friends, among them Horace Greeley, who had also befriended Cornelius Jeremiah. When she died, Greeley wrote in the *Tribune* that Sophia had lived "nearly seventy-four years without incurring a reproach or provoking an enmity." Her funeral service—Greeley was a pallbearer—was held at the Washington Square Reformed Dutch Church, which then stood on the southeast corner of Washington Place and University Place. The minister in charge was a family connection: Frederick C. Clark, brother of her son-in-law Horace F. Clark. The funeral procession wound its way down Broadway to the Staten Island ferry, where two special boats conveyed the hearse and the mourners to the island. She was buried in the Moravian Cemetery on Richmond Road with rites conducted at the cemetery by an Episcopalian minister.

Although not overcome with grief, after his wife's death the Commodore showed some interest in spiritualism; table-turning, séances, and mediumistic cures were all the rage in the 1860s and 70s. Not much is known of the Commodore's spiritualist seekings, but he is said to have been attempting to contact his mother on the other side, which, given the Commodore's well-known affection for her, rings true. He was not above consulting the ghosts on financial matters; at one sitting he ordered the shade of Jim Fisk, who had recently been fatally shot in a love triangle, summoned to give him advice on Erie shares!

The Commodore (seated on the right in the foreground) spent his summers at Saratoga Springs, New York, where he drove his trotters, watched the horse races—he was one of the incorporators of the Saratoga track—and played whist with the single-mindedness that characterized all his activities. Although there is no documentation except the sly hints of contemporaries, so vigorous a man, still handsome and very rich, could hardly have been without female companionship, particularly as Saratoga was notoriously the resort of unattached ladies.

In the course of his otherworldly investigations, the Commodore met two young sisters—then around thirty years old—named Victoria Woodhull and Tennessee Claflin. The seventh and ninth daughters of a huge, rambunctious clan of backwoodsmen from Ohio, they had been members of the family medicine show, telling fortunes throughout the Midwest. From most towns the departures of the Claflins were hasty, and they were pursued by charges of fraud, blackmail, and prostitution. Victoria became a spiritualist in 1868 when the shade of Demosthenes appeared to chat with her. The sisters soon reached New York— Demosthenes sent them—and apparently met the Commodore at a séance at which they were the mediums. According to their account, he was so impressed by the sisters and their contacts in the beyond that he asked Tennessee to marry him. This unlikely story—he was already courting his second wife, and why wouldn't Tennie, as she was called, marry one of the richest men in the world?—rests entirely on the sisters' word, and they were notorious liars.

What appears to be true is that the Commodore backed the sisters in opening "the first female brokerage house" at the

Hoffman House hotel on 24th Street and Broadway in January 1870. The newspapers delighted in calling them "the Bewitching Brokers." They also began a newspaper called *Woodhull and Claflin's Weekly,* which advocated equal rights for women and, even more scandalously, "free love." In it two years later they published the lurid news of the adultery of the Reverend Henry Ward Beecher, a preacher who commanded the almost hysterical devotion of his flock in Brooklyn. The sisters soon passed out of the Commodore's life while continuing to hint that they knew more than they were telling about his affairs.

The Commodore's mourning for Sophia was rather brief; he remarried the next year. At Saratoga in the summer of 1869, he met a young lady of about thirty who was a relation of his. Frank Armstrong Crawford, for such was the lady's unusual first name, was the great-granddaughter of his mother's brother, Jacob Hand; she was therefore the Commodore's first cousin twice removed. She was a Southern lady once briefly married to John Elliott of Mobile and now divorced, who came to New York with her mother after the Civil War. She was more than forty years younger than the Commodore and was described as "tall and queenly." She taught music for a living and was noted for her refined manners. She was extremely devout. The Commodore was not accustomed to revealing his plans, and when he decided to marry his cousin Frank, he set off for Canada with the lady and was married at the Tecumseh House hotel in London, Ontario, on August 20, 1869, before his children could protest. Some of his daughters were appalled at the marriage to a woman younger than some of their children and gave their stepmother as cold a reception as they dared. But William Henry, the heir apparent, was politic enough to congratulate the happy couple and to make friends with the new bride, who, accompanied by her mother, settled into 10 Washington Place.

An apotheosis of some sort was now due the Commodore as a tribute to his success. It took the odd but appropriate form of a freight station. The growing commerce of the city demanded a better freight station than the entirely inadequate facilities available. On the lower west side, near the commercial heart of the city, was St. John's Park, a small square bounded by Varick, Laight, Beach, and Hudson streets, part of the immense real-estate holdings of Trinity Episcopal Church. Since 1804, it had

been a public square, fenced and ornamented by trees and surrounded by solid dwellings. In 1866, Trinity was induced to sell
the park to the Commodore for $400,000; the surrounding lot
owners got $600,000 for their holdings. At once there was an
outcry that "the garden spot of downtown, one of the few breath-
ing places left to the city poor" was being sacrificed to the greed
of the railroads. The outcry did not succeed; construction of the
freight station began the following year, and in 1869 an immense
structure, three stories high, was completed.

One of the Commodore's cronies, Albert De Groot, led
the movement to create a monument "to commemorate the genius
and the vision of Commodore Vanderbilt." The official story was
that ample funds were contributed by his many admirers; in fact,
the Commodore himself paid for the monument: a pediment on
the roof, which was "a bronze biography" of him, 150 feet long
and 30 feet high. The design was by Ernest Plassman, a German-
born sculptor and teacher, and the pediment was cast by George
and Valentine Fischer, who owned a foundry large enough to
handle the immense job.

The age loved allegory, and the pediment was rich enough
in symbols to satisfy the most demanding art lover. The over-
arching theme was transportation; classical figures represented
the sailboat, the steamship, the Conestoga wagon, and of course,
the railroad. All surrounded the figure of the Commodore wearing his overcoat and carrying a stick while gazing over this
classical jumble. Helen W. Henderson, a twentieth-century critic,
wrote in *A Loiterer in New York:*

> This atrocious mass of sculpture consists of a full-length
> statue of the Commodore standing in a niche; on his right
> Ceres, on his left Neptune, lolling in abandoned attitudes.
> The intervening spaces between the statue and the mytho-
> logical figures are crammed with a mass of detail repre-
> senting ships and shipping, trains, and steam engines
> running headlong into one another in a valiant effort to
> express the stupendous activities of a life of business ad-
> venture in which the extermination of a neighborhood
> was a mere incident.

The enormous work of art was unveiled on November 10,
1869. Oakey Hall, mayor of the city, who was shortly to be

indicted for his role in the Tweed Ring scandals, orated, an ode was recited, and hundreds of sailors pulled back the long canvas that covered the statuary. Only after the ceremony was it discovered that the pediment, perched three stories above freight yards full of locomotives, could hardly be seen from the street, and its elaborate iconography could not be appreciated by passersby. Viewers were, on the whole, able to contain their admiration. The New York diarist George Templeton Strong wrote, "as a work of art, it is bestial."

Strong took the occasion in his diary to sum up the way many established New Yorkers felt about the Commodore:

> Vanderbilt began life penniless. He acquired a competence—honestly, I assume—by energy, economy, and business tact and then increased his store to a colossal fortune of sixty mills (as they say) by questionable operations in railroad stocks. Anyhow, he is a millionaire of millionaires. And, therefore, we bow down before him, and worship him, with a hideous group of molten images, with himself for a central figure, at cost of $800,000. These be thy Gods, O Israel!

Passengers on the Vanderbilt lines were the next to receive new accommodation. In 1869, the Commodore purchased all the property in a five-block area extending from 42nd Street to 47th

The Commodore's numerous enemies had their chance to satirize the entrepreneur when his statue was put atop the New York Central's freight yard in St. John's Park in 1869. Currier and Ives produced *The Statue Unveiled, or the Colossus of Roads* that year. In it, the Commodore waters the stock of the New York and Hudson Railroad while his opponent, Jim Fisk, does the same to the Erie. And the lithographers did not omit reference to the well-known passion of the Commodore for trotting horses and his beginnings as steamboat proprietor.

THE STATUE UNVEILED.
OR THE COLOSSUS OF ROADS.

The first Grand Central Terminal was used by passenger trains of the New York Central, the New York and Harlem, and the New York, New Haven, and Hartford railroads from 1871, when it opened, until 1910, when it was demolished to make way for the present station. Construction of the immense building was the first step in developing the Upper East Side of Manhattan, adding greatly to the wealth of the Vanderbilt family, who owned large tracts around 42nd Street.

Street between Fourth and Madison avenues for a new passenger terminal designed to handle not only his Hudson, Harlem, and Central lines but the non-Vanderbilt New York and New Haven, which entered the city from the Connecticut route. This was the first Grand Central Terminal.

Construction began on East 42nd Street, the site of the present-day station, in 1869. Isaac C. Buckhout was the architect. He worked with enormous dimensions: the frontage on 42nd Street was 249 feet, and the station was 695 feet long north to south; it covered five acres. The train shed was the "largest room in the country." Along the terminal's west side, a short new street was christened Vanderbilt Avenue.

The designer and builder of the first Grand Central Terminal was Isaac C. Buckhout, architect for the New York and Harlem Railroad. His great train shed in the terminal was at the time the largest enclosed space in this country. Buckhout died, at the age of only 44, just three years after the station was completed.

Unhappily, the station was a failure from the start. The grand dimensions failed to make up for extraordinary inconveniences to travelers. The public hated it and referred to it as "The Grand Swindle Depot." Each of the three lines had an entirely separate and self-contained section, which meant, incredibly, that a passenger transferring from one line to another, as thousands did each day, had to go outside in all weather. Traffic was immense: 104 trains each day in each direction and dozens of switching tracks, level with the street—an incredible tangle of tracks, locomotives, and cars, among which crosstown pedestrians had to find their way at risk to life and limb. Of the seven crosstown streets passing through terminal property only two

50

remained in use for wheeled traffic. Protests were loud. The *Times* thundered in 1871:

> The spectacle at these dangerous places, although startling in the daytime, has an additional element of the fearful at night ... While standing at 49th Street, the reporter noticed that a number of people were delayed in crossing for fear of being run over and most of those who crossed ran or walked as rapidly as they could from one side to the other. The majority of those who crossed were females, and they did so with great fear and trepidation.

There were also protests against the railroads' insistence that tickets be purchased before admission to the train shed and the trains, which was regarded as insulting. Public indignation erupted when Ulysses S. Grant, then president, was denied admission by a surly ticket collector. (The mild-mannered president humbly bought tickets for himself and his party.)

The oddest feature of the station was the arrangement of the tracks. Passing on the right hand had always been the rule on American railroads, but in the new Grand Central, outbound trains departed from the west side of the shed, the inbound arrived on the east side. The trains had to cross each other's tracks, which they did first at 53rd Street, then at the Spuyten Duyvil uptown on the Central Line and at Woodlawn on the Harlem. The road operated left-handed for the next forty years. One railroad historian described the arrangement as "lunatic." Surprisingly, due to the skill of the locomotive crews, there were few accidents.

The opening of the terminal brought a building boom to that part of New York City, with a consequent increase in value of the Vanderbilt holdings. At Fourth Avenue and 42nd Street, directly across from the station, the Grand Union Hotel, immense for its time—500 rooms—catered to travelers, offering amenities like hair curlers, hothouse roses, "hand-painted pianos," and menus with condensed timetables printed on the back; all at $1 a day for a room, $4 to $5 for a suite.

Grand Central made obsolete the New York and Harlem Station on 26th Street just above Madison Square. In 1878, William K. Vanderbilt, the Commodore's grandson, opened the depot as the first Madison Square Garden. The first National

The Commodore was portrayed in an uncharacteristically benign moment in the sitting room of 10 Washington Place with an unidentified descendant. Before his death in 1877, he had seen his family increase to almost biblical proportions. He and Sophia had 13 children (4 sons and 9 daughters), 37 grandchildren (19 boys and 18 girls), and 27 great-grandchildren (8 boys and 19 girls).

Horse Show, destined to become one of society's most important events, opened there in 1883. The Garden was not a money-maker, however, and William K. sold it in 1887 to a syndicate that hired the architectural firm of McKim, Mead & White to put up a new Madison Square Garden.

The Commodore was no more disturbed by the criticism of Grand Central Terminal than he had been disturbed by the numerous other criticisms directed against him and his operations for years. Other than the continuing problem with Cornelius Jeremiah, the old man's last years were passed in peace. He

52

On Staten Island the Vanderbilts belonged to the Dutch Reformed Church or the Moravian Brethren; later, most members of the family became Episcopalians. The Commodore had no use for organized religion, but under the influence of his churchgoing second wife he became sufficiently interested in the work of the Methodist preacher Dr. Charles F. Deems to buy outright the Mercer Street Presbyterian Church and give it to Dr. Deems, who renamed it the Church of the Strangers.

seems to have accepted that William Henry would carry on his work and to some extent turned over the management of the Vanderbilt lines to him. Daniel Torrance continued to have an important role in day-to-day office operations. The Commodore was as uninterested in paperwork as ever: a visitor noticed that his desk drawer contained only a checkbook and a box of cigars.

He rose early, had a breakfast of lamb chops, egg yolks, and black coffee, spent a few hours in the office at Grand Central, and drove his trotters in the afternoon. Evenings, he played whist at the Manhattan or Union clubs. He liked high stakes and jeered at his sanctimonious son-in-law Horace Clark, who refused to play for money. Occasionally, he invited his old antagonist Daniel Drew for two-handed euchre at Washington Place ("the lion and the lamb lie down together," said a sarcastic observer). Drew's long career as a bear had come to an end in bankruptcy. He was now too disreputable to invite to one of the Commodore's clubs.

The Commodore had never shown much interest in religion, unless infrequent attendance at spiritualist séances counted as churchgoing. Nor, as Croffut remarked, was he "naturally a philanthropist. He felt that the solicitor of charity was always a lazy or drunken person trying to live by plundering the sober and industrious." Under the influence of his young wife, Frank, who regularly attended church, he now mellowed his attitude. She was close to Dr. Charles F. Deems, a freelance Methodist clergyman who had been preaching for some years to those who were unattached to any church in New York City. (Daniel Drew was a frequent congregant.) His ambition was to build a "Church of the Strangers." According to Deems, he had his eye on the Mercer Street Presbyterian Church, which stood on the corner of Mercer and Waverly Place, near the Commodore's house, but he never asked the Commodore for money to buy it. Be that as it may, the Commodore bought the church for $50,000 and gave it to Deems, who renamed it, as he had dreamed, the Church of the Strangers. He preached there for the next twenty years. The gift was a personal one to Deems; the Commodore did not like the idea of trustees. "No, you hammer away at some of them fellows about their sins," he told Deems with homespun wisdom, "and they'll turn around and bedevil you so that you will have to quit." Despite his generosity, the Commodore never attended the church himself.

The Commodore was now softened up for a major benefaction. His first idea was that he would build a university for the education of Moravian Brethren, the church of his ancestors, but Frank introduced him to a fellow Southerner, the Reverend Dr. Holland McTyeire, a bishop in the Methodist Church South; he had been Frank's pastor in Mobile. In 1873, the Commodore offered $500,000 to found a university in the South. Dr. McTyeire suggested an already existing Methodist institution in Nashville called the Central University. It reopened in 1873 under the name

Vanderbilt University. The Commodore gave $100,000 more to the institution, then $400,000 to make up $1 million total, more than ample for the founding of a university at the time. The gift was unparalleled; these were the days before American philanthropy had reached the scale of building whole institutions.

In May 1876, the Commodore, always in such robust health, fell ill of cancer. He lingered for months; two of his doctors died while attending him, and more than once his death was falsely reported. Wall Street was on edge, wondering how the death of one of the largest investors in the United States would affect it. Reporters from the then-numerous New York newspapers rented a room across the street so that they could keep an eye on the southeast corner bedroom on the second floor of 10 Washington Place, where the Commodore lay. His horses were sometimes brought around to the street so that he could see them from his upper window. He was well aware that he was dying.

On January 4, 1877, the Commodore calmly bid members of his family good-bye in the best tradition of nineteenth-century deathbeds and joined in the singing of "Nearer, My God, to Thee." The house was packed with William Henry, his wife and children, seven of the Commodore's daughters and their husbands, and many of their numerous children. Deems, various officers of the Vanderbilt roads, and four doctors were present when the Commodore died at about 10:30 in the morning.

The Commodore had given specific and modest instructions for his funeral—no flowers, no mourning crape, no draping of the offices of the Vanderbilt roads or Grand Central Terminal. Nevertheless, the flags at City Hall and other public buildings, and the Union and Manhattan clubs flew at half-mast. Perhaps the ultimate gesture of confidence in his career was on the stock market— the Vanderbilt stocks rose several points! Deems preached the funeral sermon at his Church of the Strangers, and the body was taken to the old Moravian Cemetery on Staten Island where so many Vanderbilts were buried.

The attention of the family and the public, as soon as the Commodore was interred, was focused on his will. Everyone knew that the Commodore was rich, but few suspected, despite various boasts earlier in his career, just how rich he was. A few days after the funeral his will was read, and it was revealed that the Commodore had left an estate worth more than $100 million.

Hundreds of articles, some critical but most eulogistic, appeared about the Commodore after his death. W. A. Croffut, his first biographer, reported that "Dr. Deems said at the funeral that the deceased lacked only two things: early scholastic culture and intimate religious relations during the middle and main part of his life. The last he regretted, but Nature, by giving him a wonderful intellect, compensated for the first in part."

HARPER'S WEEKLY.

JOURNAL OF CIVILIZATION.

Vol. XXI.—No. 1047.]   NEW YORK, SATURDAY, JANUARY 20, 1877.   [WITH A SUPPLEMENT. PRICE TEN CENTS.

Entered according to Act of Congress, in the Year 1876, by Harper & Brothers, in the Office of the Librarian of Congress, at Washington.

CORNELIUS VANDERBILT.—Photographed by Howell, Broadway, New York.—[See Page 46.]

THE VANDERBILT FAMILY III

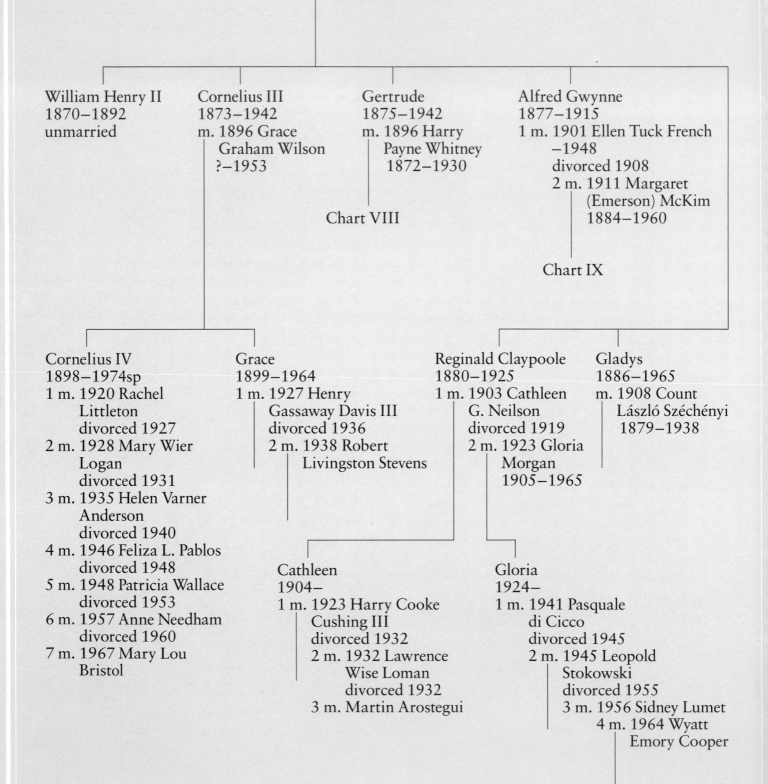

Cornelius Vanderbilt II
1843–1899
m. 1867 Alice Claypoole Gwynne
1845–1934

William Henry II
1870–1892
unmarried

Cornelius III
1873–1942
m. 1896 Grace
    Graham Wilson
    ?–1953

Gertrude
1875–1942
m. 1896 Harry
    Payne Whitney
    1872–1930

Chart VIII

Alfred Gwynne
1877–1915
1 m. 1901 Ellen Tuck French
    –1948
    divorced 1908
2 m. 1911 Margaret
    (Emerson) McKim
    1884–1960

Chart IX

Cornelius IV
1898–1974sp
1 m. 1920 Rachel
    Littleton
    divorced 1927
2 m. 1928 Mary Wier
    Logan
    divorced 1931
3 m. 1935 Helen Varner
    Anderson
    divorced 1940
4 m. 1946 Feliza L. Pablos
    divorced 1948
5 m. 1948 Patricia Wallace
    divorced 1953
6 m. 1957 Anne Needham
    divorced 1960
7 m. 1967 Mary Lou
    Bristol

Grace
1899–1964
1 m. 1927 Henry
    Gassaway Davis III
    divorced 1936
2 m. 1938 Robert
    Livingston Stevens

Reginald Claypoole
1880–1925
1 m. 1903 Cathleen
    G. Neilson
    divorced 1919
2 m. 1923 Gloria
    Morgan
    1905–1965

Gladys
1886–1965
m. 1908 Count
    László Széchényi
    1879–1938

Cathleen
1904–
1 m. 1923 Harry Cooke
    Cushing III
    divorced 1932
2 m. 1932 Lawrence
    Wise Loman
    divorced 1932
3 m. Martin Arostegui

Gloria
1924–
1 m. 1941 Pasquale
    di Cicco
    divorced 1945
2 m. 1945 Leopold
    Stokowski
    divorced 1955
3 m. 1956 Sidney Lumet
4 m. 1964 Wyatt
    Emory Cooper

III

Railroads and Riches

THE COMMODORE'S will caused universal astonishment in the United States and abroad: no other American had left so much money, nearly all of it in highly liquid railroad stocks and bonds. Sixty percent was in stock of the New York Central. The Commodore had never been attracted to real estate or valuable personal possessions. Even more extraordinary, when he left his first love, steamships, he retained no financial interest in them. When he became a railroad man, he put ships behind him.

The three richest men in America died within three years of each other: William Backhouse Astor, whose inheritance derived from his father John Jacob Astor's vast New York City real estate holdings, died in 1875, leaving about $40 million; Alexander T. Stewart, the first American merchant to make a fortune from a department store, died in 1876, leaving about the same; and the Commodore, whose estate was more than twice as large.

The New York *Herald* wrote, "The impression made upon the community by both Stewart and Astor was a faint one compared to the deep mark of Vanderbilt." Generally, the newspapers praised the Commodore for having made himself "the foremost capitalist in the country." The story of his life, one wrote, was "one honest, sturdy, fearless man against the world, and in the end the man won." The Reverend Henry Ward Beecher of Plymouth Church, earlier revealed by Woodhull and Claflin as an adulterer, continued to comment on public events from his pulpit. Noting that the Commodore was reported to have joined in family hymn singing during his last illness, Beecher said rather ungraciously, "I am glad he liked the hymns, but if he had sung them thirty years ago it would have made a great difference. He did not sing hymns as long as he could get about. We don't want to give God the tag end of our lives." The indignant Deems replied, "I confess that I do not like the tone of Mr. Beecher's talk . . . Most of the hymns were no new favorites to the Commodore. He was committing them to memory when Mr. Beecher was in his cradle."

Disputes over the Commodore's hymn-singing habits were of little significance compared to the uproar within his family when his will was published. While the newspapers and the public were astonished, impressed, or critical, most of the Commodore's numerous descendants were outraged. The Commodore had left the bulk of his property, over $90 million, to his eldest son, William Henry; of the remaining $10 million, approximately half was left to William Henry's four sons. The Commodore had, in effect, entailed the estate as the upper classes in Britain had done for centuries; he had established a dynasty.

He left his widow, Frank, a comfortable $500,000, the house at 10 Washington Place and its furnishings, two carriages, and her pick of a pair of carriage horses—and their harnesses, it was carefully stipulated—from his stable. It was then revealed that there had been a prenuptial agreement whereby Frank had given up any claim to his estate in return for this bequest. Although in love, the Commodore had not lost his head.

His eight daughters—the invalid Frances had died at the age of forty in 1868—were treated with the disdain that he had always shown for all women except his mother. They split among themselves what was, under the circumstances, the miserable sum of $2,450,000. Even that was not divided quite evenly: five (Mesdames Cross, Thorn, Clark, Torrance, and La Bau) got $250,000 each; Mrs. Osgood $300,000; Mrs. Allen got $400,000; Mrs. LaFitte $500,000. And some of the money was only in trust. The old man had not forgotten his grudge against Cornelius Jeremiah: he was left only the income of a $200,000 trust. Numerous Staten Island relations, a doctor and a clerk, and Deems received bequests; there were twenty-two of these, but they totaled less than $300,000. He left nothing to charity.

The Commodore's main concern when he wrote his will

was not the enrichment of his family, but the future of the New York Central Railroad. "I hope our people will be big enough to take care of the Central road when I am gone," he told an officer of the railroad. "The trouble will be that they will try to keep up the dividends too long. They should take care to come down in dividends as soon as there is occasion." He told his doctor that he had so provided in his will that no shares would have to be sold to settle the estate. "If I had given $3 million to one daughter and $5 million to another, the first thing that would be done would be to put Billy [William Henry] out of the road and put [Daniel] Torrance in; then they would get quarreling among themselves and throw the stock into the market and next thing it would be down to forty."

Such unequal division inevitably led to a lawsuit attempting to upset the will. Ethelinda Allen, Mary Alicia La Bau, and Cornelius Jeremiah were the plaintiffs in a suit against William Henry, alleging undue influence when the Commodore was writing his will. After various maneuvers that apparently included negotiations with William Henry to see if he would increase their shares, the plaintiffs broke up: Ethelinda Allen withdrew, then Cornelius Jeremiah fell out, but Mary Alicia La Bau, who had not spoken to William Henry in years and detested her stepmother, persisted. Her case opened on November 12, 1877.

The La Bau team of lawyers, who included the notable Scott Lord, fought rough. They attacked the character of the Commodore and did not mince words. One of the lawyers told the court: "Cornelius Vanderbilt's bump of acquisitiveness, as a phrenologist would call it, was in a chronic state of inflammation all the time . . . Morally and intellectually his mind was a howling wilderness." Other lawyers tried to show that the Commodore was a believer in spiritualism and clairvoyance. A parade of "magnetic healers," spiritualists, and assorted seers were called to testify; most of them were given a very uneasy time by the defense, and their testimony was rejected by the judge. Mary Alicia's assertions about the evil influence of spiritualists on her father backfired when testimony revealed that she herself was a frequenter of spiritualists and "magneticians."

Former New York City mayor Oakey Hall testified, rather irrelevantly, that the "public subscription" for the monument to the Commodore had never existed; the Commodore had paid for

the statuary himself. Daniel Drew, now a broken man who had lost his fortune in speculation, testified quaveringly and pointlessly. (He died the following year, bankrupt and at law with his children, leaving an estate valued at $148.51.) There was a great deal of testimony about the drunken habits of Cornelius Jeremiah, who had rejoined the suit and indignantly protested that he had health problems but led a pure life. Private detectives gave evidence to the contrary, but it was shown by the defense that they had diligently followed the wrong man for months. Thrilling testimony was expected from Victoria Woodhull and Tennessee Claflin, but the sisters opportunely sailed for England, throwing out broad hints to the press that they had been paid by William Henry to absent themselves. The trip turned out to be the best thing that ever happened to them: they both married rich Englishmen, and Tennessee became Lady Cook. They died many years later at the acme of respectability.

From November 1878 to March 1879 newspaper readers in New York and elsewhere were treated to a great deal of scandal about the Vanderbilt family, much of it untrue, while the reserved and conventional William Henry squirmed in the courtroom. Early in March, the case abruptly ended: an agreement was reached among the heirs. William Henry added to each of his sisters' shares $500,000. Cornelius Jeremiah got $200,000 in cash and a trust fund of $400,000. William Henry also had to pay the heirs of Horace Greeley $60,000, which Cornelius Jeremiah had borrowed from the editor.

The trial, with its revelations and pseudo-revelations of the Vanderbilt family problems, caused embarrassment and social damage, not the least to the young generation of the Commodore's grandchildren, whose wives were beginning to nurse ambitions of being included among the society leaders of the city. Mark Twain, who had poked fun at the Commodore and his money-making during his lifetime, was fascinated by the will and the will case. He planned at one time to publish a bogus will of the Commodore in which his enormous fortune was bequeathed as "tons of silver coin and gold coin" and "hundreds of pounds of paper known as New York Central stock."

Cornelius Jeremiah's settlement helped him little. His wife died in 1872, and he was permanently attended by a paid companion named George N. Terry, who vainly attempted to

William Henry was painted by Jared B. Flagg about the time that he assumed control of the greatest fortune in the United States. In 1880, a newspaper described William Henry as "a placid and benign looking gentleman of fifty-five, well-preserved, well-clad, well-favored, looking altogether well-satisfied with himself." As, indeed, he does.

keep him out of mischief. In 1881, Cornelius Jeremiah built an elaborate house on "Vanderbilt Hill," West Hartford Avenue, outside Hartford, Connecticut, on which he spent a great deal of money. No two rooms were alike in their woodwork and wall hangings (or, as they were called, "wall embellishments"). The parlors and the entrance hall had frescoed ceilings, and there was a billiard room and a smoking room in a tower. Furnishings were sought in Europe and at auctions in New York.

"But his true nature soon developed and exhibited itself," said one newspaper critic. "He had become more than ever a monomaniac on the subject of money, saving and borrowing in order to have more to gamble with. "Many stories were current in Hartford illustrating the petty meannesses practiced by Cornelius Jeremiah in his home life. "He carried the keys to the pantry of the house, and tea and sugar he weighed out for the household with his own hand and in stinting measure. Frequently, it was alleged, no meat was to be found on his table. His own meals he took at a restaurant."

His house had just been completed when he killed himself with a pistol shot in 1882 at the Glenham Hotel in New York. He left debts of $15,000 in Hartford alone. The estate, such as it was, was left to George Terry, who on June 29, 1883 held an auction of the house and its contents. A crystal set that Cornelius Jeremiah had bought in Europe for $1,000 sold for $41. Copies of paintings by Old Masters such as Guido Reni and Raphael were sold for $100 each. A painting of cattle by the esteemed Frederick Voltz of Bavaria sold for $29. An ebony vase and pedestal purchased at the Philadelphia Centennial for $1,200 were sold for $155. The new house itself got only a bargain bid of $15,000.

Frank Crawford Vanderbilt continued to live at 10 Washington Place with her mother. She waited for years before she emerged from mourning. On December 29, 1881, she gave her first reception since her husband's death, greeting six hundred friends, including William Henry and his entire family, who were obviously showing their support. "Mrs. Vanderbilt was dressed in a Muschowitz [a fashionable New York dressmaker] costume of pearl colored satin," wrote a newspaper reporter. "Her ornaments were black pearls set in diamonds worn in the ears, at the throat, and in the hat." Her house was filled with camellias sent by her best friend, the best-selling novelist Augusta Evans Wilson.

Just four years later, on May 4, 1885, Frank died of pneumonia caught at the funeral of the Commodore's sister, Phebe.

The breach between William Henry and his sisters caused by the will was patched over but never healed, although there was to be some contact between their numerous descendants and the main Vanderbilt line. Years later, Consuelo, Duchess of Marlborough, and her cousin Adele Sloane, both granddaughters of William Henry who knew little of the family feud, began investigating this ancient history:

> It appeared that our great-grandfather, the Commodore, had left the major part of his considerable fortune to my grandfather, each of his daughters receiving legacies that, as I remarked to Adele, would have been considered colossal as well as unnecessary in England. However, the Commodore's daughters, having already in the mid-nineteenth century acquired a decidedly American conception of women's rights, thought otherwise. Visiting their rancor on their more fortunate brother, they became estranged from him, and so formidable was their reputation that not one of his progeny had ventured a reconciliation.

They found a cousin, Adelaide Torrance, Mrs. Meredith Howland, living in Paris, a *très grande dame,* "very handsome—very arrogant—very headstrong," playing bridge in her grand townhouse with old gentlemen from the Jockey Club.

William Henry had been crown prince for a long time: he was fifty-six years old when his father died. His apprenticeship had been wearisome, but when the time came for him to assume the position as head of the greatest fortune in the United States, he was ready.

He was extremely suspicious. "He had a generally poor opinion of humanity," said one of his contemporary biographers, "and especially of the workers on his enterprises, whom he considered lazy and overpaid." Croffut wrote that, besieged by applicants for aid who knew of his vast wealth, "he looked upon every stranger as either a foe whom he had yet to meet or a suppliant whom he must yet refuse." He characterized William Henry as "a pessimist of a cheerful sort." In conversation he was abrupt and

brusque to the point of rudeness, although there was general agreement that he never equaled his father in that respect. Oddly enough, he combined this attitude with a craving for popularity and wanted to be thought a good fellow. His manner was extremely democratic, and he was ordinarily full of bonhomie unless someone crossed him or wanted something from him.

For all his caution, he had his father's bad habit of making tactless public pronouncements. Unlike J. P. Morgan, the elder Rockefeller, Harriman, Frick, and other magnates of the time, who were notoriously taciturn, William Henry spoke out even when he knew he was likely to be quoted by a hostile press; he generally put his foot in his mouth and contributed largely to the unpopularity of himself and his family.

He was methodical, slow, and industrious. He found it difficult to delegate work and wore himself out writing letters, answering with his own hand many that any clerk could have handled. Henry Clews, a Wall Streeter who knew him well, said of his railroad management: "He insisted on making himself familiar with the smallest details of every department, and examined everything personally. He carefully scrutinized every bill, check and voucher connected with the financial department of the immense railroad system, and inspected every engine belonging to the numerous trains of the roads."

Although no reader and far from being an intellectual, William Henry had some cultural interests, which is more than could have been said for his father. He collected art. He was fond of the opera, preferring the newest works, especially comedies. He was one of the founders of the Metropolitan Opera-house Company, a badly needed new house for New York.

Opera had been given on a regular seasonal basis since 1854 at the old Academy of Music on East 14th Street and Irving Place. Subscriptions to the series and especially the permanent possession of a box were the most visible indications of social position in New York, and established families regarded a box there as one of their most treasured possessions. The house, however, did not contain enough boxes to accommodate all the new rich who, by the end of the 1870s, felt their position merited one. In 1880, the directors offered to construct twenty-six new boxes, all the old building had room for, but that still would not meet the demand. The Vanderbilts alone required five.

Maria Louisa Kissam, wife of William Henry, was, like her husband, descended from English and Dutch families who settled in New York in the 17th century. In her old age her son George had John Singer Sargent paint her portrait for Biltmore, where it still hangs.

A new opera house was the solution, and a Metropolitan Opera-house Company was formed. There were seventy founders, among them William Henry, each subscribing $10,000 as warranty for their boxes. Location was important: many sites were considered. William Henry offered the block bounded by Madison and Vanderbilt avenues, 43rd and 44th streets, for a bargain $300,000, but it turned out to have a restriction on it forbidding the building of "a place of entertainment." (The Biltmore Hotel was later built on the site.) The founders then paid $605,000 for the block bounded by Broadway and Seventh Ave-

The old Metropolitan Opera House at Broadway and 39th Street opened in 1883. Its elegance belied poor sight lines, drafts, and an inadequate backstage. Still, for American operagoers it was a magical place, and the opera company's move to Lincoln Center in 1966 marked the end of a glorious old tradition.

THE CELEBRATED TROTTING MARES MAUD S. AND ALDINE, AS THEY APPEARED JUNE 15TH, 1883.
AT THE GENTLEMEN'S DRIVING PARK. MORRISANIA. N.Y. DRIVEN BY THEIR OWNER. WILLIAM H. VANDERBILT. ESQ.
TROTTING TO TOP ROAD WAGON, BUILT BY J. B. BREWSTER & CO. OF 25TH. STREET. NEW YORK. WAGON AND DRIVER WEIGHING 411 LBS.
A trial mile. "off hand." First Quarter: 32¾ seconds. - Half mile, 1:05½. - Three Quarters, 1:41. and the Full mile in the best team time on record.
2:15½.

nue, West 39th and 40th streets. Josiah C. Cady won the architectural competition for the new house. He had never been in an opera house, he boasted; in fact, he had never been to Europe. But he had been the architect of the monumental new American Museum of Natural History, and he had influential friends. The opera house he designed had poor sight lines and inadequate backstage facilities, but it held 122 boxes with 732 seats, 24 percent of the house's capacity. The Vanderbilts got their five boxes, uncomfortable though they were. One of the characters in Edith Wharton's New York novel *The House of Mirth* deplored the cold in the opera-house boxes: "And the draughts are damnable—asphyxia in front and pleurisy in the back." But for the next eighty-three years, until the Metropolitan Opera moved to Lincoln Center and the practice of owning boxes was abolished, the Vanderbilts were among the most noticed box holders in the house. Even then, Harold Stirling Vanderbilt was one of the

William Henry's favorite among all his horses was Maud S., "queen of trotters," which grazed and exercised in a square block pasture, substantially fenced and guarded, on Vanderbilt Avenue between 43rd and 44th streets, the same plot he had offered for the new Metropolitan Opera House. She was stabled there so that she could be seen by William Henry from his office in Grand Central Terminal. Maud S. was so well known and popular in New York that Currier and Ives produced no fewer than 18 separate prints in which she is portrayed, including this one showing William Henry driving her in tandem with Aldine.

principal donors to the new house and was present at the ground-breaking ceremonies in 1965.

Other than sponsoring the Metropolitan Opera and lending ten paintings from his collection for exhibition at the new Metropolitan Museum of Art, William Henry paid little attention to public affairs in the city of which he was the richest citizen. He did, however, pick up the $145,000 bill for the transportation and installation in Central Park in 1881 of "Cleopatra's Needle," a three-thousand-year-old obelisk, ninety feet tall, that the Khedive of Egypt had given to the United States. The federal government, perhaps at a loss over what to do with so unwieldy a gift, had presented it to the City of New York. William Henry contented himself with paying; he did not appear at the elaborate unveiling ceremonies.

William Henry's passion, if the term can be used for so stolid a man, was horses. Even more than his father, he was mad for what was then called "fine horseflesh." He was often seen driving his famous matched team, Aldine and Early Rose, along Fifth Avenue. His favorite among all his horses, however, was Maud S., "queen of trotters." He was sitting behind Maud S. and Aldine when on June 14, 1883 he drove a mile in a record 2:15 ½

William Henry housed his beloved horses almost as lavishly as he did his family. His 16-stall stable with carriage room and indoor riding ring on East 52nd Street and Madison Avenue were said to have cost $60,000. Lighting was from gas jets shaded with porcelain globes. Hanging on the office wall are the blankets for his famous trotting team, Aldine, a bay mare, and Early Rose, a chestnut mare, which he bought in 1882. His picture collection overflowed into the stables; on the walls are English sporting paintings.

at Fleetwood Park, a famous track situated across the Harlem River from Manhattan near 164th Street. Later that year, he was driving the same pair when he was involved in an accident and knocked unconscious. He rarely drove himself after that, but he maintained his interest in trotting horses. He bought property in 1883 at 50th Street and Broadway for the American Horse Exchange, of which he was the principal supporter.

William Henry was a member of a loosely bound group of horse fanciers, "some of the wealthiest and sportiest men in New York," a contemporary described them, called jocularly "the Sealskin Brigade." Members dressed in sealskin coats reaching to their ankles, with sealskin caps and gloves—an outfit costing between $1,500 and $2,500, then an immense sum for clothing and the yearly income of a middle-class family. Besides Vanderbilt, the sportsmen included August Belmont, E. H. Harriman, James Gordon Bennett, and Frank Work, a protégé of the Commodore and one of the leading stock speculators of his time (and great-great grandfather of Diana, Princess of Wales).

The Sealskin Brigade, often with Vanderbilt as leader, drove their trotters, harnessed to a one-man carriage known as a cutter, slowly up Fifth Avenue through Central Park to its northern end at 110th Street. Harlem Lane (now St. Nicholas Avenue), a dirt road that began at 110th Street, was used for trying out the trotters' paces. The Brigade raced a mile up the Lane to a roadhouse where "the drivers sat around the circular stove in the center of the room, drank hot Tom and Jerrys and swapped lies," wrote Frederick van Wyck in *Recollections of an Old New Yorker*.

William Henry was also one of the nine original members of the Coaching Club, founded at the Knickerbocker Club in 1875. It aimed to encourage four-in-hand driving and sponsored excursions to various inns and clubs near New York, the Westchester Country Club, or the Ardsley House at Ardsley on the Hudson, for example. From 1876 to 1884 a parade was held on Fifth Avenue during the spring, the members turning out their finest teams and coaches, brasses glittering, the horses' coats sleek. "The club was a stickler for form," said Dixon Wecter, the historian of American society, "the driver's apron had to be folded when not in use, outside out, and *de rigueur* were the artificial flowers affixed to the throat-latch of each horse. These annual spring and autumn parades, which formed at Madison

Square and drove up Fifth Avenue to Central Park, and returned for a dinner at the Hotel Brunswick, were the cynosure of fashion and the astonishment of the proletariat."

William Henry had less and less time to spend on sport, though: railroad management absorbed him. Having settled his relatives' claims on his fortune, he had to turn to running his empire. He had the misfortune to succeed to his heritage at a time when the railroads were encountering severe problems.

In the first place, there were too many railroads in the United States: by 1880 trackage had reached 115,647 miles, and it nearly doubled to 208,152 by 1890. Many of the roads overlapped territory, sometimes in a ludicrous way. The New York, Chicago, and St. Louis (the "Nickel Plate") between Buffalo and Chicago ran so close to the Vanderbilt Lake Shore and Michigan Southern that trainmen could almost talk as their trains passed. In 1880, John Moody, the great authority on railroads, estimated that there had been built "twice as much railroad as the country could employ and issued four times the securities it could pay interest on." Even traffic growing at an enormous rate—in 1881, 289 million passengers, in 1890, 520 million—could not justify so many railroads. And many of the roads approached the twentieth century staggering under a load of debt assumed during the reckless days of stock watering that boded ill for the future of the industry.

The public was outraged at the extraordinary number and horror of accidents on the railroads. During the Commodore's last illness, on December 29, 1876, occurred the Ashtabula disaster on the Vanderbilts' Lake Shore, when an entire train plunged off a bridge—which had already been denounced as dangerous—into a ravine near Ashtabula, Ohio, killing eighty-three people and severely injuring seventy-six. Because of the inaccessibility of the ravine and the bitter cold, there was great delay in rescuing the injured survivors. Descriptions of the scenes of horror and outrage at the aloof attitude of the proprietors of the road (who denied responsibility and refused to pay claims) appeared in all the newspapers. Julia Moore, the "Sweet Singer of Michigan," wrote a popular poem on the Ashtabula disaster, with the stinging subtitle, "Steam: The Seamy Side."

Accidents cause only momentary indignation, however.

The most persistent criticism of the railroads concerned their freight rates, which were haphazard, discriminatory, and favored large shippers. In the late 1860s, opposition to the railroads and their practices began slowly to organize and to bring pressure to bear on the federal and state governments, which up to that time had been the obedient tools of the railroads. In 1867, the Cheap Freight League, formed by farmers and businessmen, asked the government to intervene to stop abuses. In 1870, the Patrons of Husbandry ("the Grange") united against the railroads.

The 1870s were a period of great labor unrest in the United States, much of the protest over wages being directed against the railroads. In June 1877, the railroad owners decided to cut the wages of their workers by 10 percent across the board. At that time the brakemen, whose job was extremely dangerous, averaged about $1.75 for a twelve-hour day; firemen got about $2 a day; conductors, the princes of the road, who had ultimate responsibility for their trains, were paid about $3 a day. There were, of course, no benefits such as pensions or health insurance, nor were there any safety regulations.

The cut in wages brought about the first nationwide labor strike in American history, beginning on July 16, 1877 in New York City. Of the 75,000 miles of track in the country, about 50,000 were affected. In Pittsburgh alone dozens of buildings were burned and more than a hundred locomotives and more than two thousand cars destroyed. But the strike lasted only until the end of July when most of the militants were fired and the other workers, who had not the resources to continue the strike, returned to work at the reduced wages. The shrewd William Henry very adroitly kept the 12,000 workers on the New York Central, who had threatened to burn down Grand Central Terminal, on their jobs by distributing $100,000 among them and promising that the 10-percent wage cut would be rescinded "as soon as business improved to a point justifying such an advance."

Not only the workingmen and farmers hated the railroads; businessmen, even of the most conservative type, were furious over the railroads' practice of secretly rebating charges for carrying freight. Favored shippers paid the published tariff but received under-the-table refunds. Even the New York Board of Trade and the Chamber of Commerce protested this unfair practice. In 1879, when the New York State Legislature roused itself from its torpor long enough to form the Hepburn Committee to investigate rebating, William Henry appeared before it and flatly denied that his railroads ever engaged in the practice. Later in the investigation, however, the committee established that in the first six months of 1879 the New York Central had made more than 6,000 contracts with shippers involving rebates and that 50 percent of the Central's local freight traffic was carried at discriminatory rates.

In the midst of labor unrest and investigating committees William Henry continued to improve the Vanderbilt roads. Many trains now carried sleeping and dining cars. In 1878, the first private club car was introduced. There were even more specialized services: in 1875, the New York and Harlem built a funeral car, The Woodlawn, to carry burial parties from the city to the cemetery of that name in the Bronx, twelve miles from Grand Central.

In the mid-1870s the rail trip between New York and Chicago required thirty-six hours. But in October 1882 the Pennsylvania Railroad started a crack train called the Pennsylvania Limited, which made the trip from the Pennsylvania terminal in Jersey City to Chicago in an unbelievable twenty-six hours. The train was provided with parlor, sleeping, and dining cars. Passengers paid a $22 fare in each direction in this express as against the regular New York–Chicago fare of $14.

The New York Central had to meet the competition, of course, and speeded up its trains on the run. William Henry, who was visiting Chicago about this time, was interviewed by two reporters and discussed the rate war between the New York Central and the Pennsylvania. He said that the fare could not be reduced below $15.

One of the reporters asked, "Does your limited express pay?"

William Henry replied, "No, not a bit of it. We run it because we are forced to do it by the action of the Pennsylvania Road. It doesn't pay expenses. We would abandon it if it were not for our competitor keeping its train on."

Reporter: "But don't you run it for the public benefit?"

William Henry: "The public be damned! What does the public care for the railroads except to get as much out of them for as small a consideration as possible?"

The reporter knew immediately that he had a good thing. His story was picked up by newspapers and spread all over the world to the irritation and embarrassment of William Henry and his family. Beyond any question the phrase "the public be damned" is the best-known statement ever made by a Vanderbilt, finding its way into Bartlett's *Familiar Quotations* and other reference books. For many people, then and later, it summed up in one phrase the arrogance of the American robber barons of the nineteenth century, and for generations it was quoted with satisfaction by critics of capitalism. A few other financiers rose to William Henry's defense. Henry Clews of Wall Street insisted that the statement "was a very proper answer from a business standpoint, and the expression, when placed in its real connection in the interview, does not imply any slur upon the public. It simply intimates that he was urging a thing on the public which it did not want and practically refused." William Henry hired a public-relations man—one of the first in the country—to try to repair the damage. He was given an office in Grand Central Terminal and did his best, but "the public be damned" was irrevocably fixed in the public mind.

In his management of the Vanderbilt roads William Henry was assisted by his two grown sons, Cornelius II and William K. They were thirty-four and twenty-eight, respectively, when the Commodore died and were, as his will showed, favorites of the old man, well along in their railroad careers. Cornelius II had gone into the treasurer's office and late in his father's life became chairman of the board of directors of the New York Central and the Michigan Central. William K. was chairman of the Lake Shore and president of the Nickel Plate after it was joined to the Vanderbilt system. The third son, Frederick, went to the Sheffield Scientific School at Yale—the first Vanderbilt to graduate college—but he soon joined the railroads, too. Perennially on the scene was Chauncey M. Depew, a Yale man and lawyer who had served in the New York State Legislature and as New York Secretary of State. In 1866, he had become attorney and legislative contact man for the Commodore, in other words, the Vanderbilt lobbyist. For the remainder of his long life—he died in 1928—he was general errand boy for the Vanderbilts and president of the New York Central from 1886 to 1898. Even during two terms as

United States senator from New York, he continued to support their enterprises. A noted wit and the best after-dinner speaker of his time, he often acted as the official spokesman not only for Vanderbilt corporations but for individual members of the family. He was well rewarded for his faithfulness: at his death he left an estate of over $15 million.

Even with this assistance, the burden on William Henry was unbearable, partly because he found it so difficult to delegate. In 1879, he decided to reduce his holdings in the New York Central. He called in J. P. Morgan, then establishing himself as one of the foremost American financiers, specializing in railroad stocks, to dispose of half of his holdings. Morgan sold 200,000 Vanderbilt shares, mostly to investors in Britain, where he had important connections and a solid reputation. The sale went smoothly: the Vanderbilt roads had a reputation for good management and an unswerving 8 percent dividend. The sale brought $35 million to William Henry and still left him and his family in control of the railroad. He invested the enormous sum in United States government 4-percent bonds. For the rest of his life he bought, and occasionally sold, United States government securities. By the time of his death, he owned no less than $54 million "4 percents" as well as $4 million "3½ percents." To these were added millions of dollars of state and city bonds, most of them tax free. Also tax free at the time were the revenues from railroad bonds, of which he and his relatives owned millions of dollars' worth. William Henry was vastly increasing his father's wealth.

Money poured in on the Vanderbilts; obviously, it was high time to begin spending some of it. It cannot be coincidence that it was not until after the Commodore was safely dead and the family lawsuit settled that the Vanderbilts, headed by William Henry, began enjoying their money. In 1879, he and his two eldest sons, Cornelius II and William K., announced that they would build houses on Fifth Avenue, all filing plans on the same day. The houses were to be of a size and opulence seldom seen even in New York. The three houses were the first steps in transforming Fifth Avenue from 51st Street to Central Park into a Vanderbilt village and a public proclamation that the Vanderbilts were willing, and certainly able, to take a place in the front ranks of New York society.

New York City was two hundred years old before Fifth Avenue began to assume its reputation as the most splendid address in America, which it keeps today. The street was laid down on paper in 1811, but it had no existence in fact until much later. The lower sections from Washington Square to the 30s were "opened," meaning graded and paved, between 1824 and 1838. The section between 42nd and 90th streets was opened in April 1838. Even as late as 1869, Fifth Avenue at 59th Street was described as "a muddy dirt road which ran alongside a bog." It wasn't until 1870 that gas lighting was carried as far north as 59th Street. By the 1880s it was being said, "To live and die in a Fifth Avenue mansion is the dearest wish of every New Yorker's heart."

The Vanderbilts already had a toehold on Fifth Avenue. William Henry had bought the site at the southeast corner of Fifth Avenue and 40th Street in 1866, the previous building on that site having been burned during the Draft Riots of 1863. He paid the considerable sum of $80,000 for the lot, which was diagonally across the street from the Croton Reservoir (now the site of the New York Public Library). The house he built there was lived in by him and his family until 1880, when his grand new mansion at 51st Street was completed. (Later it became the site of the Arnold Constable department store and is now the Mid-Manhattan branch of the New York Public Library.)

The lot that William Henry bought on the northwest corner of Fifth Avenue between 51st and 52nd streets had until

After the opening of the first Grand Central Terminal in 1872, the neighborhood that the Vanderbilts and their New York Central Railroad were to make their own began to take shape. In 1876, it was still a strange mixture of the urban and the rural—a goat farm still existed on Lexington Avenue, for example. The spire on the west side of Madison Avenue is St. Bartholomew's Episcopal Church, where many Vanderbilts worshiped and Cornelius II taught Sunday school.

recently been the home of one Isaiah Keyser, who lived in a small three-story house in the middle of a vegetable garden, from which he sold produce to Fifth Avenue neighbors. He also dealt in cattle and ice. St. Patrick's Cathedral was already on its present site across the street, having been under construction since 1858. In fact, the Vanderbilts were moving into a neighborhood that was almost entirely institutional. The availability of the property was no doubt the reason for William Henry and his sons building on upper Fifth Avenue, but it seems as if they wished to distance themselves as much as possible from the old Knickerbocker aristocracy, still clustered around lower Fifth Avenue, and from the Astors at 34th Street. The Vanderbilts would build their own citadels where there was no competition. They were soon followed, however, as New York moved inexorably north, with the result that the Vanderbilt houses were the centerpiece in the "most amazing aggregation of opulent homes in the nation."

The mansion that William Henry ordered built at 640 Fifth Avenue was a double house. He and Maria Louisa and George, the youngest and only unmarried child, lived in the southern section; the northern section was divided into two houses. One, number 642, was for his daughter Emily, who in 1872 had married William Douglas Sloane, son of a immigrant Scottish weaver and founder of the carpet-making firm of W. and J. Sloane. In the other section, 2 West 52nd Street, lived Margaret Vanderbilt, who in 1868 had married Elliott Fitch Shepard.

Shepard, who was twelve years older than his wife, was a

Mother & Father on Honeymoon in Montreal 1881

lawyer who had graduated from the College of the City of New York. He was speedily drafted into his in-laws' railroad empire, becoming counsel for the New York Central. He had ambitions in politics, however, and in 1888 bought a newspaper, the *Mail and Express,* as an organ for his campaigns. But he had very little success, partly because he was given to rash gestures such as bringing a noisy party of New York ward bosses in hired dinner suits into the sacred precincts of the Union League Club for a meal. After he bought the *Mail and Express* "while devoting probably the greater part of his time to that enterprise," wrote an obituarist, "he figured in various capacities before the public as a strong churchman, the owner of a stage line, the aspirant of political honors, and as an especially able advertiser of Elliott F. Shepard." The stage line was the Fifth Avenue, and his enemies said that he had bought it solely to shut down the Sunday schedules, which as a devout Presbyterian Sabbatarian he abhorred. Shepard wasn't popular within the family, and he wasn't popular with the public either. One newspaper remarked, "Almost every-one with whom he entered into close relations personally or in

William Henry's youngest daughter, Lila, studied at Miss Porter's School in Farmington, Connecticut. In 1881, she married Dr. William Seward Webb, who had given up medicine for railroading and was working for her father. He soon became president of the Wagner Palace Car Company, which manufactured sleeping cars. Within a decade he had built the Mohawk and Malone Railroad through the Adirondack Mountains.

Lila Vanderbilt Webb was painted in 1889 with her five-year-old son, James Watson, by the American portraitist George Chickering Munzig. James Watson married Electra Havemeyer, daughter of the sugar-refining millionaire H. O. Havemeyer and his art-collecting wife, Louisine.

business came out of the ordeal with experiences to relate that found their way into current talk and furnished more or less entertainment for the community . . ."

Still another daughter of William Henry was married while the Fifth Avenue houses were under construction. At St. Bartholomew's Episcopal Church, which was becoming known as "the Vanderbilt church," on December 20, 1881 Lila Vanderbilt married William Seward Webb. A reception followed at her father's house at 450 Fifth Avenue, which he gave to the couple as a wedding present.

Webb came from a distinguished American family that had arrived in Boston from England in 1632. His grandfather had been an aide to George Washington during the Revolution. His father, James Watson Webb, was ambassador to Brazil and owner of the *Courier and Enquirer* of New York. William had graduated from the College of Physicians and Surgeons and practiced for a few years, but after his marriage he, like most Vanderbilt sons-in-law, was drafted into the family's business, becoming president of the Wagner Palace Car Company, the leading manufacturer of railroad sleeping cars, and president of the Adirondack and St. Lawrence Railroad, a division of the New York Central. He was also president of the Rutland Railroad, a small but prosperous feeder of the Central. He became a member of sixteen clubs and held such esoteric—but very social—positions as Secretary-General of the Sons of the American Revolution and Secretary-Treasurer of the American Hackney Horse Society. In 1882 he and his wife moved to 680 Fifth Avenue, next door to St. Thomas's Church, joining "Vanderbilt row."

At the same time and next door at 684 Fifth Avenue ground was broken for the home of Florence Adele Vanderbilt, who in 1877 had married Hamilton McKown Twombly. The Webb house was characterized as being in the "Gothic style" by architectural critics of the time, and the Twombly house was "Italian Renaissance."

At 660 Fifth Avenue Richard Morris Hunt was building for William K. a French château that was the most distinctive of the Vanderbilt Fifth Avenue houses. The lot was on the northwest corner of Fifth Avenue and 52nd Street with a 100-foot frontage on the avenue and 125 feet on 52nd Street. Hunt, with the very active assistance of William K.'s wife, Alva Erskine Smith, chose

the French Renaissance style of François I, although some writers referred to it as "Transitional or Later Gothic." Construction began at the end of 1879 and continued through 1882.

In 1867, Cornelius II had married Alice Gwynne, a young lady originally from Ohio whom he had met while both were teaching Sunday school at St. Bartholomew's Church. Their first home was 319 Fifth Avenue, at the northeast corner of 32nd Street. In 1881, they sold that house to the Knickerbocker Club. In 1878, they bought for $225,000 and tore down the old residences of the Bigelow and Louis Lorillard families on the northwest corner of 57th Street and Fifth Avenue. The site had once contained a series of rocky knolls through which a brook wandered, forming several shallow ponds that froze in the winter and were used for ice skating. George B. Post was the architect for their new house. His design, according to a critic, "was suggested by the seventeenth-century French château with an harmonious influence of ideas adapted from the Flemish and Jacobean schools."

J. B. Snook was the architect of 640, the double house, which was completed in late 1881. William Henry first thought of marble for the outside but soon changed to the ubiquitous New York brownstone. He seems to have felt intimations of mortality and wanted the house to be completed as soon as possible; brownstone was much easier to obtain and quicker to build with. Each of the houses had four floors. The basements contained servants' hall, the dining room, the wine cellars, laundry, drying rooms, gardeners' room, and pantries. In the butler's

Lila and Seward Webb spent winters at 680 Fifth Avenue. Summers were spent at their Shingle Style cottage built for them by the architect Robert H. Robertson at Shelburne, near Burlington, Vermont. The Webbs gradually bought up 30 small farms in the area, and in 1895 they commissioned Robertson to enlarge their house to 100 rooms. The work was completed in 1899; the building was henceforth known as Shelburne House. Frederick Law Olmsted was called upon for advice in laying out the grounds, and there was a vast barn for Dr. Webb's horses. Thirty servants were employed in the house. Shelburne, now an inn, is still owned by the Webb family.

Compared to the Vanderbilt houses at Newport, Shelburne was informal. The most imposing room was the Marble Room, used for dining, glassed on its side toward Lake Champlain and floored with black-and-white marble. Opposite was the conservatory with plants and a fountain. Breakfasts and informal dinners were eaten in the adjacent Tea Room.

pantry was a telephone connected to Grand Central Terminal, the livery stable, and William Henry's office. Bells could be used to summon messengers, the police, and the fire department.

The family lived on the two lower floors. William Henry had a bedroom and a dressing room, Maria Louisa a boudoir, a bedroom, and a dressing room, and George a library and bedroom. There was only one guest bedroom with a dressing room. The third floor was devoted to servants' bedrooms, and the fourth to trunk rooms. This arrangement met with favor from architectural writers. "This plan of living on two floors is pursued in all the great private hotels of Paris and other continental cities on which Mr. Vanderbilt's house is largely modeled," wrote one critic admiringly, "and its advantages over the common New

Opposite above left: Cornelius II and Alice Vanderbilt hired George Browne Post, a student of Richard Morris Hunt, to design a house for them at 1 West 57th Street on the corner of Fifth Avenue at a cost of $375,000 for the land and $3 million for the construction. Architectural writers struggled to describe the style, agreeing only that the inspiration was French and the result "eclectic." Post went on to design many surviving buildings in New York City, including the campus of City College and the New York Stock Exchange.

Opposite above right: Vast as 1 West 57th Street was, it was not big enough for Cornelius II and Alice and their large-scale entertaining, and in 1892 they commissioned Post to enlarge and extend the house. The five houses facing Fifth Avenue between 57th and 58th streets vanished, and the Vanderbilts could now overlook Grand Army Plaza. The house occupied 200 feet along the avenue with a new porte cochere and entrance. With 137 rooms, it was the largest town house ever erected in an American city, ample for Cornelius and Alice, their 5 surviving children, and 30 or 40 servants. Even more than before, the house defied stylistic analysis.

Opposite below: The house was embellished with the work of living American artists, including Louis Comfort Tiffany, Will H. Low, Edwin Blashfield, John La Farge, Theodore Robinson, and Augustus Saint-Gaudens. The entrance hall prepared the visitor for further splendors within. The Numidian marble mantelpiece was supported by caryatids carved by Saint-Gaudens. Many of the paintings and decorative objects had been acquired by Cornelius when he accompanied his father on shopping expeditions to Paris.

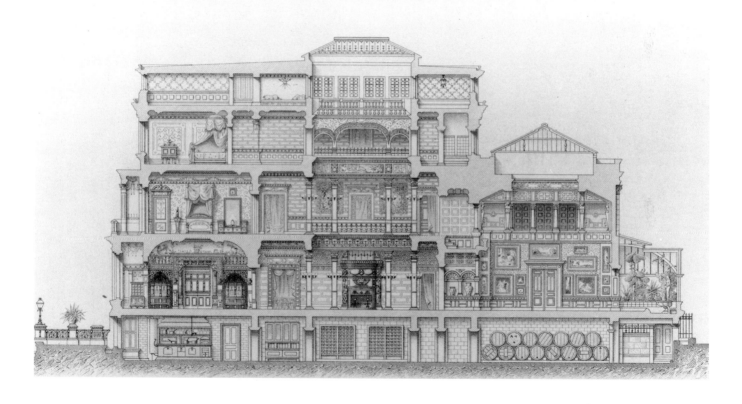

No other house of the American Gilded Age is documented like William Henry's 640 Fifth Avenue. He commissioned the art writer Edward Strahan, who wrote under the name Earl Shinn, to prepare a sumptuous four-volume work entitled *Mr. Vanderbilt's House and Collection,* which discussed in great detail every room, and, indeed, nearly every object, in the house. This sectional view from the book shows the east-west elevation of the house with the Fifth Avenue entrance on the left, the three-story central hall with skylight, and at right the picture gallery with the conservatory. The colorplates on pages 84, 85, and 87 are from chromolithographs reproduced from the Shinn Volume.

Although William Henry was no
great reader, the library was one of the
principal rooms on the first floor, with
its own anteroom (pictured here).
William M. Laffan, the art critic, saw
the house when it opened and remarked,
"One book in his 'library' was well
read: the volume of 'Successful
Americans' . . ."

Over the shelves in the library hung one of William Henry's favorite paintings, Jean-Léon Gêrome's *The Reception of the Great Condé by Louis XIV*, depicting a somewhat obscure incident in French 17th-century history when Louis, Prince de Condé, returned from the wars of the Fronde and the king is supposed to have said to him, "Do not hurry, my cousin. It is hard to walk quickly when a man is overloaded with laurels like you." William Henry commissioned the painting from Gêrome in 1878; when it was finished, the artist wrote to William Henry, "I hope I have succeeded, for my toil to the desired end has been unintermitting." The vase below it is believed to be *Science* by the great 19th-century French glassmaker M. L. E. Solon.

The American artist John La Farge established his firm of interior decorators, the La Farge Decorative Art Company, in 1880. One of his first important commissions was William Henry's house, where he was responsible for the Japanese Parlor. He also did stained-glass windows for the landings on the staircase; among the surviving examples is *Fruits of Commerce,* now installed in the winery at Biltmore, above.

A view of the northwest corner of the drawing room shows its splendor, opposite. Pierre-Victor Galland, a Salon artist, painted the ceiling to order in 1881; it depicts a procession of knights, ladies, and peasants bringing in the first grapes of the harvest. Herter Brothers hung the walls with figured velvet of pale crimson embroidered with mother-of-pearl butterflies. "When the lights are burning," an awestruck newspaper reporter wrote, "its splendor is akin to the gorgeous dreams of oriental fancy; and yet with all this dazzling opulence there is no hint of tawdriness. The effect has been perfectly massed, and the profuse decorations are harmonised with consummate taste."

South of the drawing room was the Japanese Parlor, opposite, which soon became one of the most admired rooms in New York. Decorated at the height of the craze for *japonaiserie,* the room was really an American idea of a Japanese boudoir; Shinn in his verbose account wrote carefully, "While the general effect is Japanese, nothing has been copied directly from the Japanese." The New York *Times* man wrote approvingly, "Every portion of this charming nook, the bronzes and other portable ornaments alone excepted, has been made in New York, but the effect is precisely that of the boudoir of some oriental princess."

On his shopping trips to Europe William Henry did not buy only paintings; he was a heavy purchaser of porcelain, glass, and metalwork, nearly all of it contemporary French, in fact, usually made to his order. The fashion of the time was to fill rooms with bric-a-brac, and 640 was overflowing. Even William Henry's bedroom displayed quantities against yellow walls and blue curtains, above.

One of the sumptuous pieces of furniture made by Herter Brothers for 640 Fifth Avenue was a center table for the library, above. A writer in the publication *Artistic Houses* commented, "Especially affluent and striking is the use of mother-of-pearl; very rarely, if ever, in the history of house-decoration has this material been used so generously."

Designer: Goutzwiller; maker: Herter Brothers, New York. n.d. Rosewood, carved and inlaid with brass and mother-of-pearl. H. 31¼″ W. 60″ D. 35¾″. The Metropolitan Museum of Art. Purchase, Gift of Mrs. Russell Sage, by exchange, 1972 (1972.47)

In the vestibule of the double house stood a great vase of malachite mounted in bronze by Pierre Thomire in Paris in 1819, opposite. It had been given by the Emperor Nicholas I of Russia to Nicholas Demidoff. The vase, over 9 feet tall, was bought by William Henry at the auction of the Demidoff collections in 1880. When the northern half of the double house was torn down, it was moved to the entrance hall of 640, and there it remained until 1944, when that house was torn down and the vase acquired by The Metropolitan Museum of Art.

Pierre P. Thomire. Malachite vase mounted on bronze pedestal, both decorated with gilt-bronze ornaments. H. (with pedestal) 110″. The Metropolitan Museum of Art. Frederic R. Harris Gift, 1944 (44.152a,b)

At the Demidoff sale Elliott Shepard paid $20,000 for a pair of bronze doors made by the famous Barbedienne foundry. They are a reproduction of Ghiberti's doors in the Baptistery of Florence, sometimes called "The Gates of Paradise." Shepard gave them to William Henry for the entrance to 640, opposite.

By 1883 William Henry and his family had filled the west side of Fifth Avenue between 51st and 53rd streets with their new mansions, above. On the left was William Henry's house, connected to those of his daughters Margaret Shepard and Emily Sloane by a one-story vestibule. The entrance to Mrs. Shepard's house was on West 52nd Street, indicated by the porch. Across the street was Richard Morris Hunt's house for William K. and Alva.

York method of living on four or five floors at once are great and apparent. Mr. Vanderbilt and his family and guests will have one pair of stairs and only one to go up and down."

The house at 640 Fifth Avenue was built in the form of a hollow square with a central hall or court running up to a skylight of stained glass, "which suffuses a subdued light over the court below and the surrounding galleries on which the living rooms are built." These galleries were hung with tapestries and were reached by a broad staircase. The three windows on each landing were filled with stained glass designed by John La Farge.

The interior decoration of 640 was the work of the Herter Brothers. Gustave and Christian Herter, half brothers, had emigrated from Germany and established a cabinetmaking firm in New York in 1865. They were noted for the richness of their effects and for their use of revival styles (Gothic, Renaissance, Queen Anne) and the so-called Anglo-Japanese style, one of the main components of the American Arts and Crafts movement. The Vanderbilt interiors were the last assignment undertaken by Christian Herter, who worked at it between 1879 and 1880. William Henry is said to have given the Herters a free hand and to have delighted in visiting their workshops when the decor was being prepared. He was concerned that the house be a proper setting for his most cherished possessions, his collection of paintings.

THE VANDERBILT FAMILY IV

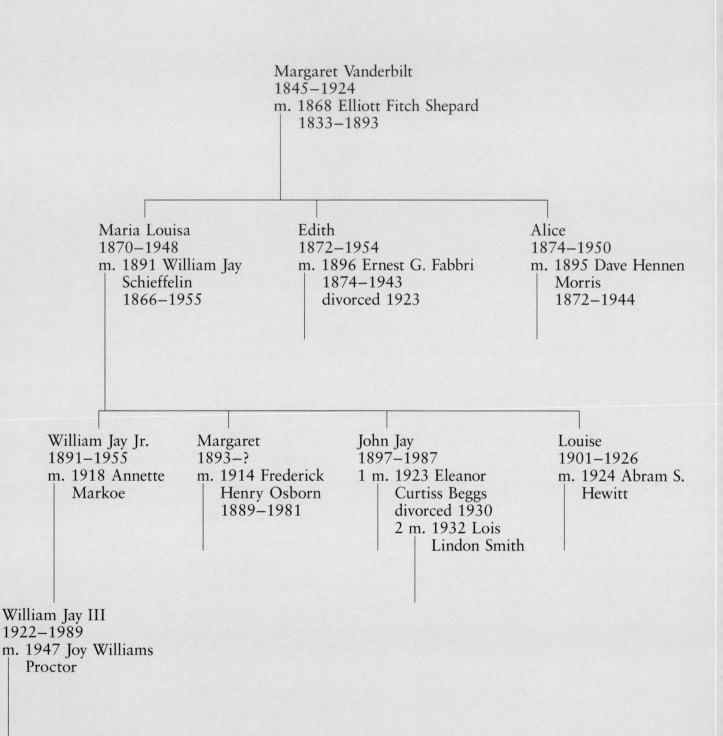

Margaret Vanderbilt
1845–1924
m. 1868 Elliott Fitch Shepard
1833–1893

Maria Louisa
1870–1948
m. 1891 William Jay
Schieffelin
1866–1955

Edith
1872–1954
m. 1896 Ernest G. Fabbri
1874–1943
divorced 1923

Alice
1874–1950
m. 1895 Dave Hennen
Morris
1872–1944

William Jay Jr.
1891–1955
m. 1918 Annette
Markoe

Margaret
1893–?
m. 1914 Frederick
Henry Osborn
1889–1981

John Jay
1897–1987
1 m. 1923 Eleanor
Curtiss Beggs
divorced 1930
2 m. 1932 Lois
Lindon Smith

Louise
1901–1926
m. 1924 Abram S.
Hewitt

William Jay III
1922–1989
m. 1947 Joy Williams
Proctor

IV

Art Collecting
on the Grand Scale

WILLIAM HENRY had always liked paintings. As early as the 1860s, when he and Maria Louisa moved from Staten Island and were living at 450 Fifth Avenue, he bought a few paintings by American artists: J. F. Cropsey's *Newark Bay from Staten Island,* the appeal of which was obvious, and *After the Sport* by Arthur Fitzwilliam Tait. He liked to visit the Tenth Street Studios, where many of America's best painters worked and received their patrons. (The building had been designed in 1857 by the youthful Richard Morris Hunt, who was to become the favored architect of William Henry's sons.) When he went to Europe on his father's *North Star* cruise, he bought paintings. At the sale of the collection of John Taylor Johnston, first president of the Metropolitan Museum of Art, in 1876, he bought William Bouguereau's *Going to the Bath,* the first acquisition in the field of contemporary French art for which his collection was to become famous.

When his tightfisted old father died, William Henry began to build a major collection of paintings. The irresistible conclusion is that the death of his father, who had confined his interest in the arts to psalm singing, freed him to be his own man, and one of the first ways in which he demonstrated his independence was in spending what he pleased on paintings. The first year in which he was in full possession of his fortune, 1878, was his

The picture gallery measured 32 by 48 feet with a ceiling 30 feet high, and when the rugs were removed, it was used as a ballroom. The paintings were hung on dull red tapestry. Lighting was provided by 169 gas jets attached to pipes that crossed the room. The large painting to the right is *The Concert* by Ferdinand Roybet, a popular Salon artist, showing a musical party in the time of Louis XIII of France with a lady singing while gallants accompany her on flute, mandolin, and bass viol.

biggest year of acquisition. In the eight years between his father's death and his own, he bought about two hundred paintings at the then staggering cost of $1.5 million. No American had ever spent so much on pictures.

William Henry was preceded in art collecting by Alexander T. Stewart, the immigrant department-store millionaire, who had bought paintings and sculpture to adorn the marble house he built in 1868 at the northwest corner of Fifth Avenue and 34th Street. Most of his collection was contemporary French school with a few paintings by American artists. He had a strange predilection for very large paintings. (William Henry was to show a leaning toward very small pictures.) He owned Albert Bierstadt's *Emerald Pool,* a White Mountains scene painted in

Through the main entrance of the picture gallery can be seen the central court and the drawing room. A year after the house was opened, the gallery proved too small for William Henry's constantly growing collection, so an addition was built to it, removing the watercolor gallery and adding a conservatory or "winter garden." The gallery had a separate entrance on West 51st Street, and for two years the public was admitted on the afternoons of certain days to see the paintings. The public misbehaved itself, however, pilfering flowers and even whole plants and pawing the costly works of art; William Henry indignantly refused further public openings.

1870, which measured 116 by 78 inches. He also owned Rosa Bonheur's masterpiece, *The Horse Fair*, which covered 96¼ by 199½ inches, but the painting of which Stewart was the proudest and for which he paid the highest price was *Friedland—1807* by Jean Louis Ernest Meissonier, a Napoleonic battle scene that cost him, with the heavy import tax then charged on the works of art entering this country, no less than $80,000. Stewart's mania for size in objects of art over-reached practical limits in a painting that he commissioned only a few years before his death from the French artist Adolphe Yvon. Entitled *The Genius of America,* it measured 35 by 22 *feet* and weighed one and a half tons. Intended for display in the Stewart house, it proved to be too large to get inside and was instead hung at the Grand Union Hotel in Saratoga, which Stewart owned. It remained there until the hotel was demolished in 1952 and was eventually presented, a rather awkward gift, to the New York State Department of Education.

Like most collectors of the time, Stewart loved sculpture, owning, for example, a copy of Hiram Powers' celebrated nude *The Greek Slave*. Old photographs of Stewart's house show endless statues lined up in the entrance hall, cemetery fashion. William Henry shared Stewart's affection for the modern French school, that is, painters who showed at the Paris Salon, but he was quite uninterested in sculpture. This rather shocked contemporary art writers. One, describing his home and collections, noted that "the Vanderbilt collection is remarkable in that it contains but little statuary. Plastic art, indeed, except of a purely decorative type, is scarcely represented in this noble mansion. An abundance of admirable carvings greets one everywhere in the friezes and cornices, but, except a small and very beautiful ivory statuette in the drawing room and superb bronzes here and there, the sculptor's art is hardly recognized at all."

The Vanderbilt collection, as it was finally memorialized in a great four-volume catalogue, was almost entirely composed of the work of the Salon painters: he owned works by Rosa Bonheur, Meissonier, Jean François Millet, and Constant Troyon. A few German, Spanish, and Italian painters, who mostly showed at the Salon, too, found a place on the crowded walls. Other than his single J. M. W. Turner and paintings by Sir Lawrence Alma-Tadema and Erskine Nicoll, the British school was not represented at all, and there were only two or three Americans.

William Henry's taste was up-to-date and fashionable. Hardly any Americans collected old pictures, and many of those who did had been stung by fake "Leonardos" and "Michelangelos" bought on European excursions. It was safer to buy the work of living artists: you knew that your painting was real. Often the buyer had met the artist and commissioned the work. That was an extra thrill and the source of innumerable anecdotes for the folks back home. Hundreds of artists, mostly French, competed in painting what the age preferred—pictures that told stories. Easily understood paintings of historical events—or, more usually, anecdotes—or scenes of contemporary life were the rage. William Henry's collection was a perfect reflection of the era in which it was formed: it was composed entirely of paintings in these two categories.

His collection remained virtually intact until 1945, and it was exhibited during his lifetime and after. As the taste for narrative paintings passed, the collection began to lose its appeal for the public and was dismissed by critics and art historians as a mere rich man's collection. But at the time of its formation, it was the height of fashion and respectability. The Salon painters were loved and admired all over the world. Paris was without doubt the art capital, and owning her best products meant, by definition, that one had the best possible collection of art.

Some of his contemporaries were suspicious of William Henry's collection just because it *was* so good: how did a millionaire railroad man come by such exquisite taste? "He knew nothing of art," sneered the socialist historian Gustavus Myers:

> and underneath his pretensions cared less, for he was a complete utilitarian, but it had become fashionable to have an elaborate art gallery, and he forthwith disbursed money right and left to assemble an aggregation of paintings. He gave orders to agents for their purchase with the same equanimity that he would contract for railroad supplies. And, as a rule, the more generous in size the canvases, the more satisfied he was that he was getting his money's worth; art to him meant buying by the square foot.

That was for long the prevailing view, but nearly a century after his death William Henry, for better or worse, was vindicated. The diaries of his principal art agents, Samuel Putnam Avery and George Lucas, were published in the 1970s and showed conclusively that in art collecting as in his business activities, William Henry was his own man. He did not give broad orders to buy pictures; he selected for himself. In their private accounts Avery and Lucas reveal that they worked principally at negotiating with artists and with other dealers and handling housekeeping chores for the collection, such as paying bills, packing and shipping, clearing customs, and installing.

Avery was the leading New York dealer of his time. Like many art dealers then, he also ran auctions of paintings, largely imports from Europe. His residence and gallery were at 86–88

Fifth Avenue at 14th Street, where he sold not only paintings and sculpture but also reproductions by the "galvano-electric process" of medieval, Renaissance, East Indian, and Persian metalwork—many of the decorative objects in William Henry's house were made by this process—prints, and objets de vertu.

Avery was born in New York City, the son of a shoemaker. He became a more or less self-taught engraver and a dealer in paintings by American artists. He acted as agent for various prominent collectors, notably Henry Walters of Baltimore. He was in the habit of spending summers in Europe, with headquarters in Paris, where he soon knew the various leading artists and bought paintings from them, both on his own account to sell in his gallery and for collectors. He was jolly and gregarious, an inveterate clubman and diner-out.

George Lucas worked closely with Avery and carried out various duties for William Henry, but he was an entirely different type, an American expatriate, reclusive and hypochondriacal, who had formed a long-time liaison with a French lady and in between visits to spas and experimenting with treatments for his fascinating ailments picked up a living by running errands for American art dealers and collectors.

Both Avery and Lucas were in awe of William Henry, as no doubt many people were in awe of one of the richest men in the world. It was a formal period, and neither man seems to have been at all chummy with William Henry, although on his trips to Paris they spent a great deal of time with him. They deferred to his judgment and were perfectly happy to carry out his instructions about the paintings he wanted. William Henry was openhanded with both the artists and his assistants: he paid well, sometimes not even inquiring the price, and quickly. The diaries are full of notes indicating that William Henry paid their bills on presentation. He always stayed at the Hotel Bristol, usually accompanied by his wife and often by some of his children and their spouses. Both Avery and Lucas met the family and did some buying for them, especially for Cornelius II and William K., who were also building houses that needed art and furnishings. They even bought lace for the Vanderbilt women.

William Henry did not restrict himself to paintings on his shopping trips to Paris. He ordered quantities of fabrics for curtains and wall hangings, porcelain, silver, and furniture. It

The Hungarian painter Mihaly Munkacsy was a stalwart of the Paris Salon, winning the medal of honor in 1878. William Henry owned two of his paintings, including this one, titled *A Gypsy Encampment.*

Paintings with a Moorish or Arab theme, vaguely known as Orientalist, were immensely popular when William Henry was collecting. One of his most expensive acquisitions, costing about $25,000—then an outrageous sum for a painting—was Mariano Fortuny's *Arab Fantasia at Tangier.* It depicts a ceremony called "making the powder talk," which Fortuny had witnessed on a trip to Morocco. Edouard Zamaçois, another leading painter of the time, described it as "a rain of jewels—a shower of fireworks." Between 1886 and 1903, it was on loan from William Henry's heirs to The Metropolitan Museum of Art.

appears that all the bric-a-brac was new, either bought in shops or made to order for William Henry. He was uninterested in antiques, least of all in previous ownership. He was quoted at the time as saying on the subject:

> There are those who are supposed to know all about these things and their intrinsic values, and of the associations connected with them. Well, I do not know all that, and I am too old to learn. If I should buy these things and take them to New York and tell my friends this belonged to Louis XVI, or to Mme. Pompadour, and should relate all the other things which make them valuable, I should be taking them from a field where they are appreciated to a place where they would not be. Perhaps I should know less about them than any one else. It would be mere affectation for me to buy such things.

When William Henry was in Paris, he and Avery made the rounds of the exhibitions, above all the Paris Salon, and the artists' studios, where William Henry bought lavishly. In those days artists held open house at their studios, and although, in most cases, they had dealers, they also sold to clients directly. The same system operated in New York, but one gets the impression that the French artists played up more to visitors than did the Americans.

From the Avery and Lucas journals and other contemporary accounts it is clear that William Henry delighted in these excursions and in chatting—usually through an interpreter—with the artists. He called on Rosa Bonheur in her house in the forest of Fontainebleau and breakfasted with her. He commissioned two paintings and urged her to paint them as quickly as possible. "I must have them," he said. "I'm getting to be an old man, and want to enjoy them." Bonheur, in fact, was a year older than he, as she pointed out laughingly. The scene must have seemed to William Henry a very long way from the offices of the New York Central Railroad.

Of all the artists whose work William Henry viewed in Paris, he was most taken with that of Meissonier; it is fair to say that he was smitten and remained so until the end of his life. William Henry was by no means alone in his admiration. Meissonier was "the king of French art," honored by the French govern-

William Henry's favorite artist was Jean Louis Ernest Meissonier, the painter of scenes from French military history who was then one of the most famous artists in the world. He bought nearly a dozen Meissoniers, often ordering works directly from the artist and competing with rich collectors in France, Britain, and Germany. William Henry once asked Meissonier which picture he thought was the finest he had painted. Meissonier answered promptly, *"Information—General Desaix and the Peasant,"* while lamenting that the painting was owned by a Mr. Meyer of Dresden. "It is lost to France!" he exclaimed dramatically. William Henry sent his agent, Samuel P. Avery, to Dresden, and he bought the painting from Meyer for $50,000 cash, at the time one of the highest prices ever paid for a painting.

ment and often called "the most popular painter in the world." Not only a superb painter, wrote one critic, "he is, like Victor Hugo, part of the *gloire nationale* of this country."

Meissonier took many of his subjects from the era of Napoleon I. Policy as much as emotion entered into that choice: the great successes of his career were during the Second Empire, and he was amply rewarded by Napoleon III for having portrayed the career of the first Napoleon. Meissonier was the first artist to become a grand commander of the Legion of Honor, and he was seconded in 1859 to the imperial staff during the Franco-Austrian War to portray the battle of Solferino.

Most of Meissonier's paintings were minute in size: he kept a large magnifying glass in his studio for patrons to examine

William Henry had a marked affection for paintings showing artists at work. Thomas Couture's *The Realist* was intended as a satire of Gustave Courbet and the realist school of the time. Couture said cuttingly in his memoirs: "I am depicting the interior of a studio of our time; it has nothing in common with the studios of earlier periods, in which you could see fragments of the finest antiquities . . . As for the painter, he is a studious artist, fervent, a visionary of the new religion. He copies what? It's quite simple—a pig's head—and as a base what does he choose? That's less simple: the head of Olympian Jupiter."

his work. Of one military scene Edmond About, a prominent journalist, said, "He stowed fifty French guards, full of life and movement, into a space where two cockroaches would not have room to stir." Not only were the paintings tiny, they were detailed and polished as though they were engraved gems. That, in fact, was part of their charm for contemporary collectors; the accepted word to use in their praise was "jewel-like."

Admiring critics said of his paintings that "you can count the threads in his doublets and the rivets in his armor." But not everyone admired all that precision, and some noticed that this adept painter had nothing in particular to say. A sharp-eyed critic wrote, "He looks through the wrong end of the telescope and paints us a world of pygmies where only the bric-a-brac is of any particular magnitude and passion. All you need to enjoy him absolutely is a good spy glass." When Edouard Manet saw *Friedland—1807,* he said, "The whole painting is tin, except the armor of the soldiers, and that is pasteboard." Emile Bernard said, "His early pictures were like well-made cakes, his late ones like gravy." And Delacroix, after visiting his studio, remarked in his journal, "His faithfulness in representation is horrible . . . there is something else in painting beside exactitude and precise rendering from the model."

William Henry was a generous patron, paying Meissonier's price without argument or, in some cases, without asking what it was. When he was in Paris in the spring of 1880, he commissioned Meissonier to paint his portrait and in May and June went almost daily from the Hotel Bristol to Meissonier's studio to sit. He even purchased a bronze sculpture portrait of the artist himself for his collection. William Henry was fascinated by artistic creation: he ordered from Meissonier a painting of *An Artist at Easel* for 85,000 francs. He also owned Charles Bargue's *Artist and His Model,* Pietro Bouvier's *Sitting for Her Portrait,* Sir John Gilbert's *Rubens Painting,* and many other depictions of artistic endeavor.

William Henry also liked scenes of the Franco-Prussian War—then fresh in memory, especially in France—turned out by painters such as Edouard Detaille. He commissioned a painting from Detaille entitled *Ambulance Corps,* which showed the arrest of a French medical group by German troops in the eastern sector of France in January 1871. A closely related painting was Alphonse de Neuville's *The Defense of Le Bourget,* which was the largest canvas in the Vanderbilt collection.

Jean François Millet's scenes of dreary peasant life in France were favorites of William Henry—he owned eleven. Millet's depictions of the soil and its unhappy workers had an enormous vogue in late nineteenth-century America. Despite his poor draftsmanship, he was considered one of the supreme artists of his time. Looking at one of William Henry's Millets, *The Water Carrier,* an observer typically remarked, "The beauty of this picture resides . . . in the quality, not of the *technique* which it displays but of the emotion it calls out."

The press soon discovered William Henry's unprecedented expenditure on paintings. The shrewd William Henry was

well aware that he was regarded as an easy mark by artists and dealers, but he persevered in paying the highest prices for what he wanted, writing home resignedly from one of his European trips, "We are being cheated out of our eye-teeth, and have to pay at least double price everywhere because we are supposed to be rich. We have to put up with the overcharges, for it is the only way to get through Europe. But it makes me mad all the same."

The most important room at 640 Fifth Avenue was the picture gallery where William Henry displayed his great collection of contemporary European paintings. On the easel at right center is the largest painting in the collection, Alphonse de Neuville's *The Defense of Le Bourget,* which depicted an incident of the Franco-Prussian War in which 8 officers and 20 men barricaded themselves in the church of the village of Le Bourget, swearing to die rather than surrender to the Germans. At the lower right is Mihaly Munkacsy's sentimental *The Two Families,* one human, one canine. Over the doorway at the rear hangs one of William Henry's few British paintings, Sir Lawrence Alma-Tadema's *Going Down to the River.*

When William Henry's painting collection was hung in two galleries—one for oils, eighty-eight in number, and one for watercolors, numbering forty-four—and the furniture and decorations supplied by the Herter Brothers and William Henry himself, now home from his European travels, were all in place, 640 Fifth Avenue was opened with a reception for art lovers and gentlemen of the press on March 7, 1882. They circulated throughout the house, gawked at the furnishings and paintings, and interviewed Mr. Vanderbilt. A few disgraced themselves by stealing some of the floral decorations and, to William Henry's annoyance, enjoying the refreshments too well.

The stories they filed reflected their astonishment at the splendor of the house. The *Times* man wrote:

There can be no possible doubt that this house with its adornment, decorations and pictures is the most superb in America . . . There is nothing exactly loud, nor anything which "swears." Still, the effect is crushing. Eyes distended to their utmost are palled as the gustatory sense is sometimes cloyed by overtasting. One longs to find out if there is not one single room where might be found some repose.

Praise for the paintings was unstinted; only a few critics were annoyed that the paintings were all European and that William Henry was not supporting the native American school. The best-informed opinion was unanimous in proclaiming the collection the finest in the United States. In a private letter, W. M. Laffan, one of the important art authorities of the day and art adviser to J. P. Morgan, wrote to a friend about the reception, "Yes, I was at the Vanderbilts and prowled around for two hours. 'Twould be magnificent, if it were not all *new*—most of the pictures included. The latter, however, *are* masterpieces. What a Millet, what a Dupré! On the whole the Mammonite interior I found to be in better taste than I had thought possible."

Some confusion, reflected in the press stories, arose over which architect could take credit for the double house. The issue has never been settled. Charles B. Atwood, an architect in the employ of the Herter Brothers, claimed that he did the designs. The Herters, however, insisted in print that they be given credit for the whole house, its architecture, interior design, and furnish-

ings; Atwood had no decision-making powers, they claimed. And John B. Snook, who was a prolific architect-builder, with other Vanderbilt houses to his credit, was the man who applied for the building permit. He introduced himself to the guests at William Henry's party as the architect. Actually, there was none too much credit to divide: while critics were impressed by the interiors, few had a good word for the exterior. One said about the Herter Brothers' claim to be the architects, "If these Vanderbilt houses are the result of entrusting architectural design to decorators, it is hoped the experiment may not be repeated." And Clarence Cook, probably the foremost architectural critic of the time, said unkindly that the double house looked like "a gigantic knee-hole table."

Before he became intrigued by the French Salon painters, William Henry patronized American artists. Seymour Guy painted *Going to the Opera— Family Portraits* and exhibited it at the National Academy of Design in 1874. Seated at far left are William Henry and Maria Louisa. Standing is Frederick, seated is George, then 12 years old, and Lila, then 14. Standing are Florence, William K., Margaret, Elliott F. Shepard, a servant, Emily, and another servant. Seated are Alice and William Douglas Sloane, and standing at far right is Cornelius II.

Ready for the Fancy-Dress Ball, commissioned in 1879 by William Henry from the Belgian painter Alfred Stevens, depicts the Chinese boudoir in the artist's Paris home. The furnishings were said to have been brought back from the imperial summer palace by the Anglo-French forces that invaded China in 1860. A contented painter of contemporary elegance, Stevens enjoyed immense popularity in his time. In 1900 he was the first living artist to have a retrospective exhibition at the Ecole des Beaux-Arts.

Alfred Stevens. *Ready for the Fancy Dress Ball.* c. 1879. Oil on canvas, 35½ × 46″. Private Collection. Courtesy of the Jordan-Volpe Gallery, Inc.

Naturally, the press was curious as to the cost of this external and internal splendor. The *Times* man guessed ". . . without estimating the value of the ground or money expended for the construction of the house, the guests . . . saw what must have cost one of the wealthiest men in the U.S. fully a million or more of dollars." Other estimates, including house and lot, ranged up to $3 million. It was certainly more than any American had ever spent on a residence.

William Henry's last years should have been happy ones. The Vanderbilt railroads increased in length and profitability, and he directed vast investments into not only government securities but the booming coal mines of Pennsylvania as well. His income was believed to be running at more than $8 million a year (other estimates placed it nearer $10 million). Fascinated, various writers like to compute his income on a time basis: his interest and dividends alone were $28,000 a day, $1,200 an hour, $19.75 a minute. But being the richest man in America was not without its dangers; he was constantly in receipt of threatening letters, and on several occasions, an "infernal machine," that is, a deadly bomb device, was delivered to his offices. He was somewhat more generous in charities than his father, although he shared the Commodore's notion that most people who needed help needed it through their own fault.

Despite expenditures on houses for himself and his daughters, art collecting, and expensive horses, he was still frugal. He counseled a friend, "Now take my advice and lay up a good nest-egg. Do away with luxuries that are really of no use until you get in position where the enjoyment of them can be indulged from your interest money rather than from the principal." His life was calm and orderly. He drove his horses, not so fast as before his accident, and played whist as constantly and as skillfully as his father had, and almost yearly he made a trip to Europe to purchase paintings. He was abstemious so far as food and drink were concerned and preferred shellfish and cereals with milk. He hardly ever drank alcohol.

But the management of his vast railroad empire wore him out. Despite having his two eldest sons working diligently in the family business, William Henry could never relax, and he continued to write his own letters. Croffut said, "William H. Vanderbilt never learned his father's knack of turning off business rapidly and easily. Whatever he had to do, he generally did in the hardest way. He could not acquire the habit of shifting his burden."

On the night of December 7, 1885, he attended the Metropolitan Opera, where he enjoyed *The Queen of Sheba,* a new comic opera by Karl Goldmark. On the 8th he got up at seven, was visited at breakfast by "the boys," Cornelius II and William K., who came the few blocks from their own houses to consult with him about some business matters, then received the treasurer of the New York Central to talk more business. About eleven he walked up to 119 West 52nd Street, the home and studio of the sculptor John Quincy Adams Ward, who was doing a bronze bust of him ordered by the trustees of the College of

A wave of interest in Japanese art and decoration passed over Europe and America in the 1880s; William Henry's Japanese Parlor was in the height of fashion. Japanese knickknacks were imported by the shipload and closely studied by the artists of the time. The French artist J. J. Tissot incorporated Japanese effects in *Le Goûter* (*The Afternoon Snack*), which William Henry bought for his collection around 1883.

THE DAILY GRAPHIC

AN ILLUSTRATED EVENING NEWSPAPER.

39 & 41 PARK PLACE.

VOL. XXXIX. | NEW YORK, WEDNESDAY, DECEMBER 9, 1885. | NO. 3

THE LATE WILLIAM H. VANDERBILT.

The death of William Henry and, even more, the announcement that his estate was worth $200 million called forth reams of periodical praise and criticism. Henry Clews wrote, "The will itself affords one of the best tests on record of the sound judgement and equitable mind of the testator. . . . William H., in accordance with his sensitive disposition, upright mind, and a due respect for the feelings, opinions and even the prejudices of others, resolved to make what public opinion would be likely to consider an approximately fair division of his immense estate."

Eulogists stressed William Henry's interest in Vanderbilt University, although his bequest to that institution was only $200,000, far less than his father's donations. The *Daily Graphic* showed on the left: the Bishop's House at Vanderbilt University, a view of the campus, and William Henry driving his trotting team; in the center, the double house and the Vanderbilt family tomb on Staten Island; on the right, his stables, the chapel at Vanderbilt University, and the Church of the United Brethren at New Dorp attended by the Vanderbilts before they moved to New York City.

SCENES CONNECTED WITH THE LATE WILLIAM H. VANDERBILT.

On a visit to Newport in the summer of 1884, William Henry and Maria Louisa posed with some of their descendants. On the porch are, left to right, William K. Vanderbilt, Jr., Frederica Webb, Lila Vanderbilt Webb holding James Watson Webb, Louise (Mrs. Frederick) Vanderbilt, William Henry and Maria Louisa, and Cornelius II. At far right is William K. Seated on steps are Dr. William Seward Webb, Alva, Frederick, Consuelo (later Duchess of Marlborough), and George Vanderbilt.

Physicians and Surgeons, of which he was a benefactor. He sat to Ward for about an hour, had lunch with his wife, George, and Florence Twombly. He then had an important visitor, Robert Garrett, president of the Baltimore and Ohio Railroad Company, who wanted to talk to William Henry about bringing in a new trunk line to the city via the Staten Island Railroad, which had been William Henry's first railroad enterprise. He and Garrett were old antagonists from more than one rate-cutting battle, but the discussion that day in William Henry's study was amicable. In the midst of it, William Henry leaned forward and died almost immediately.

The sudden death of the richest man in America caused an immense sensation. Within hours the news had been telegraphed

In the last year of his life William Henry began to think of a tomb worthy of his dynasty. Impressed by Richard Morris Hunt's design for William K.'s Fifth Avenue house, he commissioned the architect to build a mausoleum just above the Old Moravian Cemetery at New Dorp, Staten Island, where many Vanderbilts were buried. He asked Hunt for a tomb that was "roomy and solid and rich" but not "showy." Hunt gave him a Romanesque building modeled on the Church of St. Gilles near Arles, France. Work began in 1885, and the mausoleum was completed in 1889. The cost was estimated at $1 million. After William Henry's death George directed the work. He formed a friendship with Hunt and with Frederick Law Olmsted, who landscaped the grounds, that led in a few years to the collaboration of the three men in the building of Biltmore, George's North Carolina home. The bodies of the Commodore and Sophia were reinterred in the mausoleum, William Henry and Maria Louisa were buried there, and Vanderbilts are still buried in its vaults.

all over the continent and to Europe. Crowds gathered on Fifth Avenue in front of the double house; a policeman had to be assigned to keep order. A panic was expected in Vanderbilt stocks on the day following his death, and Wall Street was jittery, but the expected disorder failed to occur. Keen eyes focused on the Lake Shore Railroad, of which William Henry had been president; its activity would be an indication of what effect his death would have on the Vanderbilts' vast holdings of railroad stocks. Lake Shore had closed the previous afternoon at 88. The day after his death it opened at 85, but soon rose again to 88. Most of the Vanderbilt roads did just as well. The abhorred Jay Gould said piously, "This rapid recovery demonstrates to me very clearly the wonderful growth of this country. Its richest man is dead, but in spite of the calamity the stock market is likely to close higher than yesterday . . ."

The eulogies of William Henry were restrained. He had failed to impress the public mind as his father had, although the market-wise realized that he had controlled and expanded his inheritance in an extraordinary way. Russell Sage, known as one of the meanest traders on the street and nearly as unpopular as Jay Gould, said of William Henry in a statement that someone obviously helped him to write, "Mr. Vanderbilt was a very remarkable man, and of far more original force and financial ability than anyone imagined when he succeeded to his father's millions. I don't know that anyone ever thought of comparing him to the

Commodore, whose genius in finance was really beyond comparison. He was to finance what Shakespeare was to poetry and Michael Angelo to art."

William Henry's funeral, like that of his father, was unpretentious. Episcopal bishop Henry Codman Potter conducted the service at St. Bartholomew's in the Low Church style favored by the Vanderbilts at that time. From the church the body was taken to the 42nd Street docks where it was placed on the same ferryboat, the *Southfield,* that had carried the Commodore's body, which took it to Staten Island, where it was placed in the public vault of the little Moravian cemetery at New Dorp. Richard Morris Hunt was building a tomb for the Vanderbilts nearby, but it was not yet completed.

The 6,000-word will was brought from the Safe Deposit Vaults on December 12 and carried to the Probate Court by Chauncey M. Depew and the four Vanderbilt sons. In the previous six years William Henry had made nine wills. There are indications that he was overwhelmed by the amount of money that he had to leave and had fretted in his customary way over its division among his numerous family. When the amount of his fortune was revealed to the public, the excitement, astonishment, and indignation were much greater than at the time of the Commodore's will. His industrious but plodding son, generally thought of as capable but unimaginative, a conservator rather than an expander, had in the eight years since his father's death more than doubled the Vanderbilt fortune. William Henry's estate exceeded $200 million.

Reporters were stunned and almost, but not quite, at a loss for words. Calculations began all over: if converted to gold, the estate would have weighed five hundred tons, and it would have required five hundred strong horses to draw it from Grand Central Terminal to the Sub-Treasury Building on Wall Street. If it were in paper currency, it would have taken a man working eight hours a day thirty years to count it! The New York *Sun* declared:

> Never was such a last testament known of mortal. Kings have died with full treasuries, emperors have fled their realms with bursting coffers, great financiers have played with millions . . . but never before was such a spectacle presented of a plain, ordinary man dispensing of his own

free will, in bulk and magnitude that the mind wholly fails to apprehend, tangible millions upon millions of palpable money. It is simply grotesque.

It seems as if William Henry himself was of two minds about his fortune: he liked to affect modesty about it, but at times he was boastful. According to a New York *Times* story after his death, he once said to a friend, "I am the richest man in the world. In England the Duke of Westminster is said to be worth $200 million, but it is mostly in land and houses and does not pay two per cent." Since William Henry's income was estimated at somewhere between $8 million and $10 million a year, and his annual ordinary expenses at only $200,000, obviously he had vast sums each year for reinvestment.

Although he had been the beneficiary of the Commodore's ideas on primogeniture and had fought his brother and sister in court to retain his full share, William Henry, it seems, was disillusioned with the idea of leaving his fortune intact to one child. He said, or perhaps Croffut put the words in his mouth:

> The care of $200 million is too great a load for any brain or back to bear. It is enough to kill a man. I have no son whom I am willing to afflict with the terrible burden. There is no pleasure to be got out of it as an offset — no good of any kind. I have no real gratification or enjoyments of any sort more than my neighbor on the next block who is worth only half a million. So when I lay down this heavy responsibility, I want my sons to divide it and share the worry which it will cost to keep it.

So in his will he arranged a modified primogeniture: Cornelius II and William K. received the largest portion of the estate, about $50 million each, but his other heirs received huge legacies.

Specifically, the will gave Maria Louisa Kissam Vanderbilt, the widow, 640 Fifth Avenue and its contents, including the painting collection, an annual allowance of $200,000, and an outright gift of $500,000 for her to dispose of any way she chose (she used it mainly for the benefit of her Kissam relations). After her death, George was to inherit the house; if he left no sons, it was to go to Cornelius II's eldest son. Each of the four daughters received the house in which she lived. Then $40 million was divided among the eight children, giving each $5 million absolutely. Another $40 million was left as a trust for the eight, each to receive the income on $5 million for life, the principal to go to their children. His eldest son, Cornelius II, got an outright gift of $2 million, and his eldest grandson, William H., then fifteen years old, $3 million. Without exception and by any contemporary standard, all of William Henry's descendants were made immensely rich by the will. There were annuities and bequests to fifteen more distant relations and to old friends and employees, but these amounted to only an insignificant part of the total.

He was slightly more generous than his father had been to charities: Vanderbilt University received the largest gift, $200,000; the Metropolitan Museum of Art, the Young Men's Christian Association, and various Protestant Episcopal charities received legacies of $100,000. But all these bequests, although much praised, came to only $1.1 million, hardly a considerable proportion of so vast an estate.

The principal heirs to this stupendous accumulation of the world's goods, the sons and daughters of William Henry, were unusually young for such responsibility. Because William Henry had died when he was only sixty-four, his children were all relatively young: Cornelius II was forty-two; he and his wife, Alice, had five young children. Margaret Shepard was forty; she and Elliott had six children. William K. was thirty-six; he and his wife, Alva, had three young children. Emily Sloane was thirty-three; she and William Douglas had five children. Frederick was twenty-nine; at the age of twenty-two he had married, not to his family's satisfaction, Louise Holmes Anthony, who was not only older than he but was the divorced wife of his cousin Alfred Torrance, grandson of the Commodore. Florence Twombly was thirty-one; she and Hamilton had three children. Lila, who had married William Seward Webb, was twenty-five with two children. And the youngest of William Henry's and Maria Louisa's children, George Washington, was only twenty-three, unmarried, and living at home.

William Henry had said that his fortune had given him "no real gratification or enjoyment." This large young family, having come into the largest inheritance in America, was to set out almost immediately to prove by their expenditure that it could afford them both gratification and enjoyment.

THE VANDERBILT FAMILY V

William Kissam Vanderbilt I
1849–1920

1 m. 1874 Alva Smith   2 m. 1903 Anne (Harriman) Sands Rutherfurd
1853–1933   ?–1940
divorced 1895

Consuelo   William Kissam II   Harold Stirling
1877–1964   1878–1944   1884–1970sp
1 m. 1895 Charles Spencer-Churchill   1 m. 1899 Virginia Graham Fair   m. 1933 Gertrude
9th Duke of Marlborough   divorced 1927   L. Conaway
1871–1934   2 m. 1927 Rosamund
divorced 1921   Lancaster Warburton
2 m. 1921 Louis Jacques Balsan   1897–1947
1869–1956

John   Ivor   Consuelo   William Kissam III
10th Duke of Marlborough   1898–1956   1903–   1907–1933
1897–1972   m. 1947 Elizabeth 1 m. 1926 Earl E. T. Smith unmarried
1 m. 1920 Alexandra   Cunningham   2 m. Henry Gassaway
    Cadogan   Davis III
    1900–1961   3 m. William J.
2 m. 1972 Laura   Warburton III
    (Charteris) Canfield   4 m. N. Clarkson
    1916–   Earl

John George   Iris   Virginia
11th Duke of Marlborough   1 m. 1949 Herbert Pratt   1930–
1926–   Van Ingen   1 m. William Langdon Hutton
1 m. 1951 Susan Hornby   divorced 1964   2 m. Edwin Marston Burke
    divorced 1961   2 m. 1964 Augustus G. Paine II
2 m. 1961 Athina   3 m. 1967 Edwin F. Russell
    Mary Livanos   4 m. Donald C. Christ
    divorced 1971
3 m. 1972 Countess
    Rosita Douglas
    1946–

V

Yachts, Horses, Jewels, and Houses

ALTHOUGH WILLIAM HENRY had been a loving father and, unlike his own parent, never stinted his offspring, his death spurred his family to unparalleled spending. Yachts and horses and jewels and art were acquired at dizzying speed, but it was on houses that the younger Vanderbilts spent much of their inheritance. While in the Gilded Age many new rich families were building mansions in town and country, none came near the Vanderbilts in the number and splendor of their houses. To say that no expense was spared is insufficient; it was as though the Vanderbilts were determined to see how much they could spend. The purse strings had never been tightened on these children, yet they and their spouses surrounded themselves with luxury as though they had been brought up meagerly.

At the same time, the younger Vanderbilts wanted to be noticed. They knew that they were richer than any other American family and most British and European nobility, and they wanted to mingle with their nearest competitors. William Henry had built a superb house and filled it with works of art. He had entertained with dignity, but not frequently. Neither he nor Maria Louisa was interested in "society." The succeeding generation, although it numbered several industrious individuals who worked hard at maintaining the family fortune and even at increasing it, also numbered several, especially wives, who decided to achieve social eminence. Then, as now, playing the society game called for endurance, persistence, and a great deal of money. The Vanderbilts spent enormous sums gaining and maintaining what was then called their "social responsibilities," meaning, in the homier phrase, "keeping up with the Joneses." Thus were inculcated habits of extravagance that over the next fifty years would cost the family exchequer dearly. There were other serious financial liabilities. Though not the first members of the family to divorce—two of the Commodore's daughters had shed husbands—this was the generation of Vanderbilts that began the expensive series of divorces and costly settlements that so distinguished later generations. The fragmentation of the Vanderbilt fortune through extravagance, divorce, and inheritance, though little noticed at the time or for years to come, began with this generation. It is significant that no other Vanderbilt ever again left even half as much money as had William Henry.

The Vanderbilt to oblige New York society to take notice of the family was Alva Erskine Smith Vanderbilt, William K.'s wife. For the next half century she was to be one of the most prominent, some said notorious, members of the family. She was a Southerner, born in Mobile in 1853, the daughter of a "commission merchant," meaning a salesman. Her family claimed—in the face of considerable genealogical doubt—to be related to the historic Earls of Stirling in Scotland, fortunately extinct, and in some moods she liked to look down upon the Vanderbilts as parvenus. She gave her younger son the middle name of Stirling. After the Civil War, her family moved to France, where she was educated. Like so many members of her husband's family, she returned to France for long periods throughout her life, and the French way of doing things left its mark on her houses and her entertainments.

In the 1870s, the Smiths, who were prosperous though not "big rich," settled in New York, and on April 20, 1875 Alva married William K. Vanderbilt. Her personal attractions were few: she was plump with bulging eyes; one of her female acquaintances said she looked like a frog. She was bouncy and pushy to a degree, energetic and obsessed with getting her own way. In no time at all, she dominated her husband. He was a shrewd businessman who played a capable role in the family business, becoming chairman of the Lake Shore Railroad and president of the Nickel Plate, but he was retiring in domestic matters.

Richard Morris Hunt's first commission for William K. and Alva was Idlehour, a country place at Oakdale on the south shore of Long Island. The house was a rambling mansion in the Queen Anne clapboard-and-shingle style with more than 100 rooms. Construction lasted from 1878 to 1889 as the Vanderbilts and Hunt added greenhouses, stables, and two gatehouses. When the house burned to the ground in 1899, Hunt's son Richard Howland Hunt immediately built a new Idlehour, equally vast but in the Northern Europe Renaissance style. It survives today and is used by Dowling College.

"I always do everything first," his wife boasted. "I blaze the trail for the rest to walk in. I was the first girl of my set to marry a Vanderbilt." Although intelligent and, for a society woman of her time, well educated and well informed, she was remarkably superstitious and was absolutely terrified of ghosts. Her temper was uncertain, and she was given to tantrums that left her husband, her children, and her large domestic staff absolutely cowed. Her enemies liked to say that she was uncultured and dictated to by her architect, Richard Morris Hunt, but, in fact, she was knowledgeable about architecture and decoration. She learned a lot the hard way by almost working alongside her artisans. "She loved nothing better than to be knee deep in mortar," said a contemporary who observed her on a building site. During her long life she built or renovated at least a dozen houses in America and France.

Richard Morris Hunt is the architect whose name is always associated with the Vanderbilt family. From 1878, when he began designing a house at Oakdale, Long Island, for William K., until his death in 1895, he built for the Vanderbilts houses of a size and grandeur never before seen in the United States, as well as a family tomb, a church on Long Island, and numerous smaller commissions.

Hunt was born in Brattleboro, Vermont, in 1827. His family had been distinguished in New England for generations as

lawyers, legislators, and trustees of institutions. Hunt was always able to meet the Vanderbilts and his other clients, such as the Astors and the Goelets, as a social equal. He even owned a house in fashionable Newport.

He began studying architecture in Switzerland when he was only sixteen years old, encouraged by his cultivated and artistic family (the painter William Morris Hunt was his older brother). He spent nine years at the Ecole des Beaux-Arts in Paris, a school of art and architecture dedicated to the most rigid ideals of French classicism; it is obvious from Hunt's buildings that he never forgot anything he learned there. Indeed, he brought the lessons of the Ecole to America; in his studio young men were taught the supremacy of French architecture and the perfection of historical precedents. Rich Americans, just beginning grand-scale building, were delighted with Hunt and his designs; he was one of the most favored architects of his time by both the private and public establishments. In addition to his work for private clients like the Vanderbilts, he designed a number of important public buildings, including the Metropolitan Museum of Art, the administration building of the World's Columbian Exposition at Chicago in 1893, and the base of the Statue of Liberty.

Hunt not only worked for the Vanderbilts, he formed a close friendship with several of them, especially George, from whom at Biltmore he received his grandest private commission. He and his wife mixed with the Vanderbilts socially in Newport and New York, and the friendship was carried to the second generation: his son, Richard Howland Hunt, not only completed the assignment at Biltmore but after his father's death built houses for several other Vanderbilts.

Of the many Vanderbilt houses built on Fifth Avenue in the 1880s easily the most distinguished architecturally was the French Renaissance château created by Richard Morris Hunt for William K. and Alva. The tourelle, or round tower, above the Fifth Avenue entrance was especially admired. In it, a staircase connected Alva's bedroom on the second floor with William K.'s on the third. The outer walls of Indiana limestone were carved and embellished by a crew of 40 workmen who labored for months on the decorations. The internal dimensions of the house were enormous: a main hall 60 feet long and 20 feet wide, a dining room 50 feet long and 35 feet wide, and a children's playroom at the top of the house so large that in it the three Vanderbilt children rode bicycles and roller-skated.

On the roof of 660 Fifth Avenue was a statue of Richard Morris Hunt, nearly life-size, dressed as a stonemason and carrying a chisel and mallet, in the tradition of medieval buildings in Europe, which had often included a portrait of the architect. Legend has it that the statue was secretly carved by the workmen as a surprise for Hunt; in any event, he liked the figure so much that he included it on his personal bookplate.

Jean-Henri Riesener, one of the greatest French 18th-century cabinetmakers, made this upright secretary for the private apartments of Queen Marie Antoinette at the Château de Saint-Cloud, and it eventually was part of the furnishings of William K.'s and Alva's house at 660 Fifth Avenue.

Jean-Henri Riesener. Upright Secretary. Japanese black-and-gold lacquer and ebony, veneered on oak; white marble top; gilt-bronze mounts. H. 57″ W. 43″ D. 16″. The Metropolitan Museum of Art. Bequest of William K. Vanderbilt, 1920 (20.155.11)

The house Hunt built at 660 Fifth Avenue was completed in 1883. Informed critics mostly approved. The age loved faithful copies and admired craftmanship, and 660 was a skillfully executed copy of architecture that was especially admired at the time. Charles Follen McKim, then a young architect and later one of the country's most distinguished practitioners, who was to build houses for other Vanderbilts, used to stroll past the house in the evenings "just for refreshment." Clarence Cook, a more forward-looking critic with austere taste, called it "pretentious and fussy," however, and "a patch-work made up of bits." The

young Louis Sullivan unkindly commented, "Must I show you this *French chateau,* this little Chateau de Blois, on this street corner, here in New York, and still you do not laugh?"

Alva intended to use the house as a setting for social triumphs. New York City, which in 1880 already had two million inhabitants, was still, socially, a small town. Edith Wharton, who knew it well and was one of its severest critics, described New York society: "The sturdy English and the rubicund and heavier Dutch had mingled to produce a prosperous, prudent, and yet lavish society. To 'do things handsomely' had always been a fundamental principle . . . These well-fed, slow-moving people . . . lived in a genteel monotony of which the surface was never stirred by the dumb dramas now and then enacted underground . . ."

"Genteel monotony" was not Alva Vanderbilt's style; in all things she believed in the frontal attack. In her assault on the citadels of New York society she had certain assets: her husband's

Painted in 1835, when J. M. W. Turner was at the height of his powers, *The Grand Canal, Venice,* now at The Metropolitan Museum of Art, is a splendid example of the artist's ability to bathe architecture in shimmering light and atmospheric glow. Cornelius II bought the painting from the collection of the Earl of Dudley in 1885 for £20,000 ($100,000), then the highest price ever paid for a Turner picture.

J. M. W. Turner. *The Grand Canal, Venice.* c. 1835. Oil on canvas, 36 × 48⅛″. The Metropolitan Museum of Art. Bequest of Cornelius Vanderbilt, 1899 (99.31)

William K. was not so widely known as an art collector as his father had been, but the paintings he bought were, generally speaking, more significant. Several of the most important works in his collection were left to The Metropolitan Museum of Art, including this superb Rembrandt known as *Man in Oriental Costume* or *The Noble Slav,* painted about 1632.

Rembrandt. *Man in Oriental Costume* ("The Noble Slav"). c. 1632. Oil on canvas, 60⅛ × 43¾". The Metropolitan Museum of Art. Bequest of William K. Vanderbilt, 1920 (20.155.2)

immense wealth, her new house, her European education, and her friendship with Consuelo Yznaga, Lady Mandeville, wife of the heir of the Duke of Manchester (her sister was married to Alva's brother). Never mind that the Manchesters were among the poorest of Britain's dukes; the title was genuine, and at this period titles were still fairly rare on the New York social scene.

The first cannonade in Alva's social campaign was to open the new house with a grand party. The costume ball that Alva and William K. gave on March 26, 1883 is arguably the most famous party ever given in the United States. It was also a setback for the reigning queen of New York society—which meant American society—Caroline Webster Schermerhorn Astor, the wife of William B. Astor, an heir of the only American family that could compete in wealth with the Vanderbilts. This tall lady of few words had somehow made herself the absolute mistress of New York social life, even though her husband was neither head of his

Among the important French 18th-century paintings in William K.'s collection at 660 Fifth Avenue was *Broken Eggs* by Jean Baptiste Greuze, above, which was exhibited at the Paris Salon in 1757.

Jean Baptiste Greuze. *Broken Eggs*. c. 1756. Oil on canvas, 28¾ × 37″. The Metropolitan Museum of Art. Bequest of William K. Vanderbilt, 1920 (20.155.8)

William K. owned François Boucher's luscious *Toilet of Venus*, opposite, believed to have been painted in 1751 for the artist's patroness Madame de Pompadour to hang in her Château de Bellevue near Paris.

François Boucher. *The Toilet of Venus*. c. 1751. Oil on canvas, 42⅝ × 33½″. The Metropolitan Museum of Art. Bequest of William K. Vanderbilt, 1920 (20.155.9)

family nor its richest member. Although she herself was descended, like the Vanderbilts, from an old Dutch family, her husband was the grandson of the first John Jacob Astor, who had come to America only in 1784. Notorious for his stinginess, he had amassed a fortune first by fur trading and then by investing in New York City real estate. His methods were no better than Commodore Vanderbilt's and probably worse. Yet the Astors looked down on the Vanderbilts, probably because their fortune was derived from land, always more aristocratic than trade, even though the slum properties of the Astors were infamous for their squalor. Mrs. Astor's chamberlain and invaluable assistant in managing society was Ward McAllister, "the greatest dude of them all," who dedicated his life to social aspiration. He was given to the laying down of absurd rules of conduct, entertainment, dress, and food that were taken quite seriously by the nouveaux riches who swarmed in prosperous post–Civil War New York. According to a story hoary with age and repeated in every book on American society, the Astors were not invited to the great Vanderbilt ball because Mrs. Astor had not yet called on Mrs. Vanderbilt. But one of Mrs. Astor's daughters wanted to dance in one of the quadrilles planned for the evening and persuaded her mother to leave her card on Alva in order to get an invitation. Mrs. Astor, who was a fond mother to her distressingly plain children, left her card, and she and her daughter, Carrie, were invited to the ball. Socially, this was equivalent to the capitulation of an armed fortress. The Vanderbilts were in society.

Fancy-dress balls had been known in New York at least since the 1820s. It was claimed that during the season of 1865–1866, six hundred balls were given and $7 million spent by the ballgoers, the average cost of a striking costume being estimated at $1,000 without jewelry. But none of the six hundred equaled the Vanderbilt ball in fantasy and extravagance.

Anticipation of the evening was a delicious excitement for society. One chronicler wrote, "The ball has disturbed the . . . waking hours of social butterflies both male and female for over six weeks and has even perhaps interfered to some extent with that rigid obedience of Lenten devotions which the church makes." Rumors of elaborate costumes being constructed at incredible expense added to the excitement as did the practicing

The great costume ball given by William K. and Alva on March 26, 1883 was a housewarming for 660 Fifth Avenue, but it was also a victory ball, marking the entry of the Vanderbilts into the highest ranks of New York society over the protests of the Astor family and the old Knickerbocker aristocracy. Alva and many of her guests were photographed in the costumes they wore to the ball, not at the ball itself but in the studio at 707 Broadway of José María Mora, a Cuban-born photographer noted for the richness and profusion of his backdrops and properties—stuffed doves, in this case. Alva's gown was white and yellow brocade with a blue train. The front of her Venetian cap was ornamented with a jeweled butterfly.

Florence Adele Vanderbilt (Mrs. Hamilton McK. Twombly) was a "Watteau shepherdess" in rose embroidered with gold and silver.

Alva's Vanderbilt in-laws turned out in force. Lila Webb was dressed as a "yellow-jacket" with antennae of diamonds and stiff brocade wings.

Her husband, Dr. William Seward Webb, wore the uniform of a Hungarian hussar.

for the quadrilles to be performed at the ball by an impressive group of the younger society figures.

Quadrilles, a sort of stately square dance in five movements, were a fixture of balls at the time, but never had they been performed in New York on such a scale: six quadrilles danced by over a hundred men and women. The chief attraction was the "hobby horse quadrille" for which the dancers wore costumes that made them look as if they were mounted on horses. The life-size hobby horses took two months to construct and were covered with genuine leather hides and flowing manes. Tails were attached to the waists of the dancers and false legs placed on the outside of richly embroidered horse blankets, giving the illusion that the dancers were mounted; "the deception," one observer enthused, "was quite perfect." The other quadrilles, each with appropriate and elaborate costumes, included the "Mother Goose" and the "Dresden" in which the dancers wore court costumes of the time of Frederick the Great embroidered with the marks of the Dresden (actually Meissen) porcelain factory.

When the night of the ball finally arrived, cold and clear, a reporter noted that as early as seven in the evening, although the dancing would not begin until eleven o'clock, gentlemen returning from the hairdressers with profusely powdered heads were to be seen alighting from carriages along Fifth Avenue. "About the same time," he wrote, "the passage up the avenue of an express wagon containing the 'horses' for the hobby horse quadrille attracted a great deal of attention." The reporter was indignant that maids and valets were not permitted to enter the house and had to spend the long cold hours in carriages parked before it. They were joined by a crowd of sightseers estimated at five hundred.

When the 1,200 guests entered 660 Fifth Avenue, they found an extraordinary scene. Dancing took place in the salon lighted by the new calcium lights under a ceiling painted by the French artist Paul Baudry representing the marriage of Cupid and Pysche. "The furniture is of the bright and gracious style of that age of airy arrogance and perfumed coquetry which preceded the tragedy of the great Revolution," wrote one of the horde of reporters—in other words, the Louis XV style. The halls and drawing room were lined with roses, while upstairs the gymnasium, where supper was served, had been transformed into a tropical garden with palms, orchids, and bougainvillea.

Through these sumptuous rooms wandered Mary Stuart, the Fairy Queen from Gilbert and Sullivan's *Iolanthe,* Don Carlos, Hungarian hussars, Neapolitan fishermen, Charles IX of France, toreadors, and Circassian princes. Alva, dressed as a Venetian princess after a portrait by Alexandre Cabanel, received, joined by Lady Mandeville, who was dressed as the Princesse de Croy after a portrait by Van Dyke. The long-suffering William K., as the Duc de Guise, wore a yellow silk doublet over yellow tights.

William Henry was there, but he refused to wear a costume. He was said to be the only guest in ordinary evening clothes; Maria Louisa came as a lady-in-waiting to Marie Antoinette. Lila Webb was a marquise of the ancien régime; Emily Sloane was Bo-Peep; and Florence Twombly was described merely as dressed in rose brocade. Chauncey Depew was Father Knickerbocker. Mrs. Astor, whose presence was corporeal proof of the arrival of the Vanderbilts—she was even seen graciously chatting with Alva—wore a Venetian dress and numerous diamond necklaces; she was accompanied by the inevitable Ward McAllister dressed as a French nobleman of the time of Henri IV.

Even Alva's staid brother-in-law Cornelius II and his Alice did their part, showing family solidarity and "social responsibility" by their presence in fancy dress. Cornelius was Louis XVI while Alice was "The Electric Light" in a costume that lighted up at intervals from batteries placed in her pockets. Their two boys and daughter, aged eight to thirteen years, were dressed as "a little courtier," "Sinbad the Sailor," and "a rose."

As Proust remarked, parties do not really happen until the following day when they rivet the attention of those who were not invited. In the days following the Vanderbilt ball, the New York newspapers chronicled it as though it were the War of the Roses. The New York *World,* which took an even more piercing interest in the doings of society than the other papers, calculated to the penny what this entertainment had cost: $155,730 for costumes, $11,000 for flowers, $4,000 for carriage hire, $4,000 for hairdressing, and $65,270 for champagne, catering, music, and sundries. No doubt Alva thought it was worth every cent.

Five blocks up Fifth Avenue at 1 West 57th Street, Cornelius II and Alice were living a life as splendid and costly as Alva's and William K.'s, but much more sedate. Most people,

including their relations, found them stately and respectable to the point of dullness, and intimidating to boot. Cornelius II (he was really the third, but by common consent the unfortunate Cornelius Jeremiah was omitted in the reckoning) was Head of the House of Vanderbilt, a position he took as he did everything—very seriously. He lacked the financial imagination of his grandfather and the remarkable flair for investment of his father, but he was an excellent manager. In 1883, he had become chairman of the board of the New York Central and the Michigan Central railroads. During his administration, the Boston and Albany Railroad was added to the Vanderbilt roads on a lease from the State of Massachusetts, for which the Vanderbilts paid only $2 million a year. "The acquisition of this railroad," one historian wrote, "enabled the New York Central to make direct connection with Boston, and with much of the New England coast and added about four hundred miles to the Vanderbilt system."

Cornelius toiled daily in the offices of the Vanderbilt roads, absorbed in ledgers; he was said to be one of the best accountants in the country. He was calm, methodical, and starchy.

Never in her long life—she died at 89, having survived Cornelius II by 35 years—did Cornelius's wife, Alice Gwynne, deviate from the strictest code of social usage; she was a New York byword for formality and stiffness. In the 57th Street house she had a "colonial room" in which she preserved memorabilia of her early New England ancestors. Here she takes the air with her daughter Gladys, Countess Széchényi.

Henry Clews, an old Wall Streeter and chronicler of the American rich, wrote in *Twenty-Eight Years in Wall Street,* "The four sons of William H. Vanderbilt have had the greatest start in life of any family in all the records of history, ancient and modern, with the single exception, probably, of the five Rothschild brothers . . ." Cornelius II, dignified in mien and sober in deportment, managed his inheritance skillfully and devoted time and money to philanthropy, but to most people, including his family, he remained a remote figure.

Apparently, he was totally without humor; most people, including many of his relations, found him solemn, even grim. His niece Consuelo, Duchess of Marlborough, said frankly that she considered Uncle Cornelius "terrifying." He was puritanical, and some people considered him a saint. He had an awesome sense of what he considered to be his duty, which was to preserve, manage, and augment the family fortune and to pass it on to his children.

Cornelius II was the first Vanderbilt to assume the role of civic leader in New York and to engage in good works: he was an officer in the Young Men's Christian Association and built, at a cost of $75,000, the Railroad Branch at Madison Avenue and 45th Street "to provide the employees of the railroads which enter the Grand Central station with a modern club-house, suited to their needs." He was a trustee of the General Theological (Episcopal) Seminary, treasurer of the Episcopal Board of Foreign Missions, and a trustee of St. Luke's Hospital and the College of Physicians and Surgeons. For many years he was chairman of the executive committee of the Metropolitan Museum of Art. He was proud of his old New York ancestry: in 1885 he became president of the St. Nicholas Society. He and Alice were active members of St. Bartholomew's Church, then on the southwest corner of Madison Avenue and 44th Street. It was a very proper church. Clarence Day, Sr.—the father in *Life with Father*—liked St. Bartholomew's. "The church itself was comfortable," said his son, "and the congregation were all of the right sort . . . the place was like a good club. And the sermon was like a strong editorial in a conservative newspaper."

Despite the high-minded activities, the success both financial and social, and the praise of his peers for his charity and expert management, Cornelius II gave many contemporaries the impression that he was not happy. His rapscallion grandson Cornelius IV, not necessarily the most objective witness but keenly observant nonetheless, believed that he "suffered from some deep-seated and irradicable malaise of the soul which drove him on to an unpredictable and tragic end."

His wife, Alice, whom he married in 1867 when he was twenty-four, was equally severe. She was very small and very plain, with tight lips and cold gray eyes. Despite the best efforts of the most fashionable—and expensive—dressmakers and jewelers, she never presented an impressive appearance even when receiving guests in her superb house. Her devotion to respectability in all things was fanatical. When her daughter Gertrude sculpted a male nude, Alice's comment was, "Do give him a scarf. The fig leaf is so little!"

She was very proud of her own family: though her father was only an attorney in Cincinnati, the Gwynnes were of old New England descent, and the Claypooles, her mother's family, had Revolutionary War ancestry and membership in the Society of the Cincinnati. She sometimes gave the impression that she was trying to bring the Vanderbilts, who were of even older American stock, up to the level of the Gwynnes. It was she, for example, who began to use a Vanderbilt coat of arms, consisting of acorns surrounded by oak leaves to which they had no heraldic right. The great Vanderbilt will case, which took place when she was a young matron in the family, must have given her a permanent shock by its public mudslinging among her in-laws. Worse scandals were to come.

This serious couple, so decorous, so formal, so concerned with family, church, and appearance, enjoyed, or at least received,

When the art collection of Alexander T. Stewart, William Henry's precursor in collecting contemporary French paintings, was sold at auction in 1887, the major work offered was Rosa Bonheur's *The Horse Fair*. Painted when the artist was only 31 years old, it depicts a market day in Paris. First exhibited at the Salon of 1853, the painting won immediate acclaim and was widely regarded as one of the greatest masterpieces of the century. At the Stewart sale Cornelius II paid $53,000 for the painting, then the highest price ever paid at an American art auction, and immediately sent it to The Metropolitan Museum of Art with his compliments. A hundred years later the almost life-size work is still popular with museum-goers.

Rosa Bonheur. *The Horse Fair*. c. 1853–1855. Oil on canvas, 96½ × 199½". The Metropolitan Museum of Art. Gift of Cornelius Vanderbilt, 1887 (87.25)

an annual income conservatively estimated at $3,625,000. They found nothing incongruous in leading their conscientious lives amid settings of almost imperial splendor. Clearly then, Cornelius and Alice, especially Alice, had little in common with the rambunctious and outspoken Alva. Alice was called "Mrs. Vanderbilt" because she was the wife of the Head of the House—these things were then of great importance—while Alva was merely "Mrs. William K. Vanderbilt," and it galled her. Appearances were preserved—one could be certain of that with Alice, though not with Alva—but the rivalry existed. In the 1890s, the battlefield was to be transferred to Newport, Rhode Island, where it would produce two of the most remarkable houses ever built in America.

The little town of Newport has exercised a strange fascination on the minds of American society. By no means the most attractive place on the East Coast, even by the 1890s Newport was in its second century as the premier American summer resort. In Mark Twain's novel *The Gilded Age* some Washington, D.C. ladies are discussing resorts in 1873: a newcomer timidly submits that Long Branch or Cape May, New Jersey, might be pleasant for summering. She is immediately snubbed by a more worldly matron: "Nobody goes *there*, Miss Hawkins—at least only persons of no position in society. And the president." Another lady laments, "Newport is damp and cold and windy and excessively disagreeable, but it is very select."

It was the selectivity of Newport that turned Vanderbilt and other eyes on that resort. The Commodore and William Henry had spent summers in Saratoga, but Saratoga was raffish and full of racetrack touts and "light" ladies. The season at Newport lasted about six weeks in the high summer, giving visitors plenty of time to experience the vagaries of New England weather and to refresh themselves for the strenuous winter season in New York.

Visitors in the 90s appear to have regarded life in Newport as carefree and even giddy; by the standards of a century later, daily life was incredibly stiff and regulated. Although a resort and supposedly meant for relaxation, Newport adhered to the ceremonies of New York social life: balls and dances, morning calls (which were actually made at any time during the daylight hours), the leaving of calling cards with an elaborate protocol governing turned-down corners, and teas. The great houses—called "cottages" as a slight concession to the resort atmosphere—swarmed with servants in uniform. There was the occasional *fête champêtre,* or picnic; footmen preceded the guests to lay out a meal on damask-covered tables. After the meal, served in courses with the appropriate wines, there was dancing on the grass. Hardly anyone seems to have gone swimming. There was sailing on Narragansett Bay, of course, but that also was ceremonious and called for changing into proper yachting attire—there was a lot of clothes changing, in fact. The young ladies held archery contests. Tennis was played at the new Casino, and many hours passed watching the matches. Lively folk were addicted to four-in-hand driving in the newest and most fashionable equipages with sleekly groomed horses, although the course was somewhat limited by the dimensions of the island. One frolicsome young lady drove a three-in-hand of miniature ponies up and down Bellevue Avenue, the heart of the stylish district, lined with "cottages."

So many balls were given by competing hostesses during each of the short Newport seasons that it became difficult for the guests to devise new and original costumes. At one ball a young lady wore a headdress of small gauze balls each imprisoning a firefly. A more up-to-date guest impersonated "Lyrus" by wearing on her head a wreath of flowers while over the forehead rose a lyre composed of tiny gaslights, which were fed from a small reservoir concealed in the dress that flashed as she moved her head.

On this costly and formal social scene descended the Vanderbilts, richer than any other family and apparently determined to surpass everyone in style. Cornelius II and Alice were the first in the field. In 1885, they bought a rambling house called The Breakers, which had been built in 1877–1878 for Pierre Lorillard of the tobacco family. Oddly enough, they had bought a Lorillard house in New York to demolish for their town residence. The architectural firm of Peabody and Stearns had built for him an enormous shingle house in a style loosely called Queen Anne. The land, facing the Cliff Walk, a public pathway along the ocean side of the island, was believed to have cost Lorillard $100,000 and the house $90,000 more. Pierre Lorillard did not live there long: he was the prize mover in the development of Tuxedo Park, a planned community for the rich only forty miles from New York City, and he moved there himself in October 1885. Once he had bought The Breakers, Cornelius II hired Peabody and Stearns to make additions to the already huge house, including a new dining room measuring 40 by 70 feet, the largest in Newport at the time. Cornelius and Alice and their children spent summers and autumns at the house until 1892. In that year the family stayed unusually late, until November. The house caught fire and burned to the ground. Fortunately, since most of the family was out driving, there was no loss of life. The furnishings lost were estimated at $700,000.

By the time The Breakers burned, William K. and Alva were already building a house in Newport, the grandest ever seen, next door to Beechwood, where Mrs. Astor had been summering majestically in her sixty-two-room "cottage" since 1881. (Poor Mrs. Astor could not escape the Vanderbilts no matter where she went.) The Vanderbilt architect was, again, Richard Morris Hunt. A few years before (1878–1880) he had built them a country house near New York, Idlehour, at Oakdale, Long Island, in a style described as "Queen Anne country." There was nothing in the least Queen Anne about the house that Hunt designed and built in Newport, nor was it most people's idea of a resort residence, even in those expansive days. The building material was marble, and the little palace was given the name Marble House. Its use was not entirely ostentation; it was partly precaution, since the popular shingle houses of Newport had a bad habit of burning down.

William K., pleased with the Fifth Avenue and Oakdale houses that Hunt had built for him, apparently told the architect to spend what he needed to create the most sumptuous house in Newport. The cost was reckoned at $11 million: $2 million for the building and $9 million for the interior decoration and furnishings, which were under Hunt's supervision. Hunt was generally assumed to be building what *he* wanted. Adele Sloane, William K.'s niece, referred to Marble House as "another monument to Mr. Hunt." Such statements forgot Alva; she was not accustomed to taking the backseat for anyone, even America's most esteemed architect, and she directed the entire project. Construction was begun in the fall of 1889, and the house was ready for occupancy—and entertaining—in June 1892, just in time for the season. Although the house was sited directly on Bellevue Avenue, the main thoroughfare of the town and, like most houses in Newport, was on a relatively small plot of land, Alva did her best to keep the neighbors and the press from knowing what was going on, erecting a high fence around the construction and forbidding workmen—many of whom spoke no English anyway—from discussing their work. The neighbors, with whom the fearsome Alva was not popular, had their revenge: they referred to the building as "a marble house for a woman with a marble heart."

Alva's house is extremely formal. Critics see in it elements of both the White House in Washington and the Petit Trianon at Versailles; Hunt always quoted historical references. The grounds of the west-facing building are entered by a semicircular driveway, and in front of the portico is a fountain fed by water pouring from three carved masks.

A gold ballroom is even today a blaze of gilding with two huge bronze chandeliers and carved giltwood panels. Marine motifs such as scallops, dolphins, and stalactites were used throughout to remind guests what is easily forgotten among the splendors, that this is a seaside villa. Each parent had a special room at the head of the great staircase, a study for William K., a boudoir for Alva, marked with their initials over the doorways.

Richard Morris Hunt's majestic Marble House at Newport

The firm of Batterson and Eisele of New York supplied the marble for several of Richard Morris Hunt's Vanderbilt houses, including The Breakers, Biltmore, and Marble House. The entrance hall of the latter is lined with yellow Siena marble. Through the doorway at center is the dining room lined with dark pink Numidian marble.

One of the most unforgettable features of Marble House is the great bronze-and-steel doorway grille at the entrance, left, designed by Hunt and declared at the time to be "the finest piece of work of this character ever turned out in the United States." Although the grille weighs more than ten tons, the central doors swing easily on their hinges.

The family sitting room was the Gothic Room, opposite above left, with dark paneling and miscellaneous medieval and Renaissance objects. The fireplace was a marvel of carving with panels, figures, even crenellations. Stained-glass windows gave the only light, and no acknowledgment is made of the sea, which it faces. Consuelo remembered the room as having "a melancholy atmosphere."

The feel of Marble House is that of 18th-century France: the marble, the gilding, the stiff placement of the furnishings. The Vanderbilts' favorite sculptor, Karl Bitter, made the inspiration clear in two medallions at the head of the grand staircase, opposite above right: one (right) is of Jules Hardouin-Mansart, architect of Versailles, the other of Richard Morris Hunt. The bust in the center is of Louis XIV.

Despite the historical recollections of the architecture, very few of the furnishings of Marble House are antiques. Alva's bedroom, for example, in the Rococo Revival style, is furnished with pieces made to order by the two Paris firms of J. Allard et Fils and Henri Dasson, opposite below.

Overleaf: The dining room at Marble House. Over the fireplace is a copy of a portrait of Louis XIV. The dining-room chairs each weigh 70 pounds; footmen had to push guests up to the table.

Marble House has about fifty rooms with only one designated as a guest room; surely it must be the largest house ever to have been built with only one guest room. Many of the rooms were for the live-in servants who came from New York for the season; the Vanderbilts usually had about twenty-five in staff.

When the Vanderbilts moved in, their daughter, Consuelo, was fifteen, William K. II was fourteen, and Harold Stirling was only eight; his nursery and schoolroom are in a corridor of their own. None of the children ever spoke or wrote of the house with any affection. Alva thought of the house as a finished work of art, *her* work of art, and permitted no compromising additions. William K. gave her the house and all its contents on her thirty-ninth birthday.

But the family, even Alva, seemed eager to escape the chilly magnificence of Marble House: no sooner was it completed than they began to take long cruises on their new yacht, the *Alva*. The Commodore had built his yacht, the *North Star*, years before, but it was used only for the family's trip to Europe in 1853 and on its return was converted, in the Commodore's thrifty way, to

The Gold Room in Marble House,
opposite, considered the most opulently
decorated room in the whole of
Newport, was used for the balls and
dances given by Alva and William K.
during the short season. Karl Bitter
carved the gilt wall panels and J. Allard
et Fils supplied the sculptures. On the
ceiling is a vast painting in the style of
Tintoretto.

The enormous kitchen at Marble House,
right, with its innumerable copper
vessels and devices such as the coffee-
grinder (on the front of the table) could
prepare the lengthy and elaborate meals
of the time; according to legend, Alva
could have 200 guests to dinner without
requiring outside help.

Consuelo (Mimi) Russell, great-
granddaughter of Consuelo, Duchess of
Marlborough, in the dining room at
Marble House, below.

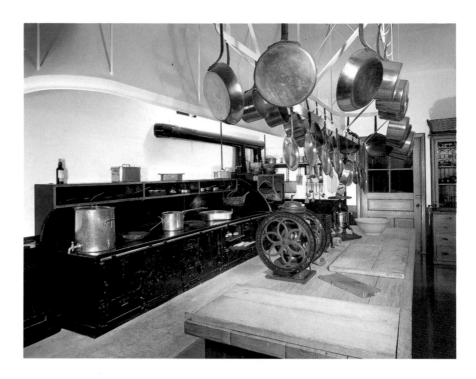

commercial purposes. William K. was the first important yachtsman in the family. In the *Alva,* the Vanderbilts traveled to faraway places, including Constantinople and India.

One of the guests on the yacht on a long 1887–1888 cruise was William K.'s friend Oliver Hazard Perry Belmont, who was usually called by his initials, O. H. P. He was the son of August Belmont, a financier who had come to the United States in the 1830s as agent of the Rothschild family and, while making a great deal of money in investment banking, had also bettered himself socially by marrying the daughter of Admiral Matthew Calbraith Perry, the man who opened Japan to the West. O. H. P. had never done much in the way of business, being perfectly willing to live on his ample inherited funds while devoting himself mainly to breeding fine horses, for which he had an obsession. He had married in 1882 but had deserted his wife on the honeymoon to go traveling in Spain with a French dancer. The horror of his family can be imagined: "dancer" was then a synonym for "adventuress," and her being French made the scandal even worse since everyone knew that morality was dead in France. The Belmonts were divorced the following year, and after that, in the disapproving words of a biographer, O. H. P. "was lost to frivolity."

After his divorce from Alva, William K. sold his yacht named in her honor and bought the *Valiant*. This photograph is inscribed to his sister Lila, "In remembrance, dear Lila, of your first ocean trip on board the Valiant, July 1897."

By the time the *Alva* had returned from a second cruise in 1889, it was obvious that O.H.P. and Alva Vanderbilt were strongly attracted to each other.

Like Belmont, William K. was interested in horses, too, and spent an increasing amount of time and money on racing. He was the principal owner of the Coney Island Jockey Club, then a fashionable organization, and was a fixture of their clubhouse, where he was generally popular. "Patrician as Mr. Vanderbilt may be," the New York *Times* remarked, "in his social life and addicted to communing with the 'howling swells' of Long Island and the grander ones of Newport and Lenox, he is a democrat of democrats when he goes to the race track."

Consuelo, daughter of William K. and Alva, was considered the most attractive of the many Vanderbilt women of the fourth generation, and during her long lifetime she was photographed often. Her portrait was painted by many artists, including John Singer Sargent, Paul Helleu, and Giovanni Boldini. She was about ten years old when this photograph was made.

Alva and William K. formally separated in 1894. Looked at askance by society, Alva turned not a hair but devoted her appalling energies and willpower to making what she considered the greatest coup of her relentless career—the marriage of her only daughter, Consuelo, into the highest European society. Consuelo was generally considered the best looking of the Vanderbilt women, but she was, by her own account, retiring and studious. Nevertheless, Alva took her to Europe and introduced her to many titled young men, including minor Balkan princes; Consuelo's presumably vast inheritance would go a long way in Eastern Europe. It was in Britain, however, that Alva found the young man who was her choice for son-in-law—Charles Richard John Spencer-Churchill, 9th Duke of Marlborough.

Consuelo's room at Marble House was an unusual one for a teenage girl, with its deep red upholstery and dark woods. Consuelo found it "austere" and in her reminiscences says that the house was so much her mother's that Alva even chose and arranged the toilet articles on the dressing table and forbade her daughter to add any personal possessions. The windows are so few and so heavily curtained that the sea could barely be glimpsed.

The Duke of Marlborough's only distinction was his ancestry. He was surly, critical, suspicious, and without intellectual qualities. He was also noticeably shorter than Consuelo—"nothing on looks," wrote her cousin Gertrude Vanderbilt. He was badly in need of funds, the extravagance and bad management of the previous dukes of Marlborough having loaded their enormous estate at Blenheim with debts. Already, art treasures had been sold from the house and, despite their undoubted social position, the family was, relatively speaking, at the wall. Marital scandals had scarred recent generations, too, in which one authority says, "All the Spencer-Churchill foibles of arrogance, quarrelsomeness, pig-headedness, and tempestuous obstinacy were brought into play."

Consuelo at about the time she met the Duke of Marlborough.

Unfortunately for Consuelo, she was already in love with someone else. Winthrop Rutherfurd was as eligible as an American young man could be. His father was Lewis Morris Rutherfurd, a distinguished astronomer. His family tree was a tangle of colonial Morrises (they gave their name to the Morrisania section of The Bronx), Winthrops (colonial governors in New England), and Stuyvesants. The Rutherfurds were "old New York" and were quite rich (Winthrop's mother had inherited much of the Stuyvesant fortune). They had always moved in circles in which the Vanderbilts were latecomers. They even had the same architect: Richard Morris Hunt had built a New York townhouse for the Rutherfurds at 175 Second Avenue and a summer house on Harrison Avenue in Newport. In addition to this sterling family background, Winthrop Rutherfurd was considered the handsomest bachelor in New York society. He proposed to Consuelo while they were on a bicycling excursion on Riverside Drive.

That was their last opportunity to meet alone. When Alva heard of the proposal, she refused to let Consuelo out of her sight. She intercepted mail and messages from Rutherfurd and forbade him to enter the house. Consuelo was taken off to Europe, and when Rutherfurd followed, they were not allowed to meet. The Duke of Marlborough came to stay in the solitary guest room at Marble House and proposed to Consuelo in the melancholy Gothic Room, where the atmosphere, as Consuelo remarked later, "was so propitious to sacrifice." She had to accept. Her father refused to intervene, apparently afraid of the wrath of his termagant wife. Her little brother, Harold, echoing other relatives and friends, informed Consuelo that Marlborough "is only marrying you for your money."

The duke set a high price on himself and his title, and his legal advisers were determined to extract as much as possible from the limitless Vanderbilt fortune to secure this rather seedy nobleman. He received a marriage settlement that gave him 50,000 shares worth $2.5 million in the Beech Creek Railway Company, which had a 4-percent annual dividend guaranteed by the New York Central Railroad. In addition, there were trusts benefitting Consuelo, and of course, her expectations were enormous.

The "Vanderbilt church" was St. Bartholomew's, but Alva showed her disdain of her husband's family by choosing St.

Consuelo soon came to know the Prince and Princess of Wales (later King Edward VII and Queen Alexandra) well and entertained them with a shooting party at Blenheim Palace in 1896. This involved finding quarters for the royal party of 30 and arranging entertainment for 4 nights. Hours were spent changing into the appropriate clothes: ladies appeared for breakfast in velvet or silk gowns, then changed to tweeds to lunch with the sportsmen in the field, then changed to elaborate gowns for tea, and finally dressed for dinner in satin or brocade with jewels and tiaras. Since the same costume was not to be worn twice, 16 dresses were required for the visit. In 1902 Consuelo was one of the four duchesses who bore the canopy of Queen Alexandra at the coronation of Edward VII. Here she is portrayed in her coronation dress.

Thomas's Episcopal Church on Fifth Avenue and 53rd Street for Consuelo's wedding. No Vanderbilts except the bride's two brothers attended. The other Vanderbilts, Sloanes, Shepards, Webbs, etc. were in high dudgeon; even the bride's grandmother, Maria Louisa, whom she adored, was excluded. Alva chose the bridesmaids from her own friends rather than Consuelo's. The honeymoon was spent at Idlehour, William K.'s house at Oakdale, Long Island. The duke then took his bride to Blenheim, where his noble relations, although welcoming her dowry and the prospect of other vast sums on the death of her father, received Consuelo coldly. The marriage was unhappy from the start.

Consuelo's parents were divorced in March 1895, before her marriage. The circumstances thrilled the public. Rumors were circulated—the New York *World,* always the first with society tittle-tattle, ran them on page one—that William K. had a mistress with the unromantic name of Nellie Neustretter, "a woman notorious in Europe," whom he had set up in a Paris apartment and a Deauville villa and allowed $200,000 a year. The *World* piously pointed out that Nellie's dozen servants "were probably better paid than the brakemen and repairmen on William K.'s railroads."

The true story, however, appears to be that William K. had the mistress for show and to establish grounds for his divorce (adultery was then the only grounds in New York State, and by tradition, it was the male partner who was accused). Henry James heard in Paris in 1895 that William K. had engaged a demi-mondaine to show off, "in order to force his virago of a wife to divorce him." James saw a story in the Vanderbilt situation:

> . . . the husband doesn't care a straw for the cocotte and makes a bargain with her that is wholly independent of real intimacy. He makes her understand the facts of his situation—which is that he is in love with another woman. Toward that woman his wife's character and proceedings drive him, but he loves her too much to compromise her. He can't let himself be divorced on her account—he can on that of the *femme galante*—who has nothing—no name—to lose.

He used the plot, with Jamesian modifications, in his short story *The Special Type* published in 1903.

William K.'s second wife, Anne Harriman Sands Rutherfurd, was in most ways the opposite of her predecessor, Alva, being known for her quiet demeanor and her charities. Her stepdaughter, Consuelo, wrote, "Visits to my Father were particularly pleasant, for I rejoiced in the happiness he had found in his second marriage. My stepmother had a gay and gentle nature."

In that same year, William K. remarried. His new wife was Anne Harriman Sands Rutherfurd, daughter of Oliver Harriman of the railroad family and widow of Samuel S. Sands, Jr. and Lewis Morris Rutherfurd, being thereby the sister-in-law of Winthrop Rutherfurd, whom Consuelo had wanted to marry.

Alva did not depart without loot. Her enormous settlement from William K. included Idlehour and a sum believed to be as high as $10 million cash. She already owned Marble House outright. She wasted little time in marrying O. H. P. Belmont—on January 11, 1896. They went to live at Belcourt, yet another Richard Morris Hunt house in Newport built for Belmont in 1891–1893, almost concurrently with Marble House. Belmont's beloved horses lived literally in the house, occupying part of the ground floor. Alva's numerous foes said with satisfaction, "She used to dwell in marble halls with Mr. Vanderbilt. Now she lives over the stables with Mr. Belmont."

Alva was unfazed. She said, "I was the first society woman to ask for a divorce, and within a year ever so many others had followed my example. They had been wanting a divorce all the time, but they had not dared to do it until I showed them the way." She summed up the social situation accurately: from about that time, divorce became common in the upper reaches of American society, and the Vanderbilts were to engage in their share.

Alva moved back into Marble House for a few years after the death of O. H. P. Belmont; she had always had her laundry done there because the facilities were better than at Belcourt. In 1912, she asked the architectural firm of Hunt and Hunt, the two sons of Richard Morris Hunt, to design a teahouse in the Chinese style for the grounds. The Hunts traveled to China for inspiration, and their design incorporated elements of the southern Chinese temples, with 10 octagonal windows and a roof with upswept eave-ends. Alva opened the teahouse in 1914 with a conference of women activists, but it was closed in 1917 and remained closed until 1981, when it was restored and opened to the public.

While William K. and Alva were attracting attention by the splendor of their new house, the wedding of their daughter, and their scandalous marital situation, Cornelius II and Alice, who must have cringed at the Vanderbilt name featuring in a divorce trial, were occupied with their good works, their social position, and yet more building. After their Newport house burned in 1892, they determined to build another house, The Breakers, on the same plot.

Cornelius II called in Richard Morris Hunt to discuss the building of a relatively simple structure. Hunt first saw the project, unlikely as it seems, as "a tent wrought in marble." Plans grew, however, as they had a habit of doing with Hunt even more than with most architects, and Cornelius II ended up with the grandest house in Newport, The Breakers. Although interfamily rivalry was naturally never mentioned by the principals, it seems clear that the demure Alice wanted to outdo her sister-in-law Alva.

Of the seventy rooms in The Breakers, more than thirty were allotted to the servants. Legend has it that the Vanderbilts could give a dinner party for two hundred without calling in

Construction on The Breakers began in the spring of 1893. Only 11 acres of land were available, but on this rather cramped space Richard Morris Hunt built the grandest house in Newport and one of the grandest ever erected in America. The house itself occupies more than an acre, measuring 150 by 250 feet, with 70 rooms, many of them extremely large. The Great Hall rises over 45 feet, and the State Dining Room is 42 by 58 feet.

The wrought-iron entrance gates to The Breakers stand 30 feet high and are topped with the CV monogram.

extra help. The kitchens are enormous and, like the rest of the house, equipped with electric light (and gas as well), telephone, and other conveniences. Both The Breakers and Marble House, despite their magnificence and overwhelming sense of the past, were typically American in that they took full advantage of the latest inventions.

Hunt seems to have had in mind the palazzi of Genoa when designing The Breakers; like them, The Breakers has high-ceilinged rooms and loggias to catch the breezes. Despite its grandeur, it is unmistakably a summer house and was never used at any other time of the year. Although there was no beach because the shore is rocky and the Cliff Walk cuts between the Vanderbilt grounds and the sea, the bathrooms in the house were piped with hot and cold running seawater as well as with fresh water.

Despite the enormous size of The Breakers, its lavish appointments, and its situation in the heart of fashionable Newport, Cornelius II and Alice were not particularly active hosts. Such parties as they gave were generally held in the Music Room, which was used for concerts and dances. The room, dazzling with silver and gold, was decorated by Richard Bouwens van der Boijen of Paris.

Various architects and designers were responsible for the interiors of The Breakers. Hunt reserved for himself two rooms to decorate—the Billiard Room and the Library, which is shown here. The woodwork is Circassian walnut and the walls are covered with Spanish leather. The principal feature is a vast 16th-century French marble fireplace. On the chimney breast is carved an inscription in old French that translates, "Little do I care for riches, and do not miss them since only cleverness prevails in the end."

The center of The Breakers is the Great Hall. Directly ahead of the arriving visitor is a wall almost entirely of glass that affords a view over the lawn and terraces to the ocean and to the reef from which the house took its name.

At The Breakers a loggia connects the two wings facing the sea. In one wing is the Billiard Room, essentially masculine, and in the other the Morning Room, opposite, essentially feminine. Both rooms are furnished in a mix of antiques and reproduction furniture made for the house.

Vinland, at Newport, above left, was the summer home of Florence and Hamilton McK. Twombly. Situated on Ochre Point, it was built in 1884 by Peabody and Stearns of Boston for the New York heiress Catherine Lorillard Wolfe and was bought from her heirs in 1896 by the Twomblys. Like the nearby Breakers and Marble House, it had at the end of its lawn the Cliff Walk, which was opened by a state law guaranteeing public access to the shoreline. So if it wanted to, the public could observe the life of the house from the lawn side, a curious exception to the valued privacy and aloofness of Newport life.

In 1891, Frederick and Louise settled into Rough Point at Newport, above right, which they opened with a ball featuring a Hungarian orchestra—Hungarian orchestras were an almost invariable accompaniment of Newport parties at the time—and the band from the Newport Casino. The grounds were decorated with Japanese lanterns and umbrellas. Passing out of the family's hands on Frederick's death, Rough Point has for many years been the home of tobacco heiress Doris Duke.

The Breakers was inaugurated by the coming-out party for Gertrude Vanderbilt, elder daughter of Cornelius II and Alice, on the night of August 14, 1895. Three hundred guests danced, with the cotillion led by Gertrude and her partner, Lispenard Stewart, a New York real-estate heir and clubman who lives in memoirs of the time as the best dancer in Newport. Supper followed after midnight, served at small tables decorated in pink and silver. Gertrude, who was tall and lanky, was described by one of her nephews as "not very attractive, or even very feminine." She appeared uninterested in society or beaux and had a friendship with Esther Hunt, daughter of Richard Morris Hunt, so intense and emotional that the suspicious Alice had ordered them not to see each other.

The Vanderbilt houses at Newport astonished the press, the public, and foreign visitors, who often felt that the prodigality of the American rich left the Old World nobility far behind. Others were predictably disgusted by the lack of moderation and restraint in these marble palaces. Many visitors then and later were struck by the strange lack of relationship between the houses and the undramatic New England shoreline in which they rise. Their reputation fell steadily in the 1920s and 30s, when Newport became a synonym for a dying society. More than one commentator suggested that they be demolished. After the Second World War, however, and especially after The Breakers and Marble House were open to the public, their historical importance as the surviving artifacts of the Gilded Age was more fully appreciated. The Breakers and Marble House are now the property of the Preservation Society of Newport County.

THE VANDERBILT FAMILY VI

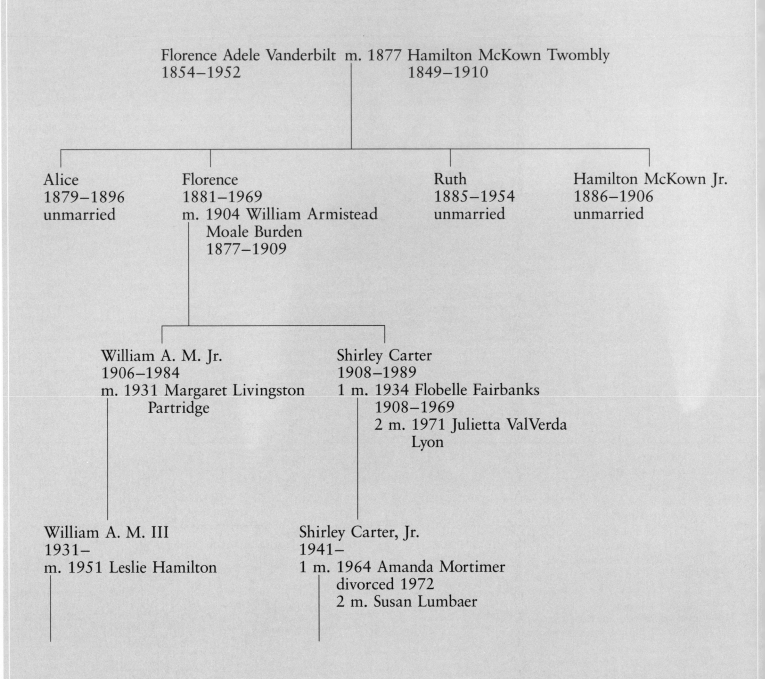

Florence Adele Vanderbilt m. 1877 Hamilton McKown Twombly
1854–1952   1849–1910

Alice   Florence   Ruth   Hamilton McKown Jr.
1879–1896   1881–1969   1885–1954   1886–1906
unmarried   m. 1904 William Armistead   unmarried   unmarried
                              Moale Burden
                              1877–1909

William A. M. Jr.   Shirley Carter
1906–1984   1908–1989
m. 1931 Margaret Livingston   1 m. 1934 Flobelle Fairbanks
        Partridge   1908–1969
                                                    2 m. 1971 Julietta ValVerda
                                                            Lyon

William A. M. III   Shirley Carter, Jr.
1931–   1941–
m. 1951 Leslie Hamilton   1 m. 1964 Amanda Mortimer
                                                    divorced 1972
                                                    2 m. Susan Lumbaer

VI

A Barony
in North Carolina

GEORGE VANDERBILT was the first intellectual produced by his family. His three older brothers, Cornelius II, William K., and Frederick, were businessmen, much involved in finance and management and sitting on the boards of numerous corporations; George was a shy scholar. Yet in combination with a serious interest in art and literature, he had more than a dash of the hereditary financial acumen. Frederick Law Olmsted, the landscape architect, who knew him well and often adopted a paternal attitude toward him, called him "a delicate, refined, and bookish man with considerable humor, and shrewd, sharp, exacting, and resolute in matters of business."

He was born in 1862 on Staten Island, where his parents were still farming. He was educated privately and from very early in his life was absorbed in books and the study of languages. When visitors were first allowed to inspect 640 Fifth Avenue in 1882, when George was twenty, it was noticed that his suite of rooms was the only one, including the library, that was lined with books. "The effect of the whole is sober and serious," wrote an awed reporter on seeing George's quarters. He eventually read eight languages and accumulated a library of 20,000 volumes.

George was only in his twenties and a bachelor when he began to build Biltmore. Gifford Pinchot, his young forester, described him thus: "George was a lover of art and of the great outdoors, a slim, simple, and rather shy young man, too much and too long sheltered by female relatives, enormously rich, unmarried, but without racing stables or chorus girls in his cosmos. . . . Biltmore was his heart's delight. To his very great credit, considering his associations and his bringing up, he had a real sense of social responsibility and was eager to do more than merely live on his money."

George was twenty-six when his father died. Under the terms of the will, he inherited $6,250,000, a pittance compared to the legacies of Cornelius II and William K. After Maria Louisa's death, he was to inherit for his life 640 Fifth Avenue and "the lots and stables on Madison Avenue and 52nd Street," as well as "all my [William Henry's] pictures, statuary, and works of art, except the portrait and marble bust of my father which I bequeath to my son Cornelius."

George was philanthropic, and with this inheritance he was able to make gifts to his favorite causes. He gave the land for the campus of Teachers College, the site between Broadway and Amsterdam Avenue, West 120th and 121st streets. Richard Morris Hunt built for him a small public library building at 251 West 13th Street, called the Jackson Square Branch, which he gave to the city, books and all. Opened in 1888, it became a branch of the New York Free Circulating Library, later absorbed into the New York Public Library. No longer a library and remodeled in 1971, the building, one of the few by Hunt remaining in New York City, still exists.

Like most of his generation of Vanderbilts, George was fascinated by architecture. While still a young man, he began to commission work from Hunt. In 1886, Hunt remodeled for him a house at 9 West 53rd Street, although George was still living with his mother at 640 Fifth Avenue. He had inherited under the terms of his father's will the old Vanderbilt homestead at New Dorp, Staten Island, where he had been born. He kept it as a working farm mainly to supply produce and flowers for 640. In 1887–1889, Hunt designed some new farm buildings there.

Supported by his inheritance, George decided to build a house outside New York City and the fashionable watering places of the East Coast where his relatives congregated. Although he had a house at Bar Harbor, Maine, which he had bought in 1889 from Mrs. Gouverneur Ogden and had the thirty acres of grounds landscaped by Frederick Law Olmsted, he determined to go farther afield for his principal country seat. In the mid-1880s he and his mother visited Asheville, North Carolina, then a new winter resort because of its relatively mild mountain climate. The region was remote—it did not have passenger railway service until 1880—and George was much struck by the beauty of the heavily forested region. Using agents so that the price would not go up on the rumor that a Vanderbilt was the purchaser, he began buying land near the town; by 1888 he had acquired about 2,000 acres. That was only a tentative beginning. In 1895 he bought the entire Pisgah Forest, comprising about 80,000 acres. By the turn of the century, he owned some 100,000 acres in the North Carolina mountains.

The land was cheap because it lay in a poor and backward part of the country. Ideas of land ownership were primitive: the deed for one of the farms that George bought gave as a boundary "the mud hole in the road." Roads were terrible, mere tracks in

most cases. Although it had an extraordinary range of species of trees, the forest was in a deplorable state, "burned, slashed, and overgrazed," in the words of Gifford Pinchot, George's chief forester.

Having accumulated a vast tract of land far from any large town, George now decided to build the largest private house in America, establish a model dairy farm, revive the forest, and establish a forestry school and an arboretum. It was an astonishing decision for a young man only twenty-eight years old, a bachelor, and without ties to the region, even though as a member of one of the richest families in the world he was able to do pretty much what he pleased. He called his new estate Biltmore, loosely deriving the name from Bildt, the town in Holland where his ancestors lived, and from an old English word, *more*, meaning rolling, upland country.

To help him in his immense project, he chose three remarkable men: Richard Morris Hunt, then age sixty-two, as architect; Frederick Law Olmsted, sixty-seven, as landscape designer; and Gifford Pinchot as forester. Hunt he had known from childhood since he was practically the official family architect. Olmsted was the head of his profession in the United States, with the triumph of Central Park behind him; Biltmore was his last major work. Pinchot was close to George's age, having been born in 1865. He was a well-connected New Yorker, his maternal

In 1889 Richard Morris Hunt began drawing plans for Biltmore, such as the west elevation from which the house overlooked the North Carolina mountains. He also had constructed a wood-and-plaster model 5 feet long and 3 feet wide. When it was completed, it was brought by wagon to Hunt's offices on Nassau Street in New York. Crowds along the way gaped as the model of the huge house passed. It is still at Biltmore.

During the building of Biltmore and the laying out of its grounds, Richard Morris Hunt, Frederick Law Olmsted, and Gifford Pinchot lived off and on with George in modest circumstances at a farm called The Brick House, opposite above left. There they were cared for by a small staff and spent daylight hours in the saddle inspecting the property and the works and evening hours discussing plans.

While Biltmore was under construction, its creators were photographed on the grounds, opposite above right: second from left is Richard Morris Hunt, sitting is Frederick Law Olmsted, and standing beside him is George.

Biltmore under construction, below, was an awesome sight with hundreds of laborers and artisans working in all seasons. Even Frederick Law Olmsted, accustomed to large-scale projects, was impressed. He wrote to his partners that Biltmore was "the most distinguished private place, not only of America, but of the world, forming at this period."

Overleaf: An aerial view of Biltmore today. The estate originally consisted of more than 100,000 acres; today there are 8,000 acres around the house. Still in the possession of George's descendants, Biltmore, with 255 rooms, is the largest privately owned house in the world.

grandfather, Amos R. Eno, having made a fortune in New York City real estate. His family and the Vanderbilts moved in the same circles. Educated at Yale, he had gone to Europe to study forestry, then unknown as a science in America. He never had to work for a living and was delighted to join George in 1891 as chief forester of Biltmore.

On the broad acres he had acquired George thought at first that he would build a large frame house along the lines of those in the Berkshire Mountains, such as sister Emily Sloane's at Lenox, Massachusetts. But he was soon converted to other, more grandiose plans by his friend Hunt. In May 1889, when Hunt was already sketching plans for Biltmore, he and his wife went to Europe with George. They visited stately homes in Britain, having lunch, for example, at Knole, one of the largest houses in Great Britain. In Paris, they found William K. and Alva Vanderbilt in residence and ready to take them to the races. At the great château of Chantilly, they were entertained by the Duc d'Aumale, son of King Louis Philippe. He had rebuilt Chantilly in the 1870s along its original sixteenth-century lines and then donated it and its incomparable collection of medieval and Renaissance art to the Institut de France in 1886. George developed under the influence of Hunt the same preference for French art and design that his relatives showed in New York and Newport. Biltmore, as completed, was little influenced by the great houses of Britain. Everywhere he went George bought furnishings for Biltmore; in London he astonished a rug dealer by purchasing at one time three hundred Oriental rugs for his new house.

Having decided on a French château, Hunt went to work with a vengeance. This was the first Vanderbilt assignment in which he was able to work within a large space: previously he had had to build on either a cramped New York City lot or within the narrow confines of oceanfront property in Newport, on little Aquidneck Island. Biltmore is enormous: it has about 255 rooms. The Banquet Hall, the largest room in the house, is 72 feet long, 42 feet wide, and 75 feet high.

The work was planned and carried out like a military operation. A private railway spur nearly three miles long and costing $77,500 was constructed to carry building materials from the main railroad line to the house site. The principal material was limestone, brought 600 miles from Indiana. Hun-

From the lodge gate, above, Olmsted laid out a winding drive, three miles in length, from which Biltmore cannot be glimpsed until the visitor arrives suddenly at the forecourt of the house. In front of the gates lay Biltmore Village.

The front entrance of Biltmore, facing east, below, with forecourt and in the distance Mount Pisgah

The west façade of Biltmore in the winter, opposite. From the arched gallery more than 50 mountains 5,000 feet or taller may be seen.

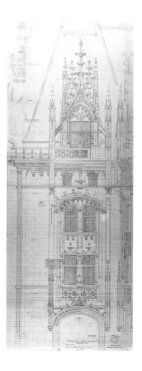

The architecture of the early French Renaissance inspired Richard Morris Hunt at Biltmore. The grand staircase to the left of the entrance to the house was modeled on that at the Château de Blois, although the spiral is in the opposite direction. Paul R. Baker, the leading authority on Hunt, says of Biltmore, "It is a highly romantic building evoking much beyond what immediately strikes the eye."

The entrance tower at Biltmore shows how Hunt skillfully adapted the architectural forms of the early French Renaissance.

dreds of workmen labored on the house. Labor was very cheap: wages were from fifty cents to a dollar a day; and a mule could be hired for about the same price!

A little town called Biltmore Village was built at the front gates to accommodate some of the workers. In addition to houses for the staff, it held offices, a railroad station, shops, sawmills, and a brick factory capable of turning out 32,000 bricks a day. All Souls Episcopal Church, designed by Richard Morris Hunt's son, Richard Howland, who worked alongside his father at Biltmore, was built for the workers.

Biltmore House, although a pretty faithful reconstruction of an early French Renaissance château, in particular the Château de Blois, was up-to-date with internal conveniences: it had central heating, plumbing, refrigeration, elevator and dumbwaiter

In the Billiard Room was exhibited part of George's vast collection of prints. He began collecting when he was in his twenties, and by 1892, when the collection was first exhibited at the American Fine Art Society in New York, it already included 251 etchings by Rembrandt, 175 woodcuts by Albrecht Dürer, and 122 mezzotints after Sir Joshua Reynolds. In the Billiard Room he hung some of his sporting and theatrical prints.

The magnificent main staircase leads from the entrance hall to the second-floor living room and bedrooms, opposite.

The Banquet Hall, above, is the largest room in Biltmore, 72 feet long, 42 feet wide, and 75 feet high. The decor is eclectic: the tapestries are 16th-century Flemish and tell the story of Venus and Vulcan; over the door are plaster studies of the statues of St. Louis and Joan of Arc carved by Karl Bitter; above the fireplace is a panoply of the flags of the great nations of Europe at the time of the discovery of America; around the walls are hung flags of the 13 original American colonies and the Revolutionary War; above the triple fireplace is a frieze called *The Return from the Chase*, carved by Bitter; and the table and two throne chairs were designed by Richard Morris Hunt.

At the opposite end of the Banquet Hall is an organ loft carved by Bitter with the entrance of the minstrels from Wagner's *Tannhäuser,* opposite. Below it, the cabinet holds a collection of Dutch, Spanish, and French brass and copper. The armor on the walls is partly antique, partly 19th century. The 67 arm and side chairs around the table are 18th- and 19th-century Italian.

The family took refuge from the grandeur of the Banquet Hall in the smaller, though still imposing, Breakfast Room, above. The walls are covered with Spanish leather with an array of family portraits. The mantelpiece is Wedgwood jasperware made from clay found about 60 miles from Asheville. The family dinner service of maroon and gold on white was made by the Minton and Spode factories in England.

Most of the meals for the family and guests were prepared in the main kitchen. The large cook stove was heated by coal or wood. Beside it stands a silver-plated server on wheels. The copper cookware shown is all original. Nearby are a pastry kitchen, a rotisserie kitchen, a canning pantry, and walk-in refrigerators.

Biltmore was furnished throughout with a mixture of antiques and later reproductions. The Chippendale Room is furnished with a mahogany full tester bed in the Chippendale style but made in the 19th century. The seating furniture is both 18th and 19th century.

equipment, and it was lighted by electricity. Even with all modern conveniences, the house and the stables, which had stalls for forty horses, required a staff of eighty servants. Several hundred more worked on the grounds.

The interiors of the house were a combination of antique and reproduction furniture, some of it made for the house. Hunt himself designed the table in the Banquet Hall and a pair of throne chairs, which were carved by the Vanderbilts' preferred sculptor, Karl Bitter. Other furniture and decorations were in various "revival" styles, Gothic, Renaissance, Baroque, Louis XV, Sheraton, and so on. Scattered throughout the rooms were nineteenth-century paintings and sculpture, many of them depicting family members, and Oriental objects of art, souvenirs of George's travels in the Far East. Unity of period, even in a single room, does not seem to have entered into the planning of the decor, with the exception of a "Chippendale Room" and a "Sheraton Room," and even in those, most of the furnishings were nineteenth-century reproductions. For all Hunt's faithfulness in recreating the Renaissance past in the exterior of his houses, he seems to have

The South Bedroom was George's, decorated in deep reds and dark woods. The dressing table, also used as a writing desk, is believed to have been designed by Richard Morris Hunt in the 17th-century Italian style. The walls are hung with old Northern European engravings. From the windows at right is an extraordinary view of Mount Pisgah.

The Old English Room's seating furniture is based on pieces found at Knole, in England. On the floor are Persian carpets from George's vast collection. On the wall at left hangs Federico Zuccaro's portrait of William and Frances Cecil, ancestors of John Francis Amherst Cecil, who married Cornelia Vanderbilt, heiress of Biltmore, in 1924.

George owned a few Impressionist paintings: Renoir's *Child with an Orange* hangs in the Chippendale Room over the fireplace.

been undisturbed by the mingling of styles in the interiors. In that respect, Biltmore is a very Victorian house. The Billiard Room—all large houses of the time had one, not so much because billiards was popular as because the gentlemen were allowed to smoke there—for example, has leather settees and chairs made by Morant & Co., London, in 1895, copies of a famous set at Knole. But it also has Flemish, American colonial, Italian, and even seventeenth-century Portuguese furniture.

The most important artist to work on the Biltmore interiors was Karl Bitter, a protégé of Richard Morris Hunt, who was born in Vienna in 1867. He came to the United States when he was twenty-one in order to escape Austrian military service. He had almost immediate success as a sculptor, due in part to his commissions from the Vanderbilt family. His work was to be found at Oakdale, Cornelius II's New York house, Marble House,

The Library at Biltmore was designed for George's vast collection of more than 20,000 volumes concentrating on art, architecture, and landscape gardening. Karl Bitter carved the vast fireplace. The furniture is Italian and English. The pair of two-tiered tables holding lamps is believed to have been made in about 1910 by Biltmore Industries, the furniture workshops set up by George to train local North Carolina craftsmen.

On the ceiling of the Library is a classical allegory entitled *The Chariot of Aurora*, painted by Giovanni Antonio Pellegrini and bought by George from the Pisani Palace in Venice.

and The Breakers. From his studio on East 53rd Street, in the midst of Vanderbilt New York houses, he poured out a stream of decorative objects for the family.

At Biltmore, Karl Bitter was responsible for carving figures of Joan of Arc and St. Louis on the exterior of the spiral staircase; copies were placed in the Banquet Hall. He made iron-and-steel andirons representing Venus and Vulcan and figures of Hestia, goddess of the hearth, and Demeter, goddess of the earth, above the fireplace in the library. But his masterwork at Biltmore was the carving of a scene from Richard Wagner's opera *Tannhäuser* on the panel of the organ gallery in the Banquet Hall. Above the mantel of the triple fireplace in the hall, he carved a limestone frieze approximately twenty-five feet long, *The Return from the Chase*. The Biltmore sculpture was among the last of Karl Bitter's private commissions; after that, he devoted himself to public monuments, of which the Pulitzer Fountain at the Plaza in New York (1914–1915) is perhaps the best known. He was killed in an automobile accident on Fifth Avenue in 1915.

The Oak Sitting Room is paneled in the Jacobean style and has an elaborate strapwork ceiling. The portrait is *Mrs. Walter R. Bacon* (a cousin of George's on the Kissam side) by John Singer Sargent. The pair of brass and copper objects with lions' masks and feet are 19th-century reproductions of 17th-century wine coolers. The bronzes on the center tables are all by the French 19th-century artists Antoine-Louis Barye, Constantin-Emile Meunier, and Pierre Jules Mène, known as Les Animaliers because they specialized in sculpting wild and domestic animals.

The Winter Garden near the entrance was filled at all seasons with flowers, palms, and ferns from the gardens and greenhouses. A trapdoor in the floor was used to bring plants up from the basement. Karl Bitter made the marble and bronze fountain with a statue of a boy struggling with geese.

With the house under construction, George began planning with Frederick Olmsted the landscaping of his vast tract. Olmsted wrote of "the exacting, yet frank, trustful, confiding, and cordially friendly disposition toward all of us which Mr. V. manifests." When Olmsted arrived at Biltmore, he found to his astonishment that George wanted him to make the entire place into a park surrounding the house. Olmsted's realistic advice, which George followed, was "to make a small park into which to look from your house, make a small pleasure ground and garden, farm your river bottom chiefly to keep and fatten livestock with a view to manure, and make the rest a forest . . ."

Olmsted had difficulties with the terrain, but he met the challenge beautifully. The house site was open to the northwest, from which a bleak wind often blew down from the mountains. Olmsted suggested that a terrace be built on the southeast and provision made below it for a sheltered ramble for outdoor exercise in blustery weather. The entrance court on the west side could be protected from the wind by extending the range of offices and stables eastward and partially concealing them by a walled court. For the entrance to the house and grounds he designed a new road to follow along the ravines through the natural forest without distant outlooks or open spaces. As one does today, the visitor would suddenly come into an open space in front of the house and would be struck by both the grandeur of the house and the beauty of the surrounding mountains.

When, in December 1891, young Gifford Pinchot took charge of Biltmore Forest at an annual salary of $2,500 and subsistence, he was anxious to put into practice the theory of forestry that he had learned in Europe. He wanted "to prove that trees could be cut and the forest preserved at one and the same time." He made Biltmore the first piece of woodland in the United States to be put under a regular system of forest management whose object was to pay the owner while improving the forest.

Pinchot entered into his task with great enthusiasm, at ease with his employer and enjoying the social life of the family. He was handsome and eligible and attracted the interest of Adele Sloane, George's niece, the daughter of Emily Vanderbilt Sloane, who made frequent trips to Biltmore. Her crush on him is charmingly chronicled in her diary, but it came to nothing. Pinchot's devotion to his work did not prevent his taking a clear-eyed view of the Biltmore enterprise. It was, he wrote:

> a magnificent château . . . its setting was superb, the view from it breath-taking, and as a feudal castle it would have been beyond criticism and perhaps beyond praise. But in the U.S. of the nineteenth century and among the one-room cabins of the Appalachian mountaineers, it did not belong. The contrast was a devastating commentary on the injustice of concentrated wealth. Even in the early nineties I had sense to see that.

The first public knowledge of Biltmore's forestry program

The Swedish artist Anders Zorn was at the height of his popularity as a painter of fashionable life when he showed *The Waltz* at the World's Columbian Exposition in Chicago in 1893. The dancer in the forefront is a self-portrait of the artist. George saw the painting in Chicago and bought it for Biltmore.

came at the Chicago Columbian Exposition of 1893. Pinchot showed greatly enlarged photographs of what the forest was like and what had already been done to improve it while making it pay. Pinchot said this was "the first exhibition of practical forestry ever made in the U.S." George also visited the Chicago exposition and while there bought *The Waltz,* a painting exhibited by the Swedish artist Anders Zorn. Pinchot also planned an arboretum to gather plants from all over the United States and most of the temperate world. A nursery for the arboretum was begun, but it was washed away during a major flood in 1902. Work on the arboretum was never resumed. However, a Biltmore Forest School to train foresters operated between 1897 and 1913. In the meantime, George's model farm was also winning accolades: he held sales of pedigreed hogs, and his Jersey cows were well known for their record-breaking milk production.

In 1895, the house was completed. The architect did not live to see it finished; Richard Morris Hunt died early that year. George had John Singer Sargent come to Biltmore and paint portraits of Hunt and Olmsted. Hunt's son Richard Howland, who had worked with his father from the beginning, supervised the completion. The housewarming began on December 26, 1895. Only members of the Vanderbilt family were invited, including Maria Louisa, Frederick and Louise, Florence and Hamilton Twombly, and Lila and Seward Webb. The party traveled down to Asheville by private railroad car attended by, as a

In imitation of medieval architects, Richard Morris Hunt embellished the outer walls and roofscape of Biltmore with gargoyles and human figures, including miniature workmen with the tools of their trades, musicians, and scholars.

The conservatory was designed by Richard Morris Hunt and rebuilt in 1957 consistent with his original plans. In the foreground is the rose garden, which now has over 3,000 varieties.

newspaper put it, "armies of servants." The guests were astonished that from the terrace of Biltmore House they could see fifty mountain peaks with summits over 5,000 feet. Between 300 and 500 employees on the estate were entertained at a party of their own, with a Christmas tree, gifts, and a dinner.

Even when the house was opened, work continued on the grounds. Olmsted, who was growing old and cranky—he was soon to retire—now had some complaints about his employer. He said it took "constant vigilance" to keep George in line. His disinclination to methodical planning was matched by a haphazard method of financing the work. He was spending about $250,000 a year for improvements and maintenance, but he rarely made a specific appropriation for a specific operation; he

George, anxious to honor the two men who had done the most to create Biltmore, asked John Singer Sargent to paint portraits of Hunt and Olmsted. In May 1895, Hunt and his wife, George, and Sargent traveled to Biltmore from New York in George's private railroad car. Sargent depicted Hunt standing outside in the front court of the house, but the weather was chilly and the posing was actually done indoors by the fire. The portrait shows Hunt frail and tired; he died two months later in Newport near some of his greatest buildings.

ordered it done and then paid whatever expense the department heads incurred in doing it. Olmsted said, "The worst feature of this casual and informal fiscal control was that inevitably much that was done proved to be wasteful and disappointing in the long run, when Vanderbilt found himself unable to maintain in a really satisfactory manner, indefinitely, what had been accomplished."

In fact, George was spending too much money on Biltmore. Hamilton Twombly, who kept an eye on the business affairs of all of his wife's extravagant relations, wrote rather highhandedly to Olmsted, reproaching him for letting George get in

Sargent wasn't too happy during the month he spent at Biltmore painting the portraits of Hunt and Olmsted, largely because Mrs. Hunt and Mrs. Olmsted insisted that he show their elderly and ailing husbands as they had been in their prime. Nor did he much like the settings: he referred to the forest background for the Olmsted portrait as "red earth stuck with specimen vegetables." Both portraits are still at Biltmore.

over his head. "The trouble with you landscape architects," wrote Twombly, "is that you don't protect your clients from their own ignorant impulsiveness about matters in which they rely on your experienced judgement." Olmsted wrote back sarcastically that he had never anticipated that a Vanderbilt could run out of money. But soon after the turn of the century, maintenance at Biltmore was reduced from $250,000 a year to $70,000.

George made Biltmore his principal residence and entertained a succession of distinguished acquaintances: the guest book shows that the American novelist Paul Leicester Ford came

in 1899, Edith Wharton in 1902, and the ubiquitous Chauncey Depew in 1903. Vanderbilts, Sloanes, Webbs, Twomblys, Kissams, and other relatives and their friends visited. They lived as they would have in an English Edwardian country house. Gertrude Vanderbilt, soon to become Mrs. Harry Payne Whitney, wrote from the opening festivities to her friend Esther Hunt, "We have walked and ridden and when we were at home sat about together and fooled and I have seldom enjoyed anything as much." In the evenings they were entertained by "darkey musicians." In truth, it was necessary for Biltmore guests to find all their amusement in the house and grounds; there were no neighbors to call on or invite in return. The extreme isolation of the house meant that it had to be self-contained.

Not all visitors were pleased with George's creation. John

Frederick Law Olmsted and Gifford Pinchot created between them a remarkably varied landscape at Biltmore, using both formal and informal elements. The stone bridges, opposite, on the grounds resemble those Olmsted designed for New York's Central Park. The azalea garden, above, today contains the world's most complete collection of native azaleas as well as many Asiatic and hybrid azaleas. It was largely the creation of Chauncy Delos Beadle, who came to work at Biltmore under Olmsted in 1890 and remained for 60 years as superintendent of the estate.

Singer Sargent, when he came to paint the Hunt and Olmsted portraits, found it lonesome and cold. The most discontented guest was the easily fussed Henry James, an old friend of George's, who arrived in February 1905 in a snowstorm, suffering from gout. His highly critical letters from Biltmore are often cited because of the eminence of their writer and their irresistible quotability. He wrote to his nephew of ". . . vast sequestered remoteness . . . huge freezing spaces and fantastic immensities of scale . . . that have been based on a fundamental ignorance of comfort and wondrous deludedness . . . as to what can be the application of a colossal French château to life in this irretrievable niggery wilderness . . ." And he told Edith Wharton that ". . . the climate is well nigh all the company in the showy colossal heartbreaking house and the desolation and discomfort of the whole thing—whole scene—as in spite of the mitigating millions everywhere expressed [is] indescribable . . ." Calling the house "a gorgeous practical joke," he soon fled to Palm Beach.

George also maintained his house at Bar Harbor. He inherited 640 Fifth Avenue after his mother's death in 1896. Across the avenue at 645 and 647 Fifth Avenue, he had Richard Howland Hunt build for him the "Marble Twins," two Beaux-Arts town houses that he apparently never intended to live in but built in order to prevent something less desirable from facing 640. Number 647 survives and is a New York City landmark. Since he was seldom in residence at 640, George leased it in 1904 to Henry Clay Frick, who lived there for ten years until he built his own mansion at 70th Street.

In 1898, he married in Paris at the age of thirty-six. His bride was an American living in Paris, Edith Stuyvesant Dresser. George and Edith had met in Paris while he was on a trip around the world with his friend Osgood Field, who a few years later would marry Lila Sloane, George's niece. The civil ceremony was held on June 1, 1898 at the town hall of the 8th arrondissement, with Cornelius II and Hamilton Twombly as witnesses. At the religious ceremony the following day at the American (Episcopal) Church, various Vanderbilts were present, including Consuelo, Duchess of Marlborough. The only child of the marriage, Cornelia Stuyvesant Vanderbilt, was born in 1900.

George and Edith bought a house at 1612 K Street, Washington, D.C. from the estate of Senator Matthew S. Quay of Pennsylvania in 1912, and for a short time they became leading hosts in the capital. But George died in 1914, at the age of only fifty-two, after an emergency appendectomy.

Edith entered into the life of Biltmore, where she made her home. She continued George's work with an industrial school for boy and girl weavers. She was president of the North Carolina Agricultural Society and State Fair and won glowing encomiums. One newspaper wrote, "The action of Mrs. Vanderbilt in excluding all gambling outfits and doubtful shows from the State Fair is receiving general approval. North Carolinians who love decency will have additional reason to be proud of the Lady of Biltmore."

But the period of expansion at Biltmore was over: in 1917 Edith sold Biltmore Industries, and in 1920 Biltmore Village and 230 acres were sold for a residential park for $1 million. Edith

Edith Stuyvesant Dresser, who married George in 1898, was the daughter of a general and a direct descendant of Peter Stuyvesant. Two years after her marriage she was painted by Giovanni Boldini, one of the most fashionable portraitists of the time. After George's death she married Peter Goelet Gerry, senator from Rhode Island.

During his long sojourns in Paris George became acquainted with many prominent artists. In 1897, his portrait was painted by the expatriate James A. McNeill Whistler.

J. A. M. Whistler. *Portrait of George W. Vanderbilt.* c. 1897–1903. Oil on canvas, 82⅛ × 37⅞". National Gallery of Art, Washington, D.C. Gift of Edith Stuyvesant Gerry

deeded about 100,000 acres of the estate to the federal government, and it became the Pisgah National Forest. Later, portions were sold for the Blue Ridge Parkway and some acreage developed into the town of Biltmore Forest. Eventually, the estate shrank to about 8,000 acres around Biltmore House.

In 1924, Cornelia, heiress of Biltmore, married John Amherst Cecil, son of Lord William Cecil and Baroness Amherst of Hackney and a descendant of Lord Burghley, Queen Elizabeth I's Lord Treasurer. The bridegroom was First Secretary of the British Legation in Washington. The wedding took place in the church at Biltmore Village.

In 1930 Biltmore opened its doors to the public, and today it is one of the most popular tourist attractions in the southeastern United States. During the Second World War Biltmore sheltered the art treasures removed from the National Gallery of Art in Washington, D.C., so as to escape possible enemy action.

In 1926, when the house was occupied by Cornelia and her husband, the Halloween Room was painted by houseguests, each assigned a section of wall to decorate; the decoration took three weeks to complete. Nearby are the bowling alley, the swimming pool—with 17 dressing rooms on separate hallways for ladies and gentlemen—and the fully equipped gymnasium.

Cornelia, only child of George and Edith, entertaining a youthful guest at tea (left), and as a young woman (right).

Cornelia's wedding in 1924 to John Cecil was held at All Souls Church in Biltmore Village. Here the ushers and bridesmaids enter the church. Their son William A. V. Cecil is the present owner of Biltmore.

After the death of Cornelia in 1976, Biltmore was inherited by both her sons, William, who today owns and manages the Biltmore enterprise, and George, who disposed of his portion of the inheritance. Founder of the Historic House Association, William is an ardent champion of preservation. He has restored the gardens at Biltmore to their original landscaping and has begun the Biltmore Winery. He believes that his grandfather George Vanderbilt always thought of Biltmore as "a working estate" and that it can best be preserved by adhering to the original concept.

THE VANDERBILT FAMILY VII

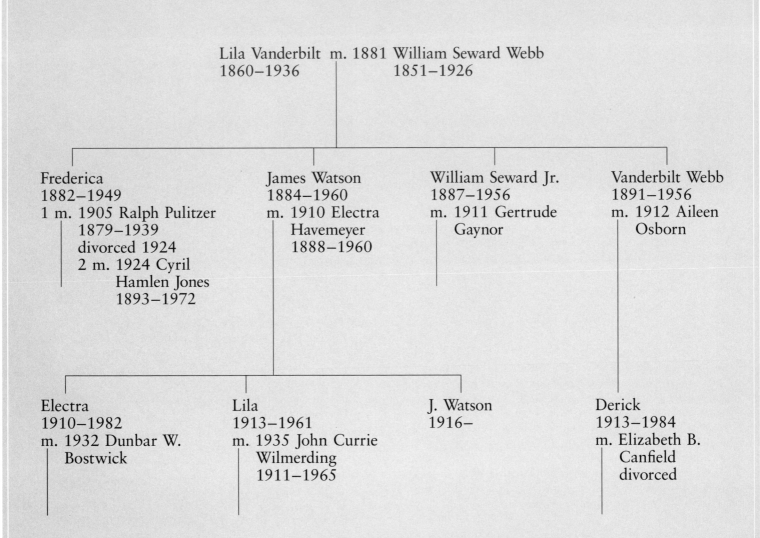

Lila Vanderbilt m. 1881 William Seward Webb
1860–1936   1851–1926

Frederica
1882–1949
1 m. 1905 Ralph Pulitzer
          1879–1939
          divorced 1924
2 m. 1924 Cyril
          Hamlen Jones
          1893–1972

James Watson
1884–1960
m. 1910 Electra
        Havemeyer
        1888–1960

William Seward Jr.
1887–1956
m. 1911 Gertrude
        Gaynor

Vanderbilt Webb
1891–1956
m. 1912 Aileen
        Osborn

Electra
1910–1982
m. 1932 Dunbar W.
        Bostwick

Lila
1913–1961
m. 1935 John Currie
        Wilmerding
        1911–1965

J. Watson
1916–

Derick
1913–1984
m. Elizabeth B.
   Canfield
   divorced

VII

Vanderbilt Country

GEORGE'S BROTHER FREDERICK, always referred to as "Fred," even in the press, and his wife, Louise, were considered the quietest of their generation of Vanderbilts, but they did their part in keeping up the family tradition of building. In addition to Rough Point, the house in Newport, and a "Japanese camp" on Upper St. Regis Lake in the Adirondacks, which had been built by fifteen craftsmen brought from Japan, they built a large house at Hyde Park in Dutchess County, New York.

In 1895 they purchased a plot of land that had belonged to Walter Langdon, the grandson of John Jacob Astor (the Vanderbilts and the Astors were often linked by properties but never by blood), consisting of 600 acres on the banks of the Hudson with a superb view of the highlands of the river. At the foot of the grounds ran, appropriately, the main line of the New York Central Railroad. The estate already had a house, and at first the Vanderbilts hoped merely to remodel it for their use. They hired the architectural firm of McKim, Mead & White to do the work of remodeling. Structural weaknesses were discovered in the old house, however, and the architects gleefully recommended that a new house be constructed on the site. There was some resistance on the part of the clients: Fred and Louise were reluctant to commit themselves, but as so often happened in the history of Vanderbilt houses, they soon found they were having a mansion

For Frederick's estate on the Hudson at Hyde Park, New York, the firm of McKim, Mead & White created a house in what was called the "Italian Renaissance style." It is a tall, rather shallow Palladian villa in the firm's most severe manner, surrounded by formal and informal gardens, stables, gate-houses, staff residences, and a pavilion to house any overflow of gentlemen guests. The house cost $660,000; the total cost of all construction and improvements was estimated at $2,250,000.

Frederick and Louise gave their first house party on May 12, 1899—the guests arriving by special train from Grand Central Terminal—and they continued to entertain until Louise's death in 1926. The main hall in which guests were greeted on arrival was reconstructed by Warren and Wetmore in 1906, and so it remains today.

built for them. When McKim, Mead & White came "to tear the old house apart," William R. Mead reported to his partner, Charles Follen McKim,

> It was found to be in as bad condition as the annex—no strength to the mortar, walls out of plumb, etc. . . . As matters stand now, we are rearranging the center on virtually the same lines but with certain changes in plan and keeping the exterior as you left it. There has been a good deal of a fight to do this because when it was found that the old house had to come down, Mrs. Vanderbilt kicked over the traces, and was disposed to build an English house as she called it. We have, however, used your name pretty freely as being much interested in this design and likely to be very much disappointed if anything happened to it, etc., etc. and when you come home you will find that you

are still master of the job and to hell with White and Mead!

The letter, with its implication that the Vanderbilts had better please their architects rather than the other way around, is a good indication of the ascendancy that the firm obtained over its clients, even the richest.

The interiors for Frederick and Louise's house were the work of George A. Glaenzer, one of New York's most noted interior decorators, and Ogden Codman, who was just beginning his career as architect and interior decorator. Their effects were French, as in most Vanderbilt houses, with occasional touches of Italian taste. The Gold Room, above, resembles an 18th-century

French boudoir. Large mirrors were inserted into the wall panels, reflecting each other so that the room seems much larger than it is.

At large dinners, above, the flatware was gold-plated and the porcelain white with a gold stripe and the Vanderbilt monogram in the center. Frederick's gold and silver yachting trophies filled

Frederick and Louise lived in an untroubled state in the midst of *dix-huitième* magnificence. Foreign visitors were unprepared for such a regal existence in Dutchess County, New York. One of the best accounts of a visit to the house was written in 1907 by Elinor Glyn, who had just published the sensational novel *Three Weeks*, which described in luscious and daring detail a Balkan love affair of that duration. The book was selling two

thousand copies a day at the time and was later banned by the Watch and Ward Society of Boston—an immense boost to sales. Mrs. Glyn was rather a surprising guest at staid Hyde Park, but she was taken there by the Duchess of Manchester (Consuelo Yznaga, the same who had been such a great asset for Alva Vanderbilt in her climb to social position).

Louise invited the author and the duchess to arrive in time for tea, which they were surprised to find served by footmen in knee breeches with powdered hair. Their hostess was wearing ropes of pearls, whose value they estimated—as foreign visitors always estimated the possessions of rich Americans—at 50,000 pounds ($250,000), and long white gloves. That scene was mod-

with flowers were often used for centerpieces.

Each of the guest bedrooms was decorated in a different color, which gave its name to the room. The Blue Room, above, was used by Margaret Louise Van Alen, Louise Vanderbilt's niece, who inherited the house after Frederick's death in 1938. The furniture throughout the house was not antique but made to order in various historical styles by Paul Sormani of Paris.

Frederick's bedroom, above, is one of the most sumptuous rooms in the house. Glaenzer covered the walls with 17th-century Flemish tapestries. The wood-work is Circassian walnut and the bed and dresser are of the same wood and were installed as part of the woodwork. The dark red rugs were made to order in India.

est compared with dinner, when the tables were decorated with American Beauty roses so enormous they seemed artificial. The company dined off gold plate. Conversation, Mrs. Glyn thought, was decorous and rather boring, "everyone speaking slowly and loudly, rarely pausing to listen for an answer."

In the bedroom assigned to Mrs. Glyn, the curtains, the dressing-table cover, the pillowcases, and the sheets were embroidered with Venetian lace. In the bathroom, the lavatory chain had a large blue satin bow tied to it. "There were no books, or any evidence that the room had ever been slept in before," she remarked.

Louise was lady of the manor at Hyde Park as Edith was at

Biltmore. She gave a club room and a library to the village, organized the Red Cross and the District Health Nurse Service, and treated the children of Hyde Park to strawberry festivals. She and Fred usually spent weekends at Hyde Park in the autumn, stopping during the week at 450 Fifth Avenue, their town residence that had once been William Henry's home. The Hyde Park house was closed on December 1. Part of the winter they spent in Florida, then it was back to Hyde Park from Easter to the Fourth of July. Then they visited Rough Point at Newport, their "Jap-

Louise's bedroom was designed by Codman to reproduce the bedroom of Louis XV's queen, complete to the balustrade, called a *ruelle,* which set off the beds of royalty in the 18th century.

205

*Dr. Webb's Special Approaching
Cheyenne, Wyoming
April, 1903.
Baxter, Supt.*

William Seward Webb liked to take his family and friends on long trips by special train. In 1889 the Webbs, their children, and 20 servants—not including the train crew—traveled between New York and San Francisco in a special 4-car train containing a gun room, a wine cellar, a bath, and a smoking room with piano. In 1903, they were again touring the West in Dr. Webb's Special.

anese camp" in the Adirondacks, or Cornfield, their house at Bar Harbor.

Between times they sailed their yacht, usually crossing the Atlantic by steamer and meeting the yacht to cruise in the Mediterranean. Between 1889 and his death in 1938, Fred owned four large seagoing vessels. The third of these, *Vedette I,* he donated to the U.S. government during the First World War. His last yacht was *Vedette II,* built in Copenhagen in 1924; it was 158 feet long and carried a twenty-three-man crew. He also helped finance contenders for the America's Cup, one of which, *Rainbow,* skippered by his nephew Harold Vanderbilt, won the cup in 1934.

Also living in calm magnificence in several houses were Florence Adele and Hamilton Twombly. In New York they occupied the house at 684 Fifth Avenue that had been a gift from her father, and at Newport they lived at their "cottage," Vinland. Even these were insufficient for the Twomblys' needs, and between 1890 and 1900 McKim, Mead & White built for them at Madison, New Jersey, another grand house, which the Twomblys called Florham, a combination of their first names. Only about twenty-five miles from Manhattan, the area was little built up, and the Twomblys were able to acquire no fewer than 1,200 acres of land. On it the architects erected an enormous Georgian house—over 100 rooms—with an indoor swimming pool and a host of outbuildings, including an orangery, a model dairy farm, and a railroad siding for private cars. William R. Mead wrote in 1895, "Twombly wants a house on the order of an English Country gentleman. I don't think he knows exactly what he means, and I am sure I don't, but as near as I can gather, his idea is that it shall be a thoroughly comfortable house without the stiffness of the modern city house. Twombly is the sort of man who, if he gets what he wants, is willing to pay for it." The final product never gained favor with architectural critics, and the house is generally considered one of the firm's least successful. There seems, in fact, almost a conspiracy to suppress mention of it; several monographs on McKim, Mead & White's work do not mention it at all. Richard Guy Wilson, an expert on the firm, has written, "The main house lacks grace, the windows are too small and too many and the front door is awkwardly proportioned to the columnar portico." Nevertheless, the Twombly family occupied it until 1955, and during Florence's long widowhood, she

Florham was furnished with a magnificence befitting its size. In the entrance hall stood carved marble busts of the 12 Caesars, and throughout the house were tapestries, which in the Great Drawing Room included a set of 10 French tapestries telling the story of Rinaldo and Armida—a gift from King Louis XIII of France to Cardinal Barberini.

Elm Court was the enormous summer house that Emily and William Douglas Sloane built at Lenox, Massachusetts. The shingle house in a vaguely Queen Anne style was placed on a white marble foundation; the marble was local.

entertained lavishly, if stiffly. Although the distance was short, the Twomblys habitually traveled from Manhattan on their private railroad car.

In the family empire, Hamilton gradually assumed the management of the financial affairs of his wife's relatives in addition to being president of several Vanderbilt enterprises. The Vanderbilt architects came to know him well because he was the overseer of expenditures and was known to protest vigorously — and rudely — when he felt the bills were becoming outrageous.

The Twomblys' family life was unfortunate: of their four children, a daughter, Alice, died at the age of seventeen; their only son, Hamilton, Jr., died in an accident at a summer camp in 1905 at the age of eighteen. One daughter, Ruth, never married, remaining her mother's companion all her life and surviving her by only two years. Another daughter, Florence, married William A. M. Burden, whose first cousin married his wife's first cousin, Adele Sloane.

Emily Sloane and her husband were among the few in their generation to build a genuine country house, albeit a huge one. Forsaking Newport, they had Peabody and Stearns of Boston build them Elm Court in Lenox, Massachusetts. Although called a "villa," it was an immense house with a main hall 35 by 22 feet and a dining room 38 by 28 feet. This house, too, has failed to find favor with critics: a typical comment is that "the house rambles across the landscape as if it were consciously mocking those 'responsible' architectural structures about unity, clarity, and focus. Its mission appears to be the consumption of maximum acreage with minimum inhibition." Nevertheless, it must have been a comfortable summer house for a growing family and innumerable summer visitors. The social columns of the day are filled with accounts of Vanderbilts, Webbs, Sloanes, Twomblys, etc. traipsing between New York, Newport, Bar Harbor, the Adirondacks, Biltmore, and Lenox on visits to each other.

As the century turned, the older generation of Vanderbilts, the children and grandchildren of the Commodore, began to die off. Maria Louisa, William Henry's widow, died on November 6, 1896 at the home of her daughter, Margaret Shepard, at Scarborough, New York. A special two-car train of the New York Central brought her body from Scarborough down Park Avenue to a siding at 51st Street, from whence it was taken to 640 Fifth Avenue. The funeral service was at St. Bartholomew's with burial in the family vault on Staten Island. She left her money mainly to her own Kissam family in trust for various sisters, nieces, and nephews. St. Bartholomew's received $250,000, and her pew there, number 17, was left to her son George, who was still living with her when in New York.

Hardly noticed by the newspapers was the death of Cornelius Vanderbilt Cross, the eldest grandson of the Commodore, who died at the age of sixty-eight on March 17, 1902. He, like the rest of the numerous descendants of the Commodore's daughters, had received almost none of the family's wealth. Trained as a mechanical engineer, he worked for the U.S. Coast Survey as an engineer but later got a job on the New York Central, where he worked for the Commodore for eight years. "For the last twenty-five years," the obituaries said, "he has traveled abroad much of the time." He and his wife lived at 24 West 56th Street, around the corner from the houses of his grand relations.

In 1902, Mary Alicia Vanderbilt La Bau, who had caused her relations so many problems during the great Vanderbilt will case, died quietly at her home, 144 Riverside Drive. She had been

The "summer people" at Lenox spent a great deal of their time driving their carriages from one house to another visiting or parading the main street of the village every afternoon. The Sloanes kept 20 driving and saddle horses, which were constantly passing through the massive porte cochere.

for years under the influence of various quacks, including "an electrician, faith healer, and heaven-born physician called Dr. Hodges, who was a spiritualist." When an article appeared in the newspapers in 1888 criticizing her beliefs, she replied indignantly to a reporter, "The article alluded to me as Mme. Berger. I will simply say that I was married in 1878 to Mr. Berger, but soon afterward left him for reasons of my own and assumed the name of La Bau . . . As to my religious belief, I have never denied and now have no intention of denying that for the last thirty years I have believed in the spiritualism of Our Master and would not therefore be deceived by such trickery as represented in the article."

THE VANDERBILT FAMILY VIII

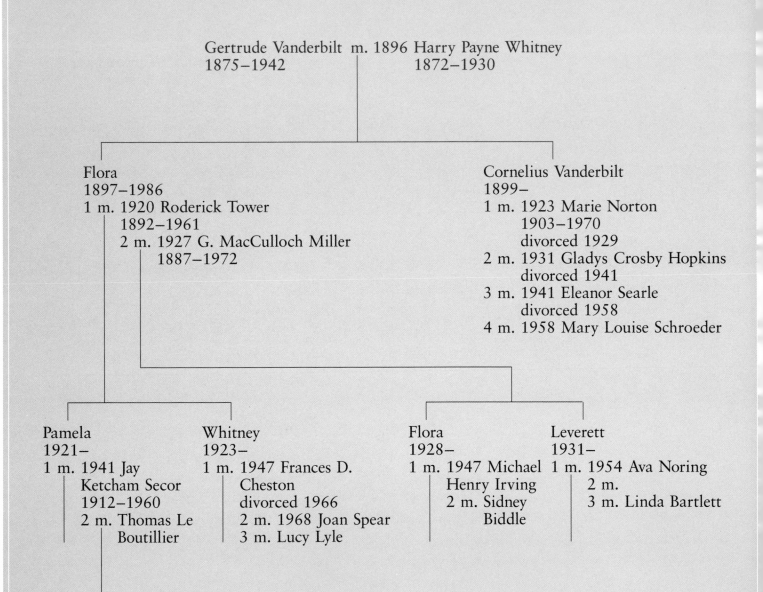

Gertrude Vanderbilt m. 1896 Harry Payne Whitney
1875–1942   1872–1930

Flora
1897–1986
1 m. 1920 Roderick Tower
        1892–1961
    2 m. 1927 G. MacCulloch Miller
            1887–1972

Cornelius Vanderbilt
1899–
1 m. 1923 Marie Norton
        1903–1970
        divorced 1929
2 m. 1931 Gladys Crosby Hopkins
        divorced 1941
3 m. 1941 Eleanor Searle
        divorced 1958
4 m. 1958 Mary Louise Schroeder

Pamela
1921–
1 m. 1941 Jay
        Ketcham Secor
        1912–1960
    2 m. Thomas Le
        Boutillier

Whitney
1923–
1 m. 1947 Frances D.
        Cheston
        divorced 1966
2 m. 1968 Joan Spear
3 m. Lucy Lyle

Flora
1928–
1 m. 1947 Michael
        Henry Irving
2 m. Sidney
        Biddle

Leverett
1931–
1 m. 1954 Ava Noring
2 m.
3 m. Linda Bartlett

VIII

The Old Guard

THE VANDERBILT HOUSES, yachts, princely entertaining, art collecting, and armies of servants were supported by a railroad empire that in the late nineteenth century grew ever larger and more prosperous. The Vanderbilts no longer had any real rivals at the apex of American society. The Astors gave them little competition after 1890, when William Waldorf Astor, disgusted at the egalitarianism of his native country, shook the dust of the New World and moved permanently to England, where he continued to spend the enormous income deriving from New York City real estate valued at $60 million. His aunt, Caroline Webster Schermerhorn Astor, was coming to the end of her reign as the leader of American society. The historian Frederick Lewis Allen wrote later, "In the early years of the twentieth century, the Vanderbilts were the most glitteringly fashionable family in the U.S." A few years before, the noted wit Ralph Curtis, traveling abroad, had replied to the question as to whether he knew the Vanderbilts, "I never knew the Vanderbilts for when I lived in New York they were still Vanderbuilding." No one would say that by 1900; the structure was complete.

The underpinning of the fortune was still the New York Central Railroad and its numerous affiliates. In the 1880s railroads in the United States grew at the rate of 7,000 miles of new track each year, in 1916 reaching the peak of 254,000 miles. In

1890, they carried half a billion passengers. Rails were being converted from iron to the stronger, longer-lasting, and safer steel rails. Track gauges were standardized, automatic car couplers were introduced, cars and locomotives were made uniform so that any train could be used on any track, and new brakes were introduced. In 1883, a regularized system of time was introduced into railroad schedules. Before that, each locality had set its own time, while each of more than a hundred railroads used its own time, usually setting it by the local time of its headquarters city. The confusion over arrivals and departures had grown unbearable as traffic increased. Under the new General Time Convention, all railroad clocks and watches were set on a standard time with four zones one hour apart. Most towns served by railroads soon adopted the new system, leaving only a residue of jokes about "railroad time" and missed trains.

Trains were also becoming much safer and much faster. The railroads, with the Vanderbilt lines in the forefront, began to introduce "name" trains and to develop around each a legend appealing to passengers. For decades, the flagship of the Vanderbilt fleet was the Central's Empire State Express, which ran between New York City and Buffalo and points beyond. On May 10, 1893 the Empire State established a record for speed: 112.5 miles per hour between New York and Buffalo. This was claimed not only to be the fastest any train had ever traveled, it was said to be the fastest *anything* had ever moved.

The New York Central then included the Lake Shore and Michigan Southern, the Michigan Central, the Boston and Albany, the West Shore, the Toledo and Ohio Central, and many smaller roads: in all, the Vanderbilt lines amounted to 10,000 miles of track. Carl Condit, the railroad historian, has said, "The New York Central, its leased properties and its numerous affiliates served the major industrial centers of Massachusetts, the entire area of New York State, the Ontario Peninsula, the basins of the Great Lakes, the Ohio Valley at strategic places from Pittsburgh to Cairo, and the broad belt bounded by the lakes and the Ohio River." By 1902, the Industrial Commission appointed by Congress revealed that the "Vanderbilt group" of railroads consisted of 19,512 miles of track, the second-largest in the country; only the "Harriman roads" were barely larger with 20,000 miles.

In 1889, the financial press estimated the Vanderbilt family's wealth at over $300 million; by 1900, the figure usually given was over $400 million. Over this railroad empire presided Cornelius II and William K. Vanderbilt, with some assistance from Frederick. Cornelius II made most of the decisions. He was as responsible and decisive as ever in business matters and deeply involved in civic affairs and philanthropy but cold and aloof. He was one of the leading citizens of the United States, and the newspapers chronicled his and Alice's stately movements between New York and The Breakers or Palm Beach, and their stays at European spas as though they were producing a court calendar.

In 1892, there occurred a family tragedy that deeply affected Cornelius. His eldest surviving child (a daughter had died at the age of five), William Henry II, the favorite of his parents and the next Head of the House of Vanderbilt, died at the age of twenty-one. A good student at St. Paul's School and Yale, he was in his junior year at the university when he came down with typhoid fever and died on May 23 in the house at 1 West 57th Street. His funeral at St. Bartholomew's was attended by the president of Yale and eighty-six classmates brought down by two special trains. In the funeral procession walked the entire Vanderbilt family, the honorary pallbearers, and the family servants.

The mantle of heir apparent then fell on the second son, Cornelius III, called "Neily," then nineteen and also a student at Yale. He was good-looking though rather small like his father and had an aptitude for mechanics and invention and was already working on improvements for locomotives. He spent his summers in the New York Central offices. Although his health was not good—he had bouts of rheumatism—he was diligent and active. On the face of it, a model young man. Neily, however, was to cause his parents the most intense public embarrassment and, at least in the opinion of some of his near relations, to contribute to his father's untimely death.

At his sister Gertrude's coming-out party at The Breakers in 1895 he met, possibly for the first time, Grace Wilson, with whom he was much taken. She moved in the same social circles as the Vanderbilts. Her father, Richard T. Wilson, was a Tennesseean who had made a substantial fortune during the Civil War in a rather unspecified manner—many people thought he was a war profiteer who had speculated in Confederate funds and cotton.

Grace Graham Wilson, one of the most popular belles in international society, married Cornelius III (Neily) despite the fierce opposition of almost the entire Vanderbilt clan. His father cut Neily's inheritance from an estimated $50 million to $500,000, and it was years before the Vanderbilts received her. In the end, Grace triumphed; for decades she was *the* Mrs. Vanderbilt.

After the war, he moved to New York with his wife and three attractive children, establishing them in comfort at 511 Fifth Avenue (formerly the home of William Marcy "Boss" Tweed). Once settled in New York, Wilson entered the railroad business, reorganizing Southern lines wrecked during the war. In 1870, he became president of the East Tennessee, Virginia, and Georgia Railway. Later, he headed his own banking firm.

The handsome Wilson children were an immediate success in New York society and married so well that they became known as "the marrying Wilsons." The son, Marshall Orme Wilson, married Caroline Astor, daughter of *the* Mrs. Astor. Warren and Wetmore built a superb town house for them at 3 East 64th Street in 1900–1903 (now the Consulate General of India). His sister May married Robert Goelet, heir to one of the great real-estate fortunes in America; their daughter became the Duchess of Roxburghe. His sister Lelia married Michael Henry Herbert, a very grand Englishman of the family of the earls of Pembroke and a diplomat who became British ambassador to the United States. That left Grace, the youngest child, who spent much of her girlhood in Europe, where she and her sisters moved with the "Marlborough House set" of the Prince of Wales (later Edward VII).

Grace Wilson's impressive financial and social background, her prettiness and popularity, and her very grand family connections did not in the least impress Cornelius and Alice Vanderbilt. From the beginning of her courtship by Neily, they were convinced that their son was being pursued by an adventuress. They believed, erroneously, that Grace was eight years older than Neily (it seems she was born in 1870, three years before Neily, but the ages of society ladies, then and now, are difficult to verify) and that alone, in those days, barred marriage. They also thought that she had pursued other rich young men, including John Jacob ("Jack") Astor and their own elder son, William Henry, and that she and her family were determined to land a rich husband for her. Above all, they believed that she was "fast," a word that, to any newspaper reader, hinted darkly at anything from hand-holding to adultery.

The senior Vanderbilts fought off a marriage between Neily and Grace with full armament, mainly the power of their money. There was a painful interview between Cornelius II and

Richard Wilson in which Wilson was told that the marriage would "alter the prospects" of Neily, meaning that he would lose the major portion of his father's vast estate. An even more painful interview followed between Alice Vanderbilt and Grace's mother, Melissa Wilson. The most painful interview of all was between Neily and his parents. Nor did Neily's siblings give him any support; Gertrude, engaged to Harry Payne Whitney and preparing for her wedding, advised him to give up Grace. The parents then fell back on that sovereign nineteenth-century remedy for everything from lumbago to a broken heart: foreign travel. Neily was sent to Europe. But Grace and her family went to Europe, too, and the sweethearts met in Paris.

Neily came back from his travels without any change in his attitude except that it had hardened: he was more determined than ever to marry Grace. The engagement was announced to the newspapers—most featured it on page one—on June 11, 1896. Richard Wilson gave an interview to the press in which he acknowledged that the Vanderbilts were opposed to the match. "It is untrue that my daughter is eight years older than Mr. Vanderbilt. She is twenty-five years old and he is twenty-three." Incredibly enough, the dour Cornelius II also made a public statement in which he said that the engagement was "against his expressed wish." In July, he suffered a paralytic stroke. His daughter Gertrude wrote indignantly of Neily to her cousin Adele Sloane, "He *knows* it is his behaviour . . . that gave Papa his stroke . . . I used to feel that it would be hard when he married her not to see him, now I don't care, I would go out of my way to avoid him. He is inhuman, crazy . . ." Despite all the pressure, Neily refused to give in to his family. He and Grace were married at her father's house on August 3, 1896. There was no wedding breakfast, no music, no dancing; for a Vanderbilt it was a hole-in-the-corner affair. But the newspapers enjoyed it. The New York *Times* society editor referred to the engagement and wedding as "a nine-day wonder" and professed astonishment at the Vanderbilt family's attitude, and the couple received hundreds of letters of support from sentimental strangers throughout the country.

The senior Vanderbilts must have consoled themselves with the eminently suitable wedding of Gertrude to Harry Payne Whitney, which took place at Newport three weeks later on August 25, 1896. The groom was the son of William C. Whitney, who was immensely rich from New York City utilities and street railways and was also a former Secretary of the Navy. His wife, Flora Payne, was even richer: her bachelor brother, Oliver, who was to leave his estate of $32 million to Whitney's children, was treasurer of Standard Oil and the dominant figure in the American Tobacco Company and Tennessee Coal and Iron. Harry Payne Whitney was a Yale man and a Columbia Law School student, but he was mainly a sportsman who became one of the world's leading polo players.

The Vanderbilt-Whitney wedding was held at The Breakers. The expected splendor was somewhat subdued because of the ill health of the bride's father—he attended in a wheelchair—but still there were sixty guests, most of them Vanderbilts, Sloanes, Shepards, Twomblys, and other relations of the bride. The wedding service was read by the Episcopal Bishop of New York and the traditional wedding music was played except that the orchestra leader, Nathan Franko, concluded with the playing of "The Star-Spangled Banner" because, he said, "It is so rarely that an American girl of fortune marries one of her countrymen that I thought the selection decidedly in keeping with the occasion."

Gifts for the bride were estimated to have cost at least $1 million and included a $200,000 pearl necklace from Uncle Oliver Payne. Bonuses were distributed to the numerous servants at The Breakers and 1 West 57th Street. The couple settled into William C. Whitney's various properties, which included an 8,000-acre farm at Lenox, a 600-acre estate, Wheatley Hills, at Old Westbury, Long Island, an immense house at 2 West 57th Street (Harry Payne was "the boy across the street"), and a "cottage" that Harry built for his bride at Newport on Bellevue Avenue near her family at The Breakers.

Neily and Grace were not invited to the wedding nor to any other festivity where his family might be in attendance. Furthermore, Alice urged her other children to boycott any occasion at which the young Vanderbilts or indeed any member of the Wilson family might be present. This imposed a heavy burden, considering the extreme sociability and wide connections of the Wilsons and their allies. Neily and Grace went to Europe immediately after their wedding and made a long stay during which an exciting rumor circulated that Grace had given birth before the proper time. This was not true; Cornelius Vanderbilt IV was born in April 1898. Cornelius II relented only to the extent that he permitted Neily to work in the engineer's office of the New York Central on his return.

Cornelius and Alice embarked on a series of trips to Europe in search of health, taking the "cures" at various spas, seeking mild weather, and doing some limited sightseeing. In true Vanderbilt style, they spent considerable time in Paris; Alice always said that she associated Cornelius even more with Paris than with New York. They were in New York, however, when Cornelius suffered his final cerebral hemorrhage on September 12, 1899 at the Fifth Avenue house.

The coroner who viewed the body said to the newspaper reporters who surrounded the house, "One could almost believe it was Julius Caesar that lies there dead. He has perfect Roman features of the most classical types." This sycophancy was nothing, however, compared to the eulogy pronounced by the Reverend David Greer, rector of St. Bartholomew's, at the funeral in which he said, "The man was more than his money. His wealth was regarded by him, not simply as something personal, not with a lavish carelessness, but with a wise and discriminating consciousness, for the benefit of his fellow men." Reverend Greer himself benefited to the extent of $50,000 under the will, and his church received a pair of bronze doors with scenes from the Old and New Testaments by a group of sculptors that included Daniel Chester French. When St. Bartholomew's moved to its present Byzantine building on Park Avenue between 50th and 51st streets, the doors were reinstalled.

Cornelius II left an estate valued at about $70 million. Dated June 18, 1896—the day when Neily announced his engagement to Grace Wilson—it showed the unyielding opposition of Cornelius and Alice to that alliance: Neily received an outright gift of $500,000 and the income from a $1 million trust. Cornelius had acted in the purest tradition of indignant Victorian fathers. The estate could not be settled until Alfred, the next son, returned from Asia, where he had been traveling at the time of his father's death. It was then found that he had received the bulk of the fortune. Rumors spread that Neily would contest the will, but an arrangement was reached between lawyers for the brothers. Chauncey M. Depew, acting as usual as the Vanderbilt spokesman ("the Vanderbilt prime minister," the press liked to call him),

Gertrude had already established herself as a sculptor with her memorial for the the victims of the *Titanic* when in 1916 she had her portrait painted—for a fee of $2,500—by Robert Henri, the American realist painter and member of the group called The Eight.

Robert Henri. *Gertrude Vanderbilt Whitney.* c. 1916. Oil on canvas, 50×72″. Collection of the Whitney Museum of American Art. Gift of Flora Whitney Miller

One of Gertrude's most ambitious sculptures was *Buffalo Bill,* commissioned by the State of Wyoming, for which she received a fee of $5,000. The 12-foot-high, 13-foot-long, 3-ton statue was cast in Brooklyn and held to be "the largest statue ever made by a woman." The Paris Salon awarded it a bronze medal, and it was unveiled at Cody, Wyoming (to which it was shipped on a New York Central flatcar) in 1924.

Gladys, youngest daughter of Cornelius II and Alice, "came out" in 1904 and four years later married a Hungarian nobleman, Count László Széchényi, in a Roman Catholic ceremony at 1 West 57th Street. The usual Vanderbilt splendor was laid on for the 400 guests; the pope sent a cable of congratulations.

Overleaf: Early in her social career Grace was photographed by Cecil Beaton wearing one of her diamond necklaces and a rose brooch that formerly belonged to Princess Mathilde Bonaparte, which she bought from Cartier in 1904. Grace always dressed for her part. Alice Roosevelt Longworth said, "I can see her now, with an enormous stomacher of diamonds pouring down her front like 'the waters coming down at Lodore . . .'"

Following page, top: Diamond *écharpe* in circular and pear-shaped diamonds commissioned in 1910 by Mrs. William K. Vanderbilt from Cartier

Middle: Diamond bandeau mounted with five pear-shaped diamonds within laurel-leaf surrounds, made by Cartier in 1909 from five hair combs dated 1905 by order of Mrs. William K. Vanderbilt

Below: Onyx bowl brooch, set with circular- and baguette-cut diamonds, two cabochon rubies, and a cabochon emerald, sold in 1925 to Mrs. William K. Vanderbilt by Cartier

issued a statement: "When Alfred Vanderbilt returned home after his father's death he decided, from brotherly affection and for family harmony, to take out of his own inheritance and give to his brother Cornelius a sum sufficient to make the fortune of Cornelius the same as that of his brothers and sisters. This has been accepted in the same spirit." The sum was not named, but appears to have been about $6 million, meaning that, compared to many in the family, Neily and Grace were poor. A peace was patched up and Alice received Grace publicly, although frigidly. Neily returned to his job at the New York Central and his inventions, which included a new furnace for the line's steam locomotives. Grace began a career of entertaining that would last fifty years and make her *the* Mrs. Vanderbilt.

Throughout the nineties and during the early years of the new century the grandchildren of William Henry and Maria Louisa Vanderbilt were taking spouses in an array of weddings that kept society editors overworked. Most of the young Vanderbilts married into families of prominence and wealth, although few, of course, exceeded the Vanderbilts in worldly goods. In 1895, Florence Adele Sloane married James Abercrombie Burden, Jr. ("J.") of a rich manufacturing family from Troy, New York (they specialized in wrought-iron spikes for railroad tracks). Four years later, her sister married John Henry Hammond, son of a successful lawyer and corporate director. Emily and William D. Sloane built houses for their daughters in Manhattan: at 7 East 91st Street the Burdens lived in a house by Warren and Wetmore, who were becoming the favorite architects of the Vanderbilts, with a staff of twenty-seven servants; at number 9, Carrère and Hastings built an equally large house for the Hammonds. Both houses, now institutions, are still standing.

Lila Sloane was married in 1902 to William Bradhurst Osgood Field at Elm Court in Lenox. The 475 wedding gifts were valued by the press at $1.3 million. The Twombly daughter, Florence, married another member of the Burden family, William Armistead Moale Burden, in 1904; their son was named ambassador to Belgium.

Gertrude, meanwhile, was making tentative first steps toward a career as a sculptor, taking lessons from James Earle Fraser, Andrew O'Connor (who worked on the Vanderbilt doors for St. Bartholomew's), and other representational and highly

At 5 East 66th Street Richard Howland Hunt built for Margaret Shepard a five-story town house in the Beaux-Arts style. She gave it to her daughter Maria, who married William Jay Schieffelin, chairman of the board of Schieffelin and Co., a wholesale drug firm founded in 1793. The Schieffelins lived in the house with their nine children until 1925. Since 1946 it has been the Lotos Club.

successful sculptors. She had a studio added to the estate at Old Westbury, Long Island, which already comprised two houses, one in American colonial style with 19 rooms and 11 baths, the other a French château of 30 rooms. The estate catered to Harry's sporting tastes, with two stables housing 65 racehorses, a training track, an indoor clay tennis court, a swimming pool, squash courts, a bowling alley, and a boxing ring. Harry was in the process of adding a polo training field and a full-size gymnasium. There were also cottages for 150 resident help. When Harry's father died in 1904, the younger Whitneys inherited more properties, including 871 Fifth Avenue—one of the finest mansions in

One of the most admired effects in the Schieffelin house was the spiral staircase.

Edith and Alice Shepard were daughters of Elliott Fitch Shepard and Margaret Vanderbilt. Edith married Ernesto Fabbri, a linguist and president of the Society of Italian Immigrants in New York. Alice eloped, marrying a man her family thought unsuitable—Dave Hennen Morris, a premedical student at Harvard. The objection to him was that his father was "head of the Louisiana lottery and some horse races," according to her cousin Gertrude, "therefore Aunt Maggie [Margaret Shepard] would have nothing to do with him." Gertrude added the most damning words of all, "We had never heard of him." Before his death Morris had become vice president of the St. Louis Southwestern Railway, United States ambassador to Belgium, and an officer of the Legion of Honor.

the fashionable district—an Adirondacks "camp" of 85,000 acres, an estate at Aiken, South Carolina, a house at Lenox, Massachusetts, and assorted farms, camps, and lodges in New York State and Kentucky. Despite all this luxury, Gertrude and Harry were not happy: he pursued other women and drank heavily while she took lovers—she preferred the muscular male nude in sculpture and in life—and became more and more Bohemian, all the while maintaining her social position and cultivating a manner so frosty that observers were reminded of her mother Alice's well-known stiffness.

By 1900 Grand Central Terminal was handling over 100,000 commuters into Manhattan every day. Even its vast train yard, photographed here in 1906, was inadequate for the constantly expanding traffic.

The death of Cornelius II left his brother, William K., as effective head of Vanderbilt affairs, since Neily had been cut out of the succession and the next in line of Cornelius II's three sons, Alfred Gwynne, was only twenty-three and showed few signs of an active interest in the family business. With the management of William K., the Vanderbilt roads prospered. Under his aegis, the greatest of Vanderbilt public buildings, the present Grand Central Terminal, was planned and built.

The old station, built in 1872, was wholly inadequate for its traffic, and a remodeling in the early years of the century was no real answer to the pressure of constantly expanding traffic. In 1899–1901, the terminal had been rebuilt under the direction of the architect Samuel Huckel. The frontage on 42nd Street, a mixture of stone, brick, and cast iron, was replaced by a finely dressed stone masonry, steam heat and electric light were added, plumbing replaced, baggage handling consolidated, and the

height of the headhouse raised 150 feet, or six stories. But still it was congested and inconvenient.

At the same time, the public demanded the electrification of the trains, which was not only cleaner than coal but safer. A terrible wreck between a New York and Harlem train and a New Haven train in 1902 in which fifteen people were killed resulted in wide and vocal indignation. The roads were hastily electrified; the first train pulled into Grand Central by electricity on September 30, 1906.

The railroad held an architectural competition for the

On the south façade of Grand Central Terminal facing Park Avenue is an immense sculptural group representing the Spirit of Transportation, principally the work of the French sculptor Jules Félix-Coutan, a professor at the Ecole des Beaux-Arts and the winner of many French government awards.

The figure of Mercury shown opposite is 28 feet high, framing a great clock, the dial of which is 13 feet in diameter; the figure VI can be opened like a window. The entire group is 50 feet wide. Above we see an early model of the central figure.

new building, which was won by the firm of Reed and Stem of Minneapolis, due not so much to their style as to the complex but imaginative engineering they proposed. To them were added the firm of Warren and Wetmore, Vanderbilt favorites. The firm's first major commission had been the 1899 building for the New York Yacht Club, in which several Vanderbilts, including William K., were active. In addition, Whitney Warren was a personal friend of William K. He was a graduate of the Ecole des Beaux-Arts and was an almost fanatical devotee of French architecture and French style in anything. The French government rewarded him for his francophilism by creating him an officer of the Legion of Honor and a member of the Institut de France. Warren and Wetmore, with the backing of William K., soon became the sole architects of Grand Central, ousting Reed and Stem in an episode of great bitterness that brought on a lawsuit eventually settled by the New York Central with a payment of over $500,000 to Reed and Stem.

Grand Central Terminal was conceived on the grandest scale: it is so enormous that except for brief periods in the 1930s and during the Second World War, when it handled troop trains, it has always been underutilized. It has sixty-seven tracks: forty-two on the first level and twenty-five on the lower level, intended for suburban trains. Over one million square feet in the terminal are devoted to railroad purposes.

The decoration of the immense terminal is splendid but restrained. On the street level was placed the bronze statue of Commodore Vanderbilt that had originally stood on the freight station in St. John's Park. It was the apotheosis of this work of art: from being ridiculed seventy-five years before it had survived to preside over one of New York's grandest and most admired buildings.

The major work of art in the terminal itself is the ceiling, designed by the French artist Paul Helleu. He was a distinctively Vanderbilt choice, known to William K. because of his interest in yachting and because he often drew Consuelo, who said in her memoirs, "He asked me to sit for him, which I did until I discovered he was doing a thriving trade on the side with the numerous pastels, etchings, and drawings he refused to let me pay for."

Helleu's assignment for Grand Central was to depict the celestial sphere. He couldn't draw the entire sphere because of inevitable distortions due to the limitations of even the vast space of Grand Central, so he restricted himself to the sphere lying approximately between the vernal and autumnal equinox. Distortions of even that area were necessary, but the artist and his craftsmen also made unfortunate errors. They painted the stars— there are 2,500 in the constellation—as though the artist stood outside the celestial sphere instead of inside, and in working from above the ceiling, they neglected to arrange objects as though they were below. The consequence is that east and west are reversed. Gold leaf and electrical illumination were used lavishly, and many observers never notice that the directions are reversed, especially as they are 125 feet above the floor of the station.

The terminal opened on February 2, 1913. Traffic soon seemed to justify the expenditure: by 1910, the New York Central had already been carrying over 48 million passengers and 47 million tons of freight into New York City. Grand Central smoothly handled incredible numbers of trains and people. A record was set on November 25, 1916, the Saturday of the Yale-Harvard football game, when the terminal accommodated 667 trains and 129,486 passengers in a twenty-four-hour period.

As Grand Central Terminal drew more and more commuters and travelers into the 42nd Street area, the New York Central developed its extensive real estate in the area, mainly with hotels and office buildings. Hotels included the Manhattan on Vanderbilt Avenue; the Belmont on Park Avenue and 42nd Street; the Biltmore, named after George's house, on Madison Avenue; and the Commodore, next to the terminal on 42nd Street, whose 2,000 rooms made it the largest hotel in the world when it opened in 1918.

The completion of the terminal began another real-estate boom in its vicinity. The Hotel Marguery was built on the west side of Park Avenue between 47th and 48th streets in 1916–1917 (it was demolished in 1957 and is now the site of the Union Carbide Building). Warren and Wetmore also built for the railroad the Grand Central Palace on Lexington Avenue between 46th and 47th streets. Their last commission for the railroad was the New York Central office building at 466 Lexington Avenue in 1917.

William K. took the lead in the planning and construction of the new Grand Central, but in the early part of the century he was gradually withdrawing from active management of the Vanderbilt railroads. In 1903, he voluntarily permitted direction of the New York Central to pass to what was known as the "Rockefeller–Morgan–Pennsylvania Railroad combination," a cartel organized by J. P. Morgan. William K. and his family were large shareholders in the Pennsylvania Railroad, ostensibly their rival, and they retained enormous holdings in the New York Central and other railroads, but from then on the executive direction of the Vanderbilt roads was essentially in other hands, although his son William K., Jr. was president of the New York Central for one year, 1918–1919.

William K. and his second wife, Anne, were notable hosts in New York City and Paris and at their château and racing stable at Poissy, twenty miles from Paris, and on their yacht, *Valiant*. Anne particularly enjoyed entertaining musical notables. Eleanor Robson Belmont recalled an evening early in 1911 when Engelbert Humperdinck, in New York for the premiere of his opera *Die Königskinder* at the Metropolitan, was at one of her parties with Giacomo Puccini, in New York for the premiere of *his* opera *The Girl of the Golden West*. After dinner Josef Hofmann played with Humperdinck and Puccini on either side of the piano.

Anne took her part in society—she was one of the founders of the Colony Club in 1903—but she was also deeply interested in philanthropy. She was responsible for the building of the "open-stair" apartment houses, four large buildings with 384 apartments on Avenue A (now York Avenue) between 77th and 78th streets, intended to house patients suffering from tuberculosis, then the scourge of New York slums, and their families in airy, sanitary surroundings. She paid the $1 million cost of the

William K. entered the offices of the New York Central while still a teenager—he did not attend college—and devoted thirty years to management and investing, increasing his already substantial inheritance. Like many members of his family, he was an ardent yachtsman, defending the America's Cup in 1895 with a yacht named *Defender*. After about 1900, when this photograph was taken, he withdrew from business and devoted himself to sport.

apartments, which were designed by Henry Atterbury Smith. Completed in 1910, the buildings still exist and are still occupied.

William K. devoted much time and money to his racing stable and became one of the major winners on the French tracks, three times taking the Prix du Jockey Club. The Aga Khan remembered that he met William K. in France in 1905 when William helped him start his long career in horse racing by allowing him to visit his stables for the trials and training of his horses. "Mr. Vanderbilt said to me," he wrote in his memoirs, "'I think you'll get more pleasure out of a free run of my stables than out of a free run of my house.'"

When William K.'s yacht the *Alva* was built in 1887, it was, at 285 feet in length, the largest steam yacht in the United States. Family quarters were a 10-room suite, and there were 7 guest bedrooms, each with a private bathroom. The crew numbered 53, including a doctor, 3 cooks, and a man to operate the ice-maker, in addition to the usual sailors. The *Alva* is shown here in the spring of 1891 on a visit to Staten Island.

William K. and Anne were living in Paris when the First World War broke out, and they became active in support of the French forces. William K. gave so much aid to the Lafayette Escadrille, the American volunteers in the French aviation service who flew between 1916 and 1918, that he was made honorary president of the group. For his services during the war he was given the cross of the Legion of Honor in 1920.

His divorced wife, Alva, had also made a career for herself. O. H. P. Belmont died in 1908; they had been married only twelve years. After his death, she discovered a new interest: votes for women. With her ample Vanderbilt and Belmont funds she soon became one of the leaders of the campaign for women's rights, which she approached in her customary steamrolling manner. To the horror of her relations, she was soon leading parades on Fifth Avenue, speaking at women's rights conventions, and getting more publicity than ever, much of it, in the eyes

During the First World War Anne worked with the American Ambulance Corps at Neuilly. Her friend Lady Decies remembered that "Mrs. W. K. Vanderbilt would glide sinuously down from the wards to join us, picturesquely attired in the white piqué uniform Worth had made for her with an impressive cap like a Russian headdress and an enormous rose as her only adornment. She was quite the most zealous person in the whole hospital."

In 1923 Alva was photographed on her return to New York from several months abroad with Consuelo Marlborough. Supported in lavish style by Vanderbilt and Belmont millions, she was able to indulge in her passion for building and restoring houses. She remained one of the acknowledged leaders of the women's rights movement, and when she died in Paris in 1933 at the age of 80, a Suffragette banner displayed at her funeral asserted "Failure is impossible."

of her peers, far from desirable. She even wrote a Suffragette operetta, *Melinda and Her Sisters,* with music by Elsa Maxwell, then beginning her career as professional companion to the upper classes. The operetta, surely one of the most unusual musical events ever staged in New York, premiered at the old Waldorf-Astoria Hotel on February 18, 1916 with what the newspapers described as "a ten-million-dollar cast." The stars were Marie Dressler and Marie Doro, with the youthful Josephine Hull and Addison Mizener, soon to be Palm Beach's favorite architect, in supporting roles. Frances Alda of the Metropolitan Opera sang a special aria, and the daughters of bankers and industrialists were among the chorus girls. In 1921, Alva became president of the National Women's Party and gave $146,000 to the group to buy a headquarters building in Washington, D.C. She endorsed the Women's Trade Union League during its strikes in the garment industry and even supported financially Max Eastman's socialist magazine *The Masses.*

William K.'s and Alva's son William K., Jr. was sent to Harvard, unlike most of the cousins in his generation, who went to Yale. When he went to Harvard, the newspapers noted, writing of him as though he were a prince, "It was thought he would live simply. He treated Harvard men in a democratic way, and they reciprocated the treatment after the manner of collegians." In addition to paying his fees, his father allowed him $1,500 a year, an enormous sum for an undergraduate at the time. After spending a few months in a dormitory, he moved into the Westmoreland Apartments "and there started what promises to be the richest apartments at Harvard." His suite had three rooms, a hall, and a bath, all in the "English style," and the walls were covered in green Japanese cloth, a newspaper remarked approvingly in September 1898.

Junior was fascinated by vehicular speed from his earliest years. In 1889, when he was only eleven years old, he rode a steam tricycle from Beaulieu on the French Riviera, where his parents were vacationing, to Monte Carlo. In 1899, at the age of twenty-one, he purchased a Stanley Steamer automobile; his first racing car was a forty-horsepower Mercedes.

He soon dropped out of Harvard and, like most males in his family, married young. On April 4, 1899, he married Virginia Graham Fair. She was a great heiress, being the daughter of James

Graham Fair, one of the discoverers of the Comstock Lode in Nevada, which between 1873 and 1878 yielded around $200 million in silver to its fortunate owners. Fair was an Irish immigrant, a diamond in the rough, noted for his total lack of finesse or even honesty in dealing with both mining rivals and friends. His two daughters, Teresa and Virginia, were introduced to New York and Newport society, and soon Teresa, called "Tessie," had married Hermann Oelrichs. The Oelrichs were not exactly in society, but due to their rapidly increasing wealth, they were arriving. The first Oelrichs came to this country in 1809 from Germany and became a merchant. His money was made in the wool trade during the Civil War, but the Oelrichs interests ranged from shipping Virginia tobacco to importing guano (the manure of sea birds used as fertilizer) from Peru. They organized the shipping firm North German Lloyd, which produced even more wealth. Hermann and Tessie Oelrichs were noted for their lavish entertaining in New York and Newport. At Newport Stanford White built for them the magnificent Rosecliff, modeled after the Grand Trianon at Versailles, between 1898 and 1900 (now the property of the Preservation Society of Newport County and open to the public).

The Oelrichs' New York home was a French château at 1 East 57th Street in the heart of the Fifth Avenue society district, and it was there that Tessie's sister Virginia Graham Fair (always called "Birdie"), who was short, plump, and spirited, with black

Jeweled bandeaux or "headache bands" were for wearing across the forehead. Virginia Vanderbilt commissioned a diamond bandeau designed as an intertwined "Byzantine" circular and rose-cut diamond plaque with triangular ends of pearls and diamonds in 1909 from Cartier, Paris. The same year she had another bandeau made from five hair combs. After her divorce from William in 1927, she called herself Mrs. Graham Fair Vanderbilt and was a well-known society figure in New York. In 1931 John Russell Pope built for her a large house in the austere Louis XV style at 60 East 93rd Street; it is now the Romanian Mission to the United Nations.

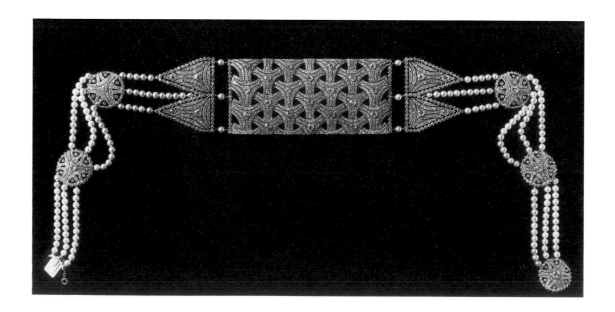

William K., Jr. and Birdie's first house was built for them by McKim, Mead & White—mainly White—in 1904–1907 at 666 Fifth Avenue on the southwest corner of West 53rd Street immediately adjacent to his father's house at 660. The most historically correct house that White ever designed, it was pure François I French Renaissance. White was a great admirer of Richard Morris Hunt, and he emulated his designs in the grillwork of the door and the carved frames of the windows so that the house seemed almost one with William Sr.'s house next door.

eyes and a mass of curly hair worn parted in the middle, and William K. Vanderbilt, Jr. were married in a Roman Catholic ceremony attended by shoals of Vanderbilts and their allies. The ballroom was converted into what the newspapers called "a typical Old English rose garden" with sundials placed here and there and flowering rose bushes, some of them ten feet high. The new Admiral Dewey rose, named after the naval hero of the recent Spanish-American War, "held the place of honor in this mimic garden."

William K.'s daughter Consuelo was on worse terms than ever with the Duke of Marlborough. In 1905, Alice Vanderbilt reported from Paris to her daughter Gertrude Whitney, "It is very

William K., Jr. took little active interest in the Vanderbilt railroads; his enthusiasm was automobile racing. In 1902 and 1903, he established world records for both the mile and the kilometer. In 1904, he sponsored the first official road race for motorcars in the United States, the start and finish being on the Jericho Turnpike, north of Westbury, Long Island. He is (right) watching from the grandstand.

Automobile races were novel at the time and extremely exciting for participants and spectators. W. Ward Smith, a young observer, wrote, "The racers would sweep around the dirt turns at East Norwich at thirty miles an hour . . . It was a thrilling sight to watch those demons come down the dirt highway, through the haze of the early morning mist, with their exhausts belching fire from motors at their engine heads."

The reward for the winner was the Vanderbilt Cup.

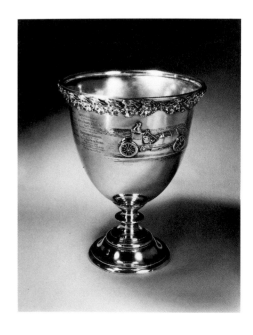

sad about Consuelo, is it not? Anne told me they were to be separated but did not explain specifically whether there is to be a divorce. . . . I hear the Churchills are furious and are going to be as unpleasant as possible." The duke was in love with another American, Gladys Deacon. This strange person was the daughter of expatriates living in France. Her father had shot her mother's lover in her bedroom, was convicted of murder and imprisoned, then pardoned by the president of France, and finally confined to an insane asylum while her mother took up with a rich Roman prince. Gladys's beauty was said to drive men mad, and she certainly had a long string of admirers, including Bernard Berenson. Her looks were becoming ravaged, however, as she could not leave well enough alone and once, to improve its shape, injected her nose with paraffin, which soon melted.

After the separation, Consuelo moved into Crowhurst Place in Surrey, a fifteenth-century house, which she bought in 1910. The contrast between this relatively modest old English house and the overblown Blenheim, which Consuelo had hated, was striking. She added more rooms and had the whole modern-

Estranged from the Duke of Marlborough, Consuelo often visited her father, William K., in Paris, where he spent much of his time in the early years of this century. Here they attend the races in Paris.

After her divorce from the Duke of Marlborough, Consuelo married Colonel Jacques Balsan, who had made a distinguished record in the French air force during the First World War, and they settled in France. At the beginning of the Second World War they came to the United States, dividing their time between New York, Palm Beach, and Southampton. Even in her old age Consuelo kept the style for which she was famous, captured in this photograph by Tony Frissell.

Alfred's first wife was Ellen ("Elsie") Tuck French, shown here with their only child, William Henry III, later governor of Rhode Island.

ized most skillfully until it was one of the most charming houses in Britain. She and the duke were finally divorced in 1921, when the duke married Gladys; they lived a cat-and-dog life with frequent separations and incessant quarrels until his death in 1934. Consuelo married Colonel Jacques Balsan, an early aviator who held French pilot license number 18 and had a distinguished war record. The Marlborough marriage was not finally dissolved until 1927. Marlborough had become a Roman Catholic and appealed directly to the pope to annul his first marriage, although it had been Episcopal. Testimony was heard before the Papal Rota. Alva, completely unembarrassed, gave evidence that she had forced her daughter to marry Marlborough, and the Rota annulled the marriage; by then the Marlboroughs were not only parents but grandparents.

Alfred Gwynne Vanderbilt, the chosen heir and Head of the House of Vanderbilt, married at the beginning of 1901 an eminently suitable bride—Ellen (called "Elsie") Tuck French, whose father had been president of the Manhattan Trust Company. The wedding was in the royal style now traditional in the

family. The bride was showered with diamonds: her mother-in-law gave her a diamond diadem and necklace; the Whitneys, a collarette of the same stones. Alfred and his bride were the first guests to register at the new Plaza Hotel, across from his family's home, on October 1, 1907. Ninety percent of the Plaza was then reserved for permanent guests. The Vanderbilt apartment rented for $25,000 a year.

Known as "the handsome Vanderbilt," he was linked with various society women, including one Agnes O'Brien Ruiz, wife of a Cuban attaché in Washington, D.C., with whom he was

Alfred Gwynne built the Vanderbilt Hotel on the southwest corner of 34th Street and Park Avenue. Designed by Warren and Wetmore, architects for Grand Central Terminal and many other Vanderbilt projects, it opened in 1909.

The showplace of the Vanderbilt Hotel was its restaurant, the Della Robbia Room. The decoration was inspired by a room in the Château de Chantilly near Paris. It was long considered one of the most elegant places to dine in New York.

alleged to have misbehaved on board his private railroad car, Wayfarer. Elsie sued him for divorce over that one and won a huge settlement of $10 million. Mrs. Ruiz committed suicide. At the same time, Margaret Emerson McKim, daughter of "Captain" Isaac E. Emerson, a self-made millionaire (he invented Bromo-Seltzer at his pharmacy in Baltimore), was being sued for divorce by her husband, Dr. Smith H. McKim, a physician of modest means. The suit was sensational: she charged that he had beaten her in a drunken rage; he cited alienation of affection, naming Alfred Gwynne Vanderbilt. The divorce was granted and Alfred gave the doctor $150,000, whereupon Alfred and Margaret Emerson were married in 1911.

Alfred Gwynne devoted himself to horses and to the revival of the sport of coaching. Once he and his friend James Hazen Hyde, heir to the Equitable Life Assurance fortune, raced from New York to Philadelphia in their coaches, using up 78 horses en route. They got to Philadelphia in 9½ hours and returned in 10. Here he drives with his first wife beside him; in the back seat is his sister Gladys, Countess Széchényi.

At Alfred Gwynne's Portsmouth, Rhode Island house, Oakland Farm, the stables were as important as the residence. Each horse had its name engraved on a plate fixed on the stall. Twenty different carriages were kept, each with its sterling silver harness polished and ready for use.

They had very few years together. In 1915, after the First World War had broken out, Alfred decided unwisely to make a trip to England. He had taken a house there and was busy reviving coaching; at this very unpropitious time, he intended to inspect some horses. He was on the *Lusitania* when it was torpedoed by a German submarine on May 7. Alfred and more than a thousand passengers drowned. Of his estate of $26,375,000, he left $8 million to his widow, $5 million in trust and the remainder to his three sons, one by his first wife, two by his second. Since Alfred had inherited approximately $42 million from his father, his estate, in a pattern becoming common among the Vanderbilts, had not increased during his stewardship.

THE VANDERBILT FAMILY IX

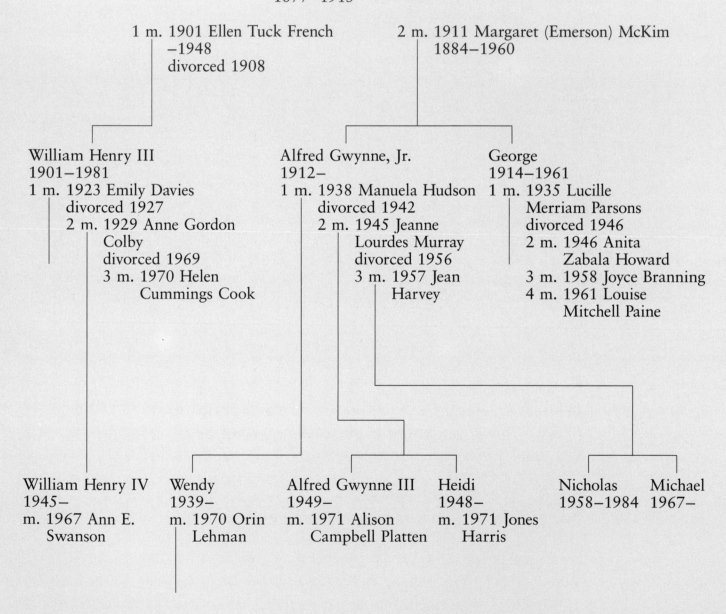

Alfred Gwynne Vanderbilt
1877–1915

1 m. 1901 Ellen Tuck French
   –1948
divorced 1908

2 m. 1911 Margaret (Emerson) McKim
   1884–1960

William Henry III
1901–1981
1 m. 1923 Emily Davies
   divorced 1927
   2 m. 1929 Anne Gordon
      Colby
      divorced 1969
   3 m. 1970 Helen
      Cummings Cook

Alfred Gwynne, Jr.
1912–
1 m. 1938 Manuela Hudson
   divorced 1942
   2 m. 1945 Jeanne
      Lourdes Murray
      divorced 1956
   3 m. 1957 Jean
      Harvey

George
1914–1961
1 m. 1935 Lucille
   Merriam Parsons
   divorced 1946
   2 m. 1946 Anita
      Zabala Howard
   3 m. 1958 Joyce Branning
   4 m. 1961 Louise
      Mitchell Paine

William Henry IV
1945–
m. 1967 Ann E.
   Swanson

Wendy
1939–
m. 1970 Orin
   Lehman

Alfred Gwynne III
1949–
m. 1971 Alison
   Campbell Platten

Heidi
1948–
m. 1971 Jones
   Harris

Nicholas
1958–1984

Michael
1967–

IX

"Thank God for the Vanderbilts!"

WHEN "CHOLLY KNICKERBOCKER," the society newspaper columnist who in real life was Maury Paul (he was also at various times for various newspapers "Dolly Madison" and "Polly Stuyvesant"), drew up lists of the Old Guard of New York society in the 1920s, 30s, and 40s he always headed his lists with the Vanderbilts. Dismissing some unfortunate climber who was trying to break into society, he wrote, "She has not dined, so far as I know, with Mrs. Hamilton McK. Twombly, lunched with Mabel Gerry, or attended one of Mrs. Henry White's musicales. And one is not really 'in' society until one has done those three things." Two of the three majestic ladies mentioned were born Vanderbilts: Florence Twombly and her sister, Emily, who after the death of her first husband, William Douglas Sloane, married in 1920 the distinguished American diplomat Henry White (his first wife had been yet another member of the Rutherfurd family).

Emily, who divided her time between 642 Fifth Avenue and Lenox, Massachusetts, was noted for her kindly disposition and her relatively light-handed attitude toward society. She had inherited one of the qualities of her father and grandfather, however: while they were noted as among the best whist players of their time, Emily White was reputed to be the best auction bridge

Florence Twombly was the last surviving granddaughter of Commodore Vanderbilt; she died in 1952 at the age of 98. To the last she kept up the style of her youth; at the time of her death she had a staff of 126 at Florham, including 30 gardeners, 4 footmen, and 8 housemaids. The sight of her arrival at the Metropolitan Opera in her maroon Rolls-Royce with chauffeur and footman in maroon liveries was unforgettable.

player in New York. Florence Twombly, on the other hand, was patrician to her fingertips. She never relaxed what she considered the standards of society. The fate of this lady has been to be chronicled by social historians as one of the most aloof dowagers in American social history. Even Dixon Wecter, the most serious historian of American society, refers to her as "Mrs. Hamilton McK. Twombly, vastly rich, proud, frosty granddaughter of the Commodore." Her arrival at the opening night of the Metropolitan Opera in her maroon limousine with maroon-liveried attendants was watched with closer attention than the proceedings on the stage. Society reporters, even the brashest, were quite frankly terrified of her: Mrs. Twombly did not give interviews or acknowledge the existence of the press. Since he could never do any firsthand reporting of her activities, Maury Paul avoided the question by saying lamely of her and Mrs. Marshall Orme Wilson (Caroline Astor, sister-in-law of Grace Wilson Vanderbilt), ". . . they are now so well established in the smart world, they scorn newspaper mention and rarely do anything interesting enough to cause a society reporter to glance twice in their direction." Plenty of other Vanderbilts featured in the columns, however; Paul used to say to his secretary when news of other celebri-

Grace as a young matron with her two children, Grace, born in 1899, and Cornelius II (Neil), born in 1898. In 1901, during a serious illness of her husband, Grace's honey blond hair turned white and she left it that way for the next fifty years.

ties was thin, "Thank God for the Vanderbilts!" Some member of the family was sure to be worth a column.

Mrs. White and Mrs. Twombly were eclipsed by their niece-in-law: Grace kept the family on a social peak until the end of her life. Beginning soon after her marriage and continuing for the next fifty years, she waged a campaign to achieve and keep her position as the leading American hostess, the only woman to take the place of *the* Mrs. Astor. Despite the circumstances of her marriage, her husband's disinheritance, and the snubs of his relations, she succeeded in making herself an unrivaled place. Achieving and maintaining her rule demanded qualities of toughness and perseverance and, of course, the commitment of lots of money. Under her fluffy appearance beat the heart of a drill master. She directed her social campaigns like military operations. Despite a strange indecisiveness in everyday matters — choosing which gown she would wear for a party might take hours — when she was inviting guests and arranging for their feeding and entertainment, she was sure-handed and prompt.

She began giving parties soon after her marriage. After living at 511 Fifth Avenue with her parents and at 608 Fifth at her sister May Goelet's house, she and Neily settled into 677 Fifth

Cecil Beaton photographed Grace in the library of 640, where she received guests for tea every afternoon, in 1940. The antique French furniture was upholstered in raspberry silk and yellow-green damask. The tapestry behind Grace was woven in Brussels in the 17th century and represented the visit of Alexander the Great to Diogenes. There were few books, and Grace only skimmed the newspapers. Frank Crowninshield of *Vogue*, a gushing admirer of Grace, wrote that the ". . . library tables are loaded with bibelots, with ornaments in mutton-fat jade, with vases filled with flowers . . . A beautiful jumble of damasks, petit-point, tapestry, and velvets, this room is thoroughly lived in." Beaton, who was inclined to poke fun at Grace, related in his diaries the possibly apocryphal story that when Grace told a well-informed visitor, "This is my Louis Seize room," the visitor replied, "What makes you think so?"

Grace entertained most European royalty who visited America between the wars, among them Elizabeth, consort of King Albert of the Belgians. This invitation was sent to Henry Fairfield Osborn, paleontologist and president of the American Museum of Natural History and an old friend of the Vanderbilts.

Avenue, a huge brownstone that was formerly the home of the Belmont family and in the midst of the Vanderbilts who had snubbed her, the heart of the enemy's country. Her first big dinner party and ball in the winter of 1901 was held, rather daringly because ladies had only recently begun to dine in public places, at Sherry's Restaurant. The 166 guests included Mrs. Astor in spangled purple velvet and diamonds. Grace's first major triumph was to snare Prince Henry of Prussia, brother of the Kaiser, who visited the United States in 1901. Excitement was great in New York society: although many Americans, including Grace, had hob-nobbed with royalty on their own grounds, no one had had the opportunity to entertain a Hohenzollern. Grace's home was

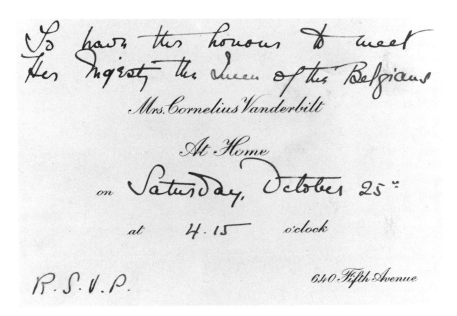

the only private American house where the prince dined during his stay. She pulled this off by reminding the prince that she knew many of his relations, including the British royal family, from her long visits in Europe before her marriage. Other hostesses were mad with envy, and the newspapers let their readers share vicariously in the imperial pleasures, noting pointedly that not a single Vanderbilt was invited.

In 1901, Grace invaded Newport. The William Waldorf Astors had moved permanently to Britain, where he soon was created a viscount, to his infinite satisfaction. Grace and Neily bought his Newport house, a large square building of two stories with a mansard roof; they called it Beaulieu and made a number

One of Grace's dinner parties at 640 Fifth Avenue was photographed in the late 1940s. The damask tablecloth was 18 yards long, the candelabra, flower and fruit vases, and fingerbowls were gold. Grace never drank alcohol, and it was rather sparingly served to her guests. She had a sweet tooth, however: her favorite dessert was raspberry and vanilla ices covered with mint-flavored chocolate sauce, and eight kinds of candy were available to guests—the household candy bill ran $300 a month in the 1930s. Grace always sat at the center of the dinner table. Here (tenth on right) she is talking to Elmendorf Carr, who gave a lecture on South American affairs after dinner that evening. Although Grace entertained hundreds of people whom she scarcely knew at her large parties, at "small" dinners such as this her guests were drawn from select old-time New York society: around the table were Burdens, Hammonds, Frelinghuysens, Harrimans, Berwinds, and Biddles.

Beaulieu, Grace and Neily's house in Newport, had been built about 1850 by the Peruvian ambassador to the United States. By the standards of other Vanderbilt houses in the resort it was simple, but it did have 16 bedrooms and 13 baths with 10 servants' rooms over the stables. Grace disdained what she called "birthday-cake colors" such as bright yellow and green and redecorated the house in peach and coffee-and-cream shades. She favored the well-worn look and seldom if ever had her antique furniture regilded or reupholstered.

of changes. The house was unusual in that it had a wide veranda around the first floor, giving it an almost rustic look in distinction to other palatial Newport houses. The Breakers was in sight—surely no accident. Alice continued to reign there after having mourned her husband in black crepe for a year, hardly leaving 1 West 57th Street, then in black and white for six months, after which she wore shades of lavender for six months, according to the most rigid rules for widows. A truce between her and Grace had been achieved and Alice had received the errant son and his wife, but there was no warmth in the relationship and contact between the two branches of the family was infrequent and chilly.

Grace's first great party in Newport was "The Fête of Roses" in August 1903. The hit of that New York theater season was a musical—of only temporary fame—called *The Wild Rose*. Grace brought the entire show from New York to Newport to perform at her party, which entailed closing it on Broadway for two days. The performance, abbreviated to an hour in order not to try the patience of the guests, was only one feature of an extraordinary evening. A very select group of only two hundred guests, including a few Vanderbilts who had come around, among them Consuelo Marlborough, entered the grounds through a midway 275 feet long, lined with fairground booths at which guests had their fortunes told, shot at wooden ducks, or tested their strength at weight-lifting machines. After these amusements and a Punch-and-Judy show palled, they entered a temporary wooden theater to see *The Wild Rose*. Supper was served on the piazza, decorated and made fragrant in the summer night with thousands of American Beauty roses. While the guests were eating, workmen were converting the theater into a ballroom, and at one in the morning dancing began. At breakfast gifts were distributed to the guests: silver atomizers and cigarette cases and other costly trifles. The sun was coming up when the last guests departed.

Grace and Neily had been considering building a house in New York, but in 1914, on the death of George Vanderbilt, they inherited 640 Fifth Avenue. William Henry had bequeathed it to George with the provision that if he had no son, which he did not, it would pass to the eldest surviving son of Cornelius II. Since the eldest son, William, had died, Neily inherited. Grace compared the house to the Black Hole of Calcutta and wanted it lightened in atmosphere. She called in Horace Trumbauer, the Philadelphia architect who was still practicing the fading tradition of the Ecole des Beaux-Arts in New York and Newport. He did not finish his work until 1917, but the house was more gorgeous than ever, with Louis XV and XVI furniture, tapestries, and needlework. A staff of thirty, under the direction of an English butler and including six footmen in maroon livery, was necessary.

Although Grace was an imaginative and frequent hostess — she gave two dinner parties a week and a ball at least once a month even at the beginning of her career — she was no ground-breaker in the matter of guests, seldom straying from the *Social Register* and the *Almanach de Gotha*. In his memoirs, *Farewell to Fifth Avenue*, her son, Cornelius IV (called "Neil"), listed her regulars: Goelets, Rhinelanders, Millses, Morrises. To these were agreeably mixed visiting royalty and nobility and American politicians and diplomats if they were prominent and refined enough. She took great pride in having statesmen dine at her table; as *The Dictionary of American Biography* cuttingly remarks, "She was inclined to overestimate the value of the contacts made there."

Not everyone approved of this extravagance, of course, but most of the complaints came from people who were not invited. The young Elsa Maxwell, who was definitely not invited, said, "The 'young' Mrs. Vanderbilt . . . was trying to prove to her jealous mother-in-law, the 'old' Mrs. Cornelius Vanderbilt, that she could pack more deadly bores into her drawing room than any other hostess on the North American continent." And Maury Paul, in a moment of peevishness at being ignored by Grace, once wrote, "One thing is certain—Mrs. Neily manages to antagonize the majority of the people she meets. She lives for society—and society alone. That, in itself, is not conducive to outward graciousness." Grace made no effort to cultivate Paul or any other reporter: she never gave interviews or furnished lists of her guests for parties in her box at the opening of the Metropolitan Opera, yet her activities were tirelessly noted and discussed. People, including some of her own relatives, thought this a calculated policy; by making herself unavailable, Grace continually captured the attention of the press.

Most of her guests liked her, although at the same time they tended to laugh at her a little. For instance, Theodore Roosevelt, a frequent guest, liked her. Perhaps as his daughter, the observant Alice Longworth, said, "because she was pretty and feminine and appeared so helpless. Everything was a fairy story for her. There she was, the pretty Southern belle, queen of society, married to a Vanderbilt; she seemed to sail along on a wave of fantasy . . . She was never quite sure whether the joke was at her expense or not. She once gave me what she probably thought was an affectionate nibble on the ear, and I gave her my bull ape imitation and let out such a howl of rage that she ran from the room screaming."

Grace soon eclipsed Neily. A dinner guest noted when they had been married just ten years: "Poor Cornelius Vanderbilt looked bored to death. It seems he hates this sort of thing and all during dinner he looked liked one treading water and calling for help." In 1910, Neily asked President William Howard Taft if he could represent the United States at the coronation of King George V, whom he and Grace already knew. The President refused and said to an aide, "I would not mind having Mrs. Cornelius to represent us at that time, but I hardly think the husband has either the presence or the importance for such a mission."

Grace's hospitality climaxed each Christmas when there was a giant tree at 640 Fifth with a small gift for each guest.

When the United States entered the First World War, Neily assumed command of the 102nd Engineers Corps. He served in France and was promoted to brigadier general in the field. Later he served in the mobilization program at Camp Lewis in Washington State. Grace made the supreme sacrifice and joined him there. She soon returned for the last of the Metropolitan Opera's season, vowing never to travel west again. She never did. But she was so proud of Neily's rank that she referred to him for the rest of his life, against military protocol, as "the General."

Although considered snobbish by many, she was famous for her loyalty to old friends and invited to her parties people who had been thought dead for years. "Frequently [the guests] emerged from unsociable retirement," said Eleanor Robson Belmont, "you had a feeling that the Angel Gabriel had blown his horn." Mrs. Belmont added, "Occasionally people accused her of over emphasis on royalty and titles, but to my definite knowledge she was loyal to old friends, even when their fortunes had changed for the worse."

Neily sought solace in his railroad work, his laboratory, in writing articles for learned journals, and in numerous philanthropies. After the war he ensconced himself for long periods on his yacht, which was equipped with a laboratory for his experiments. He steadily battled Grace to keep the decor from becoming "too chintzy." As the years passed, he spent more and more time at sea. His first steam yacht, purchased in 1903, was called the *North Star* after the Commodore's famous vessel. It was 233 feet long and 30 feet wide and had a drawing room 26 feet long. Grace had her way in the cabins, which were hung with silk made in France and even boasted of wicker wastebaskets lined with pink silk. "The handrails were ropes of velvet," her son wrote, "and everywhere on fragile rosewood tables stood Chinese porcelain vases, Imari bowls, heavy crystal flower vases, and tortoise-shell cigarette boxes filled with Turkish cigarettes that bore the blue and white pennant of the *North Star* with its two crossed V's."

In the 1920s Neily bought for $750,000 a sailing yacht, the *Atlantic,* 188 feet long with three sailing masts over 100 feet tall and also diesel-powered; she was considered one of the fastest and sleekest of her class ever built. He sailed all over the world. In 1929, despite heavy losses in the stock market, he bought an even more expensive and faster yacht, the *Winchester,* 225 feet long. On this vessel he spent most of his time. Grace, no great fan of yachting, seldom traveled with him. She spent her holidays at the Homestead in Warm Springs, West Virginia, where she took mineral-water baths, ate lightly, was massaged, and planned new parties for the New York and Newport seasons.

Neily became increasingly bitter about his wife's social life. "Father remarked that her hospitality had become a kind of blind overpowering instinct," their son wrote. "'Your mother has become a waltzing mouse.' Gradually I began to understand that being a leader of society was not a hobby with my mother, or even an avocation, but a full-time profession which taxed all her resources every waking moment."

Her two children, Neil and Grace, were disillusioned with their mother's absorption in society. Both were bored with the life of society and its innumerable rules. Neil wrote, "At the beginning Mother's careful adherence to social protocol may have grown out of a desire to outdo her mother-in-law, who was known to be a stickler for rules and propriety. Before long, however, the rigid forms and stilted patterns of gentility — which all too often lack all heart or meaning — came to assume a larger and larger part in Mother's life." She was a remote parent, sometimes not writing her children for months while she was in Europe chumming with the titled.

Neil served in the First World War and was discharged a lieutenant. To the horror of his parents, he decided to become a newspaperman — Neily and Grace detested the press for what they considered its unwarranted interest in the Vanderbilts' private lives. He was a staff member of the New York *Herald,* then the New York *Times.* His parents considered him a Bohemian and there were frequent clashes, but Neil nevertheless made an eminently proper marriage.

Neily named his first oceangoing steam yacht *North Star* after his great-grandfather's vessel. On it he and Grace entertained King Edward VII and Queen Alexandra, Kaiser Wilhelm II and the Kaiserin, Theodore Roosevelt, and innumerable members of European and British nobility.

Grace was a poor sailor and never felt any great affection for the *North Star,* but she insisted that it be fully equipped for entertaining, which included two complete sets of china made by Copeland specially for the yacht — the dinner service included 108 plates. The sheets were of the finest Irish linen and the blankets French, bound in silk. Other comforts included a well-stocked library and a wine cellar.

Grace and Neily's only son, Neil, spent most of his life as a working newspaperman. He made headlines himself, too, with his outspoken memoirs *Farewell to Fifth Avenue,* his society novels like *Palm Beach,* and his seven marriages. After his mother's death he wrote an affectionate but clear-eyed biography of her called *Queen of the Golden Age.*

In 1923, Neil launched his own "clean tabloid to sell for a penny [that] would uphold the highest standards of journalistic excellence." This was the Los Angeles *Illustrated Daily News,* which was followed by another tabloid in San Francisco, then one in Miami; they lasted just two and a half years when Vanderbilt Newspapers, Inc., died, with losses of up to $6 million. Neil went to the New York *Daily Mirror* as assistant managing editor.

His private life was exuberant. His friend W. Ward Smith, whose scabrous diary, *A Letter from My Father,* was published decades later, describes Neil when he was "on the rocks" in 1926 and living in a renovated brownstone on Fifth Avenue across the street from his Vanderbilt grandmother. He entertained largely, especially girls. The atmosphere of Neil's place, Smith said frankly, "was fornicatious." Neil, though no drinker, enjoyed midnight parties, especially those that ended up in Harlem. He liked to scramble eggs for everyone late in the evening and relate his war experience—Smith was convinced many of these were imaginary—to an admiring female circle.

In 1927, his sister Grace eloped with Henry Gassaway Davis, a Princeton graduate and mining engineer. The ceremony

Neil, like most Vanderbilt males, married young; he became engaged to Rachel Littleton, a well-connected New Yorker whom he had met at the party his mother gave for his twentieth birthday. Three thousand guests attended their wedding at St. Thomas's Church in 1920, and his parents gave Rachel a laurel-leaf bandeau of diamonds worth $300,000. The couple were divorced in 1927, and Neil remarried—six times! He described his mother's attitude toward his various wives, "... often her clear gray green eyes looked through the junior Mrs. Vanderbilts simply as though they did not exist."

at the Little Church Around the Corner was attended only by her brother. Her parents were disappointed but soon came to terms, and Davis joined a brokerage firm. That marriage ended in divorce in 1936; Davis married another Vanderbilt, Consuelo, daughter of William K., Jr. and Birdic Fair.

William K. Vanderbilt died in 1920. The appraisal of his estate submitted in Suffolk County, New York, in 1923 totaled $54,530,000. From its summary it was learned that he owned $29 million in stock of the New York Central, the Delaware, Lackawanna, and Western, and the Pittsburgh and Lake Erie railroads; $1.4 million in the Delaware, Lackawanna, and Western Coal Company; more than $2 million in the Chicago and Northwestern Railroad; and over $1 million in the Pullman Company. He had $2 million in cash on hand, and shortly before his death he had given his daughter, Consuelo, no less than $15 million, and in his will he left her $1.6 million more as well as $1 million to each of her two sons, Lord Blandford and Lord Ivor Churchill.

His son William K., Jr. was mainly engaged in yachting. At various times he owned nine different yachts, but the most

William K., Jr. was a skilled sailor; in 1920 he passed the examinations for a ship master's certificate endorsed for all oceans and unlimited tonnage. The grandest of his many yachts was the *Alva*, named for his mother, 259 feet long and equipped with a seaplane cradle on the afterdeck. An awed reporter noted that "The $75,000 plane carried is half the size of the China Clipper." The ship's equipment included motorboats and express cruisers that could be rapidly launched.

imposing was the *Alva*. The nine-hole golf course at Eagle's Nest, his Suffolk County home, had each hole named for one of his yachts. During the First World War he commanded the U.S.S. *Tarantula*. In 1941, he gave the *Alva*, then valued at $3 million, to the U.S. Navy.

His brother, Harold, was an even more serious yachtsman, who three times defended the America's Cup. He was chairman of the board of trustees of Vanderbilt University and took an active role in the management of the New York Central, of which he chaired the executive committee. He owned only 60,000 shares and his cousin, William H., owned 8,000 shares in 1949, a

William K. III was a traveler and big-game hunter. When he died in an automobile accident in 1933 at the age of 26, his father built a memorial wing onto Eagle's Nest filled with trophies and memorabilia of his son's expeditions. One wall contains a mural showing William K. III shooting in the Sudan two years before his death.

relatively minor holding in a railroad known as "the Vanderbilt Road." One of the Vanderbilts' opponents in an ownership struggle remarked sarcastically that their yachts cost more to maintain than the value of their holdings. Perhaps Harold's most famous accomplishment was the invention of contract bridge while he was on a cruise in 1925. The new game swept the world, vanquishing the prevailing auction version of the game. The grandest prize for players was called the Vanderbilt Cup.

Among the few who refused to play the new way was William K.'s and Harold's mother, Alva, who lived until 1933. Age had not mellowed her, and she scorned the system devised by

William K., Jr. was a serious student of marine biology; many of his yachting cruises were undertaken to gather specimens. A number of species of marine life were identified and named by him and his staff of biologists, and he was accompanied by artists who sketched the specimens as they were brought up. On the grounds of Eagle's Nest he built a Hall of Fishes (left) in the same Spanish Revival style as the house. It also catered to his other interest: on the roof is the first tee of his private golf course.

William K., Jr. chose Centerport, Long Island, for the site of his summer home because the harbor there is the deepest on the North Shore of the island and his yacht could anchor very near the house. Eagle's Nest, opposite, one of the last great Vanderbilt mansions, was built for him over a period of 20 years by Warren and Wetmore in a style called Spanish Revival. At the entrance are two massive black iron eagles that stood atop of the first Grand Central Terminal.

Harold or, as she called him, "the Professor." "The Professor goes crazy when I'm his partner," she said, "but he cannot make me obey his hidebound rules. As long as I pay my losses, I'll bid any way I please." Alva divided her final years between her house at 477 Madison Avenue and a fifteenth-century castle at Auganville-la-Rivière in France and extensive travels throughout the world. She said before she died, according to her friend Elsa Maxwell, "I had too much power before I knew how to use it, and it defeated me in the end. It drove all sweetness out of my life except the

266

Most Vanderbilt men were active yachtsmen, but the most prominent and the most successful in racing was Harold Stirling, who defended the America's Cup three times. The *Enterprise,* above left, was the 1930 winner.

Portrait of Harold Stirling at the wheel of his yacht *Ranger,* winner of the 1937 America's Cup, above

At the age of 49, Harold Stirling married for the first time in a quiet ceremony in New York. Immediately after the ceremony he and his bride, the former Gertrude Conaway of Philadelphia, sailed for France. Here they are honeymooning in Cannes. Harold was the last Vanderbilt to play a role in the New York Central Railroad. He was a trustee and major benefactor of Vanderbilt University and one of the first donors to the Lincoln Center for the Performing Arts in New York.

Iris Smith Christ is chairman of the trustees of Eagle's Nest, her grandfather William K., Jr.'s home at Centerport, Long Island, which is now opened to the public. Here she is (far left) in the library at Eagle's Nest, opposite, with her daughter, Serena Van Ingen McCallum; daughter-in-law, Julie Gordon Van Ingen; son, H. Peter Van Ingen, Jr.; and granddaughters Olivia Morgan McCallum, Serena Alexandra McCallum (standing), and Kelly Vanderbilt Van Ingen (on chair), seventh-generation descendants of the Commodore.

affection of my children. My trouble was that I was born too late for the last generation and too early for this one. If you want to be happy, live in your own time."

In the 1930s another scandal broke over the heads of the children and grandchildren of Cornelius II. The youngest son of Cornelius II and Alice was Reginald Claypoole Vanderbilt. He

had attended Yale University, where he acquired a reputation for dissipation and no diploma. His escapades made lively reading in the tabloids. Although he did not neglect women and drinking, his special vice was gambling. He was reputed to have lost as much as $70,000 at a sitting at Canfield's, a gambling house on 44th Street, and was once picked up in a raid there. Despite his trust funds, he was virtually insolvent most of the time. He was, as one might expect, his mother's favorite child, and she often bailed him out. To the relief of his relations in 1903 he married an acceptable bride, Cathleen Gebhard Neilson, but he did not mend

Alva had not used Marble House for years, and shortly before her death she sold it to Frederick H. Prince, president of Armour and Company. The Prince family retained it until 1963, when Harold Vanderbilt provided funds for its purchase by the Preservation Society of Newport County, which opened it to the public. The house is often the scene of concerts and charity events such as the Tiffany Ball of 1957.

his ways, and divorce followed in 1919. Four years later he took an eighteen-year-old bride, Gloria Morgan, by whom he had one daughter, Gloria. Two years later he died of a bad liver brought on by alcoholism. He was broke and left only an inviolable trust fund bequeathed to him by his father amounting to $2.5 million, which went to his infant daughter, Gloria. Her mother began to live the high life in Europe and New York, spending the large income—about $112,000 a year—from her daughter's trust.

The baby's aunt Gertrude became a widow in 1930, when Harry Payne Whitney died leaving $47 million in securities and

In 1919 Addison Mizener, Palm Beach's eccentric architect of the 1920s, built for himself El Solano on South Ocean Boulevard. Less than a year later he sold it to Harold, who immediately commissioned him to make additions, including one of the first private swimming pools in Palm Beach. In the years since Harold's death the house, which is still standing, has had a variety of owners, including John Lennon and Yoko Ono.

Maury Paul, the society columnist who wrote under the name Cholly Knickerbocker, christened them "the Magnificent Morgans." The twin daughters of a very minor American diplomat, Gloria (left) and Thelma Morgan were well known on the international society circuit when they were still teenagers. At the age of 18 Gloria married Reginald Vanderbilt, who was 43, and became the mother of a second Gloria. Thelma married Lord Furness but was better known as the mistress of the Prince of Wales (later Edward VIII).

Reginald's interests were Thoroughbred horses, dog breeding, automobiles, and dissipation. At Sandy Point, his 280-acre farm adjoining his brother Alfred Gwynne's Oakland Farm, he kept 60 horses and innumerable dogs in kennels that occupied nearly an acre. He was said to be an expert at four-in-hand driving. At automobiling he was not so expert; he injured several pedestrians.

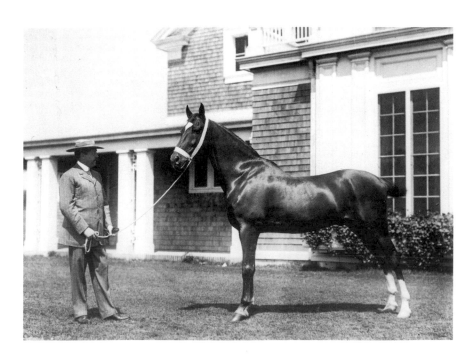

Reginald and Gloria spent much of their short married life in restless travel. Here they are on their arrival in Cherbourg, opposite below, aboard the S.S. *Leviathan*.

Gertrude seated among her sculpture. Standing is Juliana Force, first director of the Whitney Museum of American Art.

$16 million in federal, state, and municipal bonds plus real estate, works of art, and more than two hundred valuable racehorses. Gertrude had continued her sculpting and had received quite a number of commissions, mostly for public statuary. Convinced that her niece Gloria was not being properly brought up, she sued, seeking her guardianship. The suit, which was tried in 1934, was contested by Gloria Morgan Vanderbilt, and again family secrets—most of them deliciously unsavory—were aired in public. Newspaper coverage was plentiful and scandalous. The case has been brilliantly reconstructed and narrated by Barbara Gold-

smith in her book *Little Gloria . . . Happy at Last.* Gertrude won custody of her niece but, according to both Goldsmith and the younger Gloria's memoirs, hardly seemed to know what to do with her once she had won.

Gertrude had become absorbed in the collecting of art by American painters and sculptors and in 1930 founded the Whitney Museum of American Art, which opened its doors in a building on Eighth Street in 1931. Gertrude died in 1942, leaving an estate valued at $11 million, surprisingly small, but she had given her three children many gifts in her lifetime. The Whitney Museum received a bequest of $2.5 million. The contents of the vast Whitney town house at 871 Fifth Avenue were auctioned and the house soon demolished.

The Vanderbilt roads flourished. During the First World War the railroads were run by the federal government from January 1918 to March 1920. After the war, the New York Central claimed that the government administration had caused damage to the rolling stock and tracks totaling nearly $11 million. The claim was not upheld by the courts; on the contrary, the railroad ended by paying the government $23 million for improvements while the road was under federal control.

Grand Central Terminal proved its worth. A record for first-class traffic was set on January 8, 1923: twenty-six trains carrying 4,028 sleeping-car passengers arrived at the terminal before noon. The occasion? The first day of the annual automobile show at the Grand Central Palace. The irony of this was not then appreciated, but soon automobiles began to cut seriously into rail traffic with dire consequences for the great railroading fortunes.

The years between the two world wars were years of glory for Grand Central and for the Vanderbilt roads. New name trains were introduced: the Southwestern Limited, the Knickerbocker, the Iroquois, the De Witt Clinton, the Fifth Avenue Special. The first high-speed through train to Chicago running on a daily basis, the Lake Shore Limited, had been placed in service in November 1897, making the trip in twenty-four hours. It was succeeded and surpassed by the most famous Vanderbilt train, indeed the most famous train in American history, the Twentieth Century Limited. From the first the train caught the public's attention and retained it for fifty years as a symbol of speed and style. For years it was difficult to get reservations. On January 7, 1929 it operated eastbound in seven sections carrying 822 pampered passengers. The Commodore Vanderbilt was put into service in the 1930s to handle the overflow of passengers from the Twentieth Century, but traffic increased so rapidly that the Advance Commodore Vanderbilt had to be added. All these trains had dining cars famous for their cooking and service, showers, maid service, stenographers, libraries, club cars, and other comforts. The last luxury train to make its debut before the Second World War was the streamliner Empire State Express, which made its first run on the ill-fated date of December 7, 1941. The lounge was equipped with pigskin banquettes, and the diner was decorated with murals depicting early New York history.

Grand Central Terminal continued to fascinate the American public with dazzling statistics: the average clerk at the information booth answered 167,440 questions each year; the Oyster

1826 ~ APRIL 17 ~ 1926
NEW YORK CENTRAL LINES
CENTENNIAL

On April 17, 1926 the New York Central celebrated its centenary with a dinner. The menu showed the Commodore surrounded by other founders of the line, opposite, and both the first and second Grand Central terminals.

In 1932 the Pennsylvania Railroad scheduled the trip from New York to Chicago on its Broadway Limited at 18 hours. The Twentieth Century soon matched that time. New York mayor Jimmy Walker shook hands with passengers departing on the first trip, above. That same year Ben Hecht and Charles MacArthur used the glamorous train as the setting for their classic farce *Twentieth Century.*

Bar restaurant served 25,000 oysters a day during the winter season. The station had a newsreel theater, an art gallery, and the Grand Central School of Art, which held classes between 1924 and 1941 and sometimes enrolled over a thousand pupils a year. In 1946, the Columbia Broadcasting System installed its television station on one of the upper floors.

American railroads, however, were in trouble, although only a few people recognized it. The burden of debt that they had accumulated in the nineteenth century, together with the competition from automobiles and, increasingly, airplanes, was shortly to plunge them into desperate straits. The Depression of the 1930s was their death knell. In 1929, the net profits of the major railroads of the United States amounted to $1,252,698,000; Class I railroads had 226,703 miles of track; they carried 17 percent of all travelers in the country. Their revenues accounted for an amazing 6 percent of the gross national product. At that time, the Vanderbilt family, according to a federal survey, owned

589,000 shares of common and preferred stock in five important railroads, and that figure did not include bonds. As late as 1936, four Vanderbilts held a total of 76 directorships in a variety of railroad corporations.

But by 1932, when the Depression had already struck hard, the net profits of the major railroads had shrunk to $326,298,000. In that year the companies that operated 72 percent of the nation's trackage did not earn enough money to meet their fixed charges. By 1938, 650,000 railroad employees had been fired. Thirty-eight Class I railroads, operating 31 percent of the country's mileage, were in bankruptcy or receivership. By 1937, more than $3 billion worth of railroad bonds had ceased paying their interest.

The Depression also ended the life of many great American houses. Even before it broke, the Vanderbilts were beginning to leave Fifth Avenue where they had so long been the principal residents. The area was becoming commercial, and the great houses were stranded among the office buildings and smart shops, amid the noise of street traffic and crowds of pedestrians. The first to move was Margaret Shepard, who left 2 West 52nd Street, one of the double houses, to her sister Emily Sloane and moved to an apartment on Fifth Avenue near the Metropolitan Museum of Art. Emily Sloane, by that time Mrs. Henry White, sold both their houses and bought another, smaller house farther up Fifth Avenue in an area that was still residential—854 between East 67th and 68th streets, formerly the R. Livingston Beekman House, built in 1905 by Warren and Wetmore (now the Yugoslav Mission to the United Nations). Lila Webb sold her house at 680 to the Mutual Benefit Society. In 1929, Florence Twombly sold her home, 684 Fifth Avenue, to John D. Rockefeller and went to live in an Italian Renaissance palace built for her at 1 East 71st Street. That house had a short existence; it was demolished in 1944 to build the apartment building now occupying the site.

Alice left 1 West 57th Street in 1925. She died nine years later. Under her will, her daughter, Gladys Széchényi, received The Breakers, her house at 1 East 67th Street, and about two-thirds of a trust fund of $7 million, and Neily received a building in Cincinnati worth about the same amount. A trust of about $1.25 million was left to Reginald's daughters, Cathleen and Gloria. Bequests of smaller sums went to a dozen other relatives,

Alice clung to her house at 57th Street and Fifth Avenue until 1925, when the taxes on it had risen to $130,000 a year. She sold it then for $7 million and gave the great wrought-iron gates from the courtyard to the city, which installed them on the Fifth Avenue side of Central Park near 105th Street. By the time Alice departed, her enormous house was overlooked by the Plaza Hotel on the right and the Heckscher Building on the left.

Alice then took up residence in the hardly less grand house at 1 East 67th Street, opposite, a neo-Italian Renaissance palazzo designed by Horace Trumbauer and built in 1907–1908 for George J. Gould. She died there in 1934.

servants, and charities. One of the peculiarities of Alice's estate is that it contained $10,184,587 in cash.

Gladys Széchényi leased The Breakers to the Preservation Society of Newport County for the token sum of $1 per year; it was opened to the public to raise funds for the restoration of other houses in Newport. Gladys's daughter, Sylvia, married to the Hungarian Count Anthony Szápáry, has continued to occupy an apartment in the house.

The Head of the House of Vanderbilt was now Alice's grandson Alfred Gwynne II. He attended St. Paul's School and spent a year and a half at Yale, dropping out in 1933. On his twenty-first birthday, his mother, who was a noted owner of racehorses, gave him Sagamore Farms in Maryland, where he also devoted himself to the turf on a grand scale. In 1936, Sagamore Farms was described as having twenty-four exercise boys who gave the horses their workouts, four jockeys, eight foremen, two blacksmiths, a veterinarian, a bookkeeper, grooms, cooks, and stable workers—seventy-five employees in all—to care for 166 Thoroughbreds on the farm. The annual expense of the establishment was reportedly $200,000.

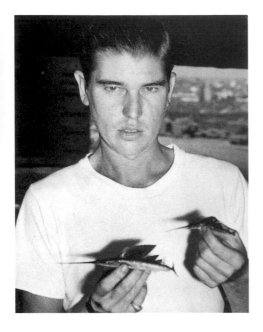

George, younger son of Alfred Gwynne I, was an avid yachtsman, shown here with a rare specimen of sailfish brought back from an expedition off the Mexican Pacific coast in 1941.

Both Alfred Gwynne II and his brother, George, served on PT boats in the South Pacific during the Second World War. George's first wife, Lucille Parsons, and their daughter, Lucille ("Lulu"), are shown in 1944 in their Palm Beach home. After the war Alfred was active in the World Veterans Federation.

Alfred Gwynne II was the youngest member ever admitted to the legendary Jockey Club. In 1936 he became the largest shareholder and later the president of the Pimlico track in Baltimore. In 1940 he became president of Belmont Park in Queens, New York. Among his horses was Native Dancer, who won 22 starts in 1952, his first year of racing. Here (left) is Alfred with Native Dancer's trainer on the morning of a big race.

Alfred Gwynne II leads Native Dancer into the winner's circle at Belmont Park after the horse won the Futurity Stakes in 1952. Native Dancer retired to Alfred's 580-acre breeding farm at Glyndon, Maryland.

In 1939 Alfred, then married to Manuela Hudson, bought a Sands Point, Long Island, estate with a residence containing twenty-three rooms and ten baths. When he divorced and then married Jeanne Lourdes Murray, daughter of one of the first commissioners of the New York–New Jersey Port Authority, he was dropped from the *Social Register;* he promptly named one of his best horses Social Outcast.

The last of William Henry's sons was Frederick, who died at Hyde Park on June 29, 1938. To everyone's astonishment he had quietly but efficiently managed his assets and increased them dramatically—even in retirement he was a director of twenty-two railroads and many other corporations—and his estate amounted to more than $78 million. Of that he left $14 million to the Sheffield Scientific School at Yale University, where he had been educated, and $10 million to Vanderbilt University. Taxes,

Alfred Gwynne II's third wife was Jean Harvey of the Chicago restaurant family. *Life* magazine showed them honeymooning in Florida in 1957.

Alfred Gwynne II and his wife, Jean Harvey, at Truman Capote's black-and-white ball at the Plaza Hotel, New York, in November 1966

federal and state, took $41 million. To the dismay of his Vanderbilt relations, they got none of the estate. His wife, Louise, had died in Paris twelve years earlier. They were childless but had become very attached to Louise's niece Margaret ("Daisy"), who had married James Van Alen of New York and Newport; she spent much of her time with them at Hyde Park, and she received the entire residue of the estate.

Neil Vanderbilt described with some relish the effect of the will on his parents:

> Uncle Fred had been a widower for many years before he died, and since he and Aunt Lulu had no children, there was much speculation about his fortune and to whom he would leave it. Although Mother and Father were feting the Crown Prince and Princess of Sweden at Beaulieu, they canceled the affair to attend the funeral . . . Uncle Fred had owned nine mid-Manhattan properties, including a large Fifth Avenue mansion. All of these, plus the Hyde Park estate and all his furniture and paintings and tapestries and silver, all his yachts and automobiles and jewelry . . . he bestowed on the pretty head of his wife's niece, Mrs. James Van Alen. He did not leave a single penny to any of the Vanderbilts. It was quite the scandal of the year.

Mrs. Van Alen did not want the house in Hyde Park, and after some attempts to sell it, she gave it in 1940 to the federal government. It was designated a National Historic Site and ever since has been open to the public under the administration of the National Park Service.

At 640 Fifth Avenue Grace entertained as enthusiastically as ever: one year she had thirty thousand guests! The cost of this was about $250,000 a year. Neily had received offers to buy the house; at one point it was considered as part of the site for Rockefeller Center. In 1940, taxes on the house were $168 a day, and Neily sold it for $1.5 million with the provision that Grace could continue to live there until three years after his death. Although there was no public acknowledgment, the couple were virtually separated, Neily living on the yacht *Winchester*. When war broke out, he gave the yacht to the Canadian government for conversion to a war vessel and moved to a 100-foot chartered yacht tied up at the Miami Yacht Basin. He was there when he

Grace had to give up 640 Fifth Avenue in 1944. For years it had been an anachronism: a Gilded Age mansion in the heart of a shopping and entertainment district. Her friend Elizabeth Drexel Lehr said, ". . . her house on Fifth Avenue was the perfection of taste, yet in my fancy it seemed to be resisting something. It was like a citadel of another age. The ever-encroaching skyscrapers around it, the nearby Radio City were an advancing army. Modernity on the march." Grace's final home was 1048 Fifth Avenue, built in 1914 in the Louis XIII style by the distinguished architectural firm of Carrère and Hastings.

died in February 1942. He left only about $4 million divided among his wife and children.

Grace held on at 640 for two more years, beleaguered by skyscrapers on every side. Finally, even she had to give up. The final party was held in 1944, when the house was open to the public for the benefit of the Red Cross, and for the last time guests danced in the Louis XV rooms beneath the French paintings collected by William Henry sixty years earlier. Then she moved out and the following year the paintings were sold at auction. The buyer of the house, who promptly tore it down for a bank building, was Lord Astor of Hever. In the greatest of American society rivalries, the Astors in a sense had the last word.

Since 1875, when the Commodore's endowment transformed it from a struggling local school into a major educational institution, the Vanderbilt family has continued to make major gifts to Vanderbilt University in Nashville, Tennessee. Here some of the Commodore's descendants gather before his statue on the campus.

Afterword

AFTER THE CLOSING of the house at 640 Fifth Avenue and its speedy demolition, Grace found another house on Fifth Avenue, number 1048 on the southeast corner of 86th Street, an area that fifty years before had been considered a social no-man's-land but was now in the heart of the fashionable district. The handsome limestone-and-brick French Renaissance town house had been built by Carrère and Hastings in 1914. Grace referred to the house as "the gardener's cottage," although it had twenty-eight rooms. Her staff was now down to eighteen, but she continued to entertain: thirty guests for lunch and a hundred for dinner were not at all unusual. She always said that interesting and attractive men were the key to any successful party, and her secretary kept a list of 138 eligible males divided into categories such as "men who will dance," "men who can lunch," and "men who will go to the theatre, but not the opera."

Grace kept her maroon Rolls-Royce and maroon-liveried driver and footmen. Legend has it that when she called on her friend Mrs. Morton Plant, who lived directly across the street, Grace entered her Rolls in front of her house, was driven around the block, and solemnly alighted in front of the Plant mansion.

She claimed to loathe being photographed, but hers had become one of the best-known faces in New York. Although like

Grace never missed the opening of the Metropolitan Opera. At the November 1939 first night she appeared, as in every year, wearing her three trade-marks: the bandeau, or "headache band," on her forehead, her diamond stomacher, and the famous silver fox wrap. And, as always, she was the focus of awed attention. Ten years later she made her final appearance in a wheelchair.

many great hostesses she was ill at ease in other people's houses, she occasionally dined out and attended the more important debuts. In appearance, Grace had now gone well beyond fashion; she had her own style. Her hair had gone white early in life, and she left it alone except for rinsing it in a rare tea, which gave it a faint golden sheen. Around her forehead she wore one of her famous bandeaux, or "headache bands"; she owned about two hundred of these, many embroidered with jewels, and she never appeared in the evening without one. She was much attached to a silver fox scarf, which she wore year after year, the head resting on her bosom. The scarf grew somewhat seedy through the years, but Grace, who like most rich people had her small economies, never replaced it.

She still ignored the press, but the press never ignored her. When she finally met Maury Paul after he had been writing about "Her Grace" for about twenty years without ever actually meeting her (he had been very sarcastic about the silver fox), she had the last word. Paul said nervously, "I'm not such a terrible person as you think, Mrs. Vanderbilt." Grace replied sweetly, "Judging from what you write, I get the impression that *I* am the terrible person."

In her seventies Grace's eyesight deteriorated until in her last years she was virtually blind. She made her final appearance at the opening night of the Metropolitan Opera in 1949 in a wheelchair. Her last two years she was bedridden, entertained by a companion who used to retell to her the social triumphs of the past. She died at eighty-three in 1953 and was buried in the Vanderbilt Mausoleum on Staten Island, surrounded by the family who had once refused to receive her and finally, however ruefully, had acknowledged her social supremacy. The house on Fifth Avenue and 86th Street was sold and is now the Yivo Institute for Jewish Research.

Frank Crowninshield, who had watched her career first-hand in his years at *Vanity Fair* and *Vogue*, wrote kindly, "While she may have erred as Mrs. Astor did in allowing her ritual to become a shade too rigid; in placing an overemphasis on magnif-icoes and distinguished personages, her qualities of heart have more than made up for her preoccupation with ceremony. All in all, her influence has been restorative, her loyalties unswerving, and her hospitality at all times unbounded."

Her son, Neil, made his home in Reno, Nevada, as far as one could well get, in every way, from Fifth Avenue. He continued writing and lecturing on world affairs, becoming a strong supporter of the new state of Israel. He died, childless, in 1974. His sister, Grace, after her divorce from Henry Gassaway Davis, married Robert Livingston Stevens, a direct descendant of Commodore Vanderbilt's ancient rival in the early steamboating days.

Florence Twombly, the last surviving granddaughter of the Commodore, died in 1952 at the age of ninety-eight. She had never lost one jot of her stateliness, and to the last lived in the splendor of a bygone day at Florham. Even as late as the Second World War she had a staff of 126 at Florham, including thirty gardeners, twelve dairymen, four footmen, eight housemaids, her famous chef, Josef Donnen, who had four assistants, painters, bricklayers, furniture repairmen, and chauffeurs. Her daughter, Ruth Vanderbilt Twombly, survived her by only two years. Ruth had dearly loved Paris, and she died there at the Ritz Hotel. She left an estate of $22 million. The following year an auction was held at Florham, and the Chippendale furniture, the Oriental rugs, and two sets of Gobelins tapestries that once belonged to the Roman Princes Barberini were sold. The house became the administration building of Fairleigh-Dickinson University.

As the older generation of Vanderbilts died off, the mainstay of the fortune, the New York Central Railroad, was itself nearly moribund.

The all-time high for the stock in the road was recorded in 1929: 256½. By 1931 it was down to 25. The all-time high in passenger traffic was reached by the Central in 1945, when it carried over 78 million passengers—many of them returning servicemen—and 180 million tons of freight. The biggest single day in Grand Central's history was July 3, 1947, when 252,288 passengers arrived or departed from the terminal. The railroads, however, were in irreversible decline: in the next decade the number of passengers fell to a third of what it had been in 1929.

In 1946, after the New York Central's revenues and profits had been falling steadily for years, the Texas-born financier Robert E. Young began a vigorous campaign to gain control of the railroad. Having already taken the Baltimore and Ohio Railroad, he thought he could wield it and the New York Central into a vast and profitable rail network in the eastern United States. He launched an advertising campaign against the Central's inefficiency and indifference to passenger comfort. For a time, his advertisement about the necessity of changing trains in Chicago when traveling from New York to the West Coast—"a hog can cross the country without changing cars, but you can't!"—became one of the best-known slogans in the country.

The battle for the Central climaxed at the annual meeting held in Albany on May 26, 1954. The atmosphere was that of a circus; special trains filled with stockholders supporting Young or the current management (which included Harold S. and William H. Vanderbilt) left Grand Central Terminal, their passengers waving flags and chanting "We want Young!" or "We want White!" (William White, president of the Central). More than two thousand people jammed the National Guard Armory in Albany and ate a box lunch while nominations proceeded for the election of a new board of directors. Stockholders' proxies were counted—it took more than three weeks—and Young was pronounced victor. The New York Central was no longer the Vanderbilt road.

But even the able and determined Young could not save it. In 1957, his through passenger cars from New York to Los Angeles were canceled, and in that same year the proud New York Central, Commodore Vanderbilt's creation, slid into the red. On January 20, 1958 at a meeting at Young's Palm Beach home, the directors decided to omit the coming dividend. Five days later Young committed suicide.

The railroad limped on with continually declining revenues. In January 1968, the Central joined with its historic rival, the Pennsylvania. Just three years later, the National Railroad Passenger Corporation acquired the passenger-carrying plant of the nation's railroads under the name Amtrak. In 1976, the Consolidated Rail Corporation ("Conrail") was formed; it included the Penn Central among many other railroads. Grand Central Terminal is today owned by Conrail but operated under lease by the New York Metropolitan Transit Authority, the National Railroad Passenger Corporation, and the Connecticut Department of Transportation.

In December 1967, the grand old Twentieth Century Limited was discontinued after more than sixty-five years of

service, and the famous red carpet was no longer laid down for passengers at six in the evening.

Between 1952 and 1979, a total of fifteen hotels, apartment houses, and office buildings around Grand Central Terminal were torn down. They were replaced by much taller buildings; the first was the Union Carbide, designed by Skidmore, Owings, and Merrill, which opened in 1960. There were plans to build a tower over Grand Central Terminal, or even tear it down. After a historic landmark-preservation battle, which went to the Supreme Court, the station was preserved, but the huge Pan Ameri-

When the present Grand Central Terminal was completed in 1913, the statue of Commodore Vanderbilt that had once stood atop the New York Central freight building in St. John's Park was discovered in storage and placed in front of the station. Today the figure gazes down Park Avenue, where over a century ago horses pulled the cars of the Commodore's first railroad.

An era in transportation came to an end on December 2, 1967 when the New York Central's grand old Twentieth-Century Limited made its final New York-to-Chicago run after 65½ years of service. No event better symbolized the decline of American railroads.

can Airways Building was erected just north, towering over the station, in 1963. The neighborhood created by the Vanderbilts and the New York Central was changing beyond recognition.

Vanderbilt descendants have cut across a wide spectrum of activities and have included politicians, scientists, businessmen, and writers, among them William Douglas Burden, the explorer and naturalist; William B. Osgood Field, the geographer; and Derrick Webb, Republican member of the Vermont State Senate.

One of the most unexpected scions was Frederick Vanderbilt Field, who in the 1940s was a member of numerous organizations later declared to have been Communist fronts, and an assistant to Owen Lattimore on the controversial *Pacific Affairs*. He was once jailed for refusing to answer questions about his Communist party membership. Whittaker Chambers remem-

Electra Havemeyer began collecting Americana at the age of 18, when she bought a cigar-store Indian. After her marriage to J. Watson Webb, she bought quilts, decoys, weather vanes, and painted furniture, which they stored in the Webb house at Shelburne, Vermont. By 1950 the Webbs were acquiring entire New England buildings and even a 892-ton steamboat, the *Ticonderoga*. The collection was opened to the public as the Shelburne Museum. Exhibits now include a room from the Webbs' New York City apartment with Old Master and Impressionist paintings.

Like his father Harry Payne Whitney, Cornelius Vanderbilt Whitney has been a notable polo player on the Old Westbury team, opposite above. At Yale he rowed on the varsity crew. He has also been a successful owner of racehorses: in the 1930s and again in 1960 his blue-and-brown colors topped the list of winning purses on American tracks.

J. Watson Webb, opposite below, of the American Polo Team practicing at the Piping Rock Club on Long Island for an international match

bered that when he met Field to discuss left-wing activities he was given a lavish lunch in the Vanderbilt Hotel on Park Avenue.

John Hammond, the jazz critic, talent scout, and record producer, was the grandson of Emily and William Douglas Sloane. He brought public renown to a long string of important musical performers, including Billie Holiday, Count Basie, Aretha Franklin, Bob Dylan, and Bruce Springsteen. In 1934, he helped Benny Goodman organize his famous jazz band. His sister, Alice, later married Goodman.

Among the living descendants of the Commodore—who today number between 800 and 1,000—only a few keep up the grand old style of Vanderbilt life. The most prominent socially is Cornelius Vanderbilt Whitney, Gertrude's son, who has had careers in mining and aviation and was president of Hudson Bay Mining and Smelting Company and chairman of the board of Pan American Airways. He was an investor in motion pictures and, with his cousin John Hay ("Jock") Whitney, backed the produc-

tion of *Gone With the Wind*. In Cody, Wyoming, he and Gertrude's other children built the Buffalo Bill Historical Center and Whitney Gallery of Western Art. He and his fourth wife, the former Mary Louise (Schroeder) Hosford, have for many years kept up the lavish life of an earlier time, "a throwback," one magazine wrote, "to the Gilded Age" in their eight homes—each ready for a visit at any time—a Fifth Avenue apartment, a

Banker Timothy Proctor Schieffelin and his wife, Susan, stand in the library of the landmark house at 5 East 66th Street, New York, which was designed for his great-great-grandmother Margaret Vanderbilt Shepard by Richard Howland Hunt. Since 1946 the house has been home to the Lotos Club.

Alexander Stewart Webb, great-grandson of Lila Vanderbilt and William Seward Webb, is president of Shelburne Farms Resources, which has turned his great-grandparents' home on Lake Champlain into an inn and cultural center, home to the Vermont Music Festival. He is also an active preservationist. Here he is shown in the game room of Shelburne House with his wife, Marilyn, and daughters Anna (left) and Heidi.

Saratoga house for the racing season, a farm in Lexington, Kentucky, a lodge at Lake Placid, a house in the Adirondacks, two houses in Florida (one at Marineland, which the Whitneys own, and one at Palm Beach), and a vacation house in Majorca, Spain.

Gertrude's descendants have maintained their interest in the museum she founded: her daughter, Flora Whitney Miller, was president of the Whitney Museum of American Art in New

Mary Lou Whitney, wife of Cornelius Vanderbilt Whitney, is one of America's best-known hostesses. At Saratoga, New York, she opens the August racing season with a gala ball followed by a garden party for the townspeople and benefits for the National Museum of Racing and the National Museum of Dance. Here she attends the Saratoga polo matches, above.

At the age of 17 Gloria married Pasquale ("Pat") di Cicco, a Hollywood agent and employee of Howard Hughes, who had previously been married to movie actress Thelma Todd. The wedding was held at the mission at Santa Barbara, California, opposite above. Left is the bride's mother.

Gloria's second husband was conductor Leopold Stokowski; her third was film director Sidney Lumet. In 1975 she was photographed at a gala at the Imperial Theatre, New York, opposite below, with her fourth husband, writer Wyatt Cooper.

York, a post in which she has been succeeded by her daughter, Flora Miller Biddle.

The best-known Vanderbilt today is Gloria. For sixty years the press has chronicled her life. The celebrated custody trial, her four often stormy marriages—one to conductor Leopold Stokowski, who was forty-two years older than she—have been the stuff of tabloids. A poet, memoirist, and briefly, an actress, she began an entirely new and extraordinarily successful career in the 1970s as a designer of jewelry, table linen, scarves, and china followed by the even greater success as a designer of jeans for the Murjani Company. In the 1980s she introduced new lines of fragrances called "Glorious" and "Vanderbilt." The energy and talent she has shown together with the willingness to change careers remind one in the late twentieth century of the same qualities that her great-great-grandfather the Commodore showed in the early nineteenth century. The unique saga of the Vanderbilt family, which began with the birth of the Commodore on a Staten Island farm nearly two centuries ago, continues to unfold.

William Henry III was active in cancer research and in Planned Parenthood. One of the few Vanderbilts to show an interest in politics, he was governor of Rhode Island in 1938–1940. William Henry III died in 1981 at the age of 79. Here he sits with his wife and three daughters beneath a portrait of the Commodore.

BIBLIOGRAPHY

Soon after the death of William Henry Vanderbilt, W. A. Croffut published *The Vanderbilts and the Story of Their Fortune* (Chicago: Belford, Clarke & Co., 1886), the first book entirely devoted to the Commodore and his children. Although generally eulogistic, it was not entirely uncritical. All later writers on the Vanderbilts draw on its wealth of first-hand facts. Another view by a contemporary is Henry Clews's *Fifty Years in Wall Street* (New York: Irving Publishers, 1908). The Commodore's best biographer is Wheaton J. Lane, who wrote *Commodore Vanderbilt: An Epic of the Steam Age* (New York: Alfred A. Knopf, 1942).

The origins and history of the Vanderbilt fortune are chronicled, not always fairly, by Gustavus Myers in his *History of the Great American Fortunes* (New York: The Modern Library, 1964) and *The Ending of the Hereditary American Fortunes* (New York: Julian Messner, 1939); by Ferdinand Lundberg in *America's 60 Families* (New York: The Citadel Press, 1946); and by Frederick Lewis Allen in *The Lords of Creation* (New York: Harper & Brothers, 1935).

The best histories of the New York Central Railroad are Alvin F. Harlow's *The Road of the Century: The Story of the New York Central* (New York: Creative Age Press, Inc., 1947) and Edward Hungerford's *Men and Iron: The History of the New York Central* (New York: Thomas Y. Crowell, 1938). For the history of the Vanderbilt railroads and Grand Central Terminal, I have also relied on Carl Condit's unrivaled two-volume *History of the Port of New York* (Chicago: University of Chicago Press, 1980–1981). For the decline and bankruptcy of the New York Central a good source is Peter Lyon, *To Hell in a Day Coach: An Exasperated Look at American Railroads* (Philadelphia: J. B. Lippincott, 1968).

Quite a few Vanderbilts have spoken for themselves. The youthful diary of Florence Adele Sloane was edited, with a charming commentary, by Louis Auchincloss as *Maverick in Mauve: The Diary of a Romantic Age* (Garden City: Doubleday & Co., 1983). Consuelo Vanderbilt Balsan's *The Glitter and the Gold* (New York: Harper Brothers, 1952) is one of the best firsthand accounts of life in the Gilded Age as well as

a sincere and engaging autobiography. Cornelius IV wrote frankly—too frankly, according to his relatives—of himself and his family in *Farewell to Fifth Avenue* (New York: Simon and Schuster, 1935). He wrote an equally frank and absorbing biography of his mother, *Queen of the Golden Age: The Fabulous Story of Grace Wilson Vanderbilt* (New York: McGraw-Hill, 1956). Gloria Vanderbilt has written two volumes of memoirs, *Once Upon a Time: A True Story* (New York: Alfred A. Knopf, 1985) and *Black Knight, White Knight* (New York: Alfred A. Knopf, 1987). Shirley Burden's *The Vanderbilts in My Life: A Personal Memoir* (New Haven and New York: Ticknor & Fields, 1981) is a book of photographs with a brief text. In *On Record: An Autobiography* (New York: Summit Books, 1977) John Hammond gives glimpses of his Vanderbilt relations.

B. H. Friedman's massive biography, *Gertrude Vanderbilt Whitney* (Garden City: Doubleday & Co., 1978), is not easy reading—it is inexplicably written entirely in the present tense—but it contains valuable extracts from Gertrude's diaries and letters. The story of the custody trial of Gloria has been told with skill and verve in Barbara Goldsmith's *Little Gloria . . . Happy at Last* (New York: Alfred A. Knopf, 1980), which is well researched and compulsively readable.

The important sources for William Henry's art collecting are Samuel P. Avery, *The Diaries, 1871–1882*, edited by Madeleine F. Beaufort *et al.* (New York: Arno Press, 1979), and George A. Lucas, *The Diary . . . An American Art Agent in Paris, 1857–1909* edited by Lillian M. C. Randall (Princeton: Princeton University Press, 1979).

Some of the Vanderbilt houses have been well chronicled, others have had little written about them. Undoubtedly the most complete study ever made of a Vanderbilt house, its interior, and objects was commissioned by William Henry from Edward Strahan, who wrote under the name Earl Shinn. He prepared a four-volume study of the house at 640 Fifth Avenue entitled *Mr. Vanderbilt's House and Collection* (New York: privately printed, 1883–1884). Wayne Andrews's *Architecture, Ambitions and Americans* (New York: The Free Press, 1978) is a good overview. Paul R. Baker's *Richard Morris Hunt* (Cambridge: MIT Press, 1980) is the definitive study of the architect who built so much for the Vanderbilts. *The Architecture of Richard Morris Hunt* (Chicago: University of Chicago Press, 1986), edited by Susan R. Stein, is also useful. The work of the Vanderbilts' favorite sculptor is described by James M. Dennis in *Karl Bitter: Architectural Sculptor, 1867–1915* (Madison: University of Wisconsin Press, 1967).

Contemporary photographs accompanied by a detailed and extremely well-written text are found in Arnold Lewis, *American Country Houses of the Gilded Age* (New York: Dover Publications, 1982), and Arnold Lewis *et al., The Opulent Interiors of the Gilded Age* (New York: Dover Publications, 1987). Two books on an architectural firm that did much work for the Vanderbilts are Leland M. Roth's *McKim, Mead and White, Architects* (New York: Harper & Row, 1983) and Richard Guy Wilson's *McKim, Mead & White, Architects* (New York: Rizzoli, 1983). Thomas Gannon's *Newport Mansions: The Gilded Age* (Dublin, N.H.: Foremost Publishers, 1982) has been useful. Joe Sherman's *The House at Shelburne Farms: The Story of One of America's Great Country Estates* (Middlebury, Vt.: Paul S. Erikson, 1986) is one of the few books devoted to a single Vanderbilt house. Gifford Pinchot described his work at Biltmore in his autobiography, *Breaking New Ground* (New York: Harcourt, Brace and Co., 1947), and Olmsted's work there is described by Laura Wood Roper in *FLO: A Biography of Frederick Law Olmsted* (Baltimore: The Johns Hopkins University Press, 1973).

On the social activities of the Vanderbilts in this century Eve Brown, in her *Champagne Cholly: The Life and Times of Maury Paul* (New York: E. P. Dutton, 1947), is lively and knowledgeable. For the Vanderbilt interest in horse racing, I have used Bernard Livingston's *Their Turf: America's Horsey Set & Its Princely Dynasties* (New York: Arbor House, 1973). And all students of American society must rely on Dixon Wecter's superb *The Saga of American Society: A Record of Social Aspiration, 1607–1937* (New York: Charles Scribner's Sons, 1937).

The American press has been fascinated by the doings of the Vanderbilts for over a century. Hundreds of articles have appeared, but they must be used judiciously. I found the best to be those in the New York *Times, Life,* and *Vogue.*

By far the best of the older books on the dynasty is Wayne Andrews's *The Vanderbilt Legend: The Story of the Vanderbilt Family, 1794–1940* (New York: Harcourt, Brace and Co., 1941), and I have relied heavily on that scholarly and entertaining work.

The most complete genealogy of the family to have appeared was compiled by Verley Archer: *Commodore Cornelius Vanderbilt, Sophia Johnson Vanderbilt and Their Descendants* (Nashville: Vanderbilt University, 1972).

ACKNOWLEDGMENTS

Many descendants of Commodore Vanderbilt have talked to me about the history of their family. They include William A. V. Cecil, Iris Smith Christ, Serena Van Ingen McCallum, Alexander F. Milliken, Consuelo (Mimi) Russell, Timothy P. Schieffelin, Alexander S. Webb, and J. Watson Webb. The interpretations of family history and personalities are, of course, my own.

At the Vanderbilt houses I am indebted to Craig Jessup, Vanderbilt Mansion, Hyde Park; G. Carroll Lindsay, Vanderbilt Museum, Centerport; Susan Ward, Michael K. Smith, and Travis Ledford at Biltmore; and John A. Cherol and Monique Panaggio at the Preservation Society of Newport County.

I am most grateful to James F. Carr for locating rare books and periodicals dealing with the Vanderbilts.

Mary Louise Norton of *Town & Country* aided the project from the beginning and I am most appreciative. Also at *Town & Country* I want to thank Frank Zachary, Arnold Ehrlich, John Cantrell, and Lois Taylor.

My editor at Abrams, Mark Greenberg, and my picture editor, John Crowley, have been everything editors should be, and the book is better for their help. Also at Abrams I have to thank Dirk Luykx, who designed the book, and Margaret Kaplan, Paul Gottlieb, and Elizabeth Robbins.

My agent, Susan Zeckendorf, possesses the best of all agent's qualities, enthusiasm, and I am grateful to her for support since the book was first proposed.

Thanks also to Terry Ariano, Museum of the City of New York; Susan E. Linder, New York Public Library; Waldo Maffei, Robert Nikirk, Thomas E. Norton, Elizabeth Sims, Karen Sinapi, Mr. and Mrs. James Van Alen, Mr. and Mrs. William Van Alen, and Professor Barbara Welter, Hunter College.

Most of my research was done at the New York Society Library, and I am appreciative, as I have been for years, of the staff of that great New York institution.

INDEX

PHOTOGRAPH CREDITS